W9-ATE-686

ACCOUNTABILITY AND PRISONS

Accountability and prisons

Opening up a closed world

Edited by
Mike Maguire
Jon Vagg
Rod Morgan

Tavistock Publications
London and New York

*First published in 1985 by
Tavistock Publications Ltd
11 New Fetter Lane, London
EC4P 4EE*

*Published in the USA by
Tavistock Publications
in association with Methuen, Inc.
29 West 35th Street, New York
NY 10001*

*Printed in Great Britain by
Richard Clay, the Chancer Press,
Bungay, Suffolk*

British Library Cataloguing in Publication Data

*Accountability and prisons:
opening up a closed world.*
*1. Prisons 2. Prisons – Law and legislation
I. Maguire, Mike II. Vagg, Jon
III. Morgan, Rod
365 HV8665*

*ISBN 0-422-79600-X
ISBN 0-422-79610-7 Pbk*

Library of Congress Cataloging in Publication Data

Accountability and prisons.

*Bibliography: p.
Includes index.
1. Prison administration – Great Britain – Addresses, essays, lectures. 2. Prisoners – Legal status, laws, etc. – Great Britain – Addresses, essays, lectures. 3. Prison discipline – Great Britain – Addresses, essays, lectures. 4. Prisoners – Legal status, laws, etc. – Addresses, essays, lectures. I. Maguire, Mike.
II. Vagg, Jon.
III. Morgan, Rodney.
HV9646.A28 1985
365'.64'0941 85-14746
ISBN 0-422-79600-X
ISBN 0-422-79610-7 (pbk.)*

Contents

Editors' acknowledgements

The idea for this book grew out of a Home Office-financed study of Boards of Visitors, undertaken at the Oxford University Centre for Criminological Research. Mike Maguire and Jon Vagg would like to thank again the many members of the Home Office Research Unit and the Prison Department (particularly P4 Division) who gave advice and support on that project, which provided the stimulus for a subsequent exploration, with Rod Morgan, of wider issues of accountability in the prison system. They would also like to thank the Centre Secretary, Carol McCall and her assistant Janet Larkin, for their many hours of uncomplaining work, and Jay Kynch for her patient proof-reading.

Rod Morgan would like to thank Sir James Hennessey, Chief Inspector of Prisons, and Mr Gordon Lakes, formerly Deputy Chief Inspector of Prisons and now Deputy Director General of the Prison Service, for their assistance and advice on the chapter concerning the work of Inspectorate. He would also like to thank the Nuffield Foundation, in particular James Cornford, for making possible his visit to the USA in the autumn of 1983 on the basis of which Chapter 18 was prepared. During that visit he received hospitality and information from lawyers (including Al Bronstein at the ACLU National Prison Project in Washington) and wardens too numerous to mention, but without whose help the chapter included here would not have been possible.

Finally, the editors would like to thank all the contributors for producing their chapters within a relatively short period of time, and the Home Office for allowing members of its staff to contribute original material to this book.

Mike Maguire
Jon Vagg
Rod Morgan

Notes on contributors

CLAIRE AUSTIN, Senior Research Officer, Home Office Research and Planning Unit. Co-author of *Board of Visitor Adjudications* (Home Office Research Unit Paper 3 1981) and *A Study of Prisoners' Applications and Petitions* (Home Office 1985).

PATRICK BIRKINSHAW, Lecturer in Law, University of Hull. He has published widely on issues relating to public law and central government, local government and prison administration. He is the author of *Grievances, Remedies and the State* (Sweet and Maxwell 1985). He is a member of the Legal Action Group's working party on prisoners' rights.

ALVIN J. BRONSTEIN, a lawyer, has been Executive Director of the National Prison Project of the American Civil Liberties Union Foundation since 1972. He has been involved in much of the prisoners' rights litigation in the US and has been the editor or author of numerous publications in the field, most recently: *Representing Prisoners* (Practising Law Institute, New York 1981); (with Rudovsky and Koren) *The Rights of Prisoners* (Bantam Books, New York 1983); contributor to *Our Endangered Rights* (ed. N. Dorsen, Random House, New York 1984).

SILVIA CASALE, Consultant to the National Association for the Care and Resettlement of Offenders and the VERA Institute of Justice, London office. She is author of *Fines in Europe* (German Marshall Fund Report 1981); *The Fine Process* (National Institute of Justice 1984) and *Minimum Standards for Prison Establishments* (NACRO 1984). She is currently engaged on a study of magistrates' courts for the VERA Institute.

JOHN DITCHFIELD, Senior Research Officer, Home Office Research and Planning Unit. Author of *Police Cautioning in England and Wales* (Home Office Research Study No 37 1976); co-author of *Board of Visitor Adjudications* (Research Unit Paper 3 1981) and *A Study of Prisoners' Applications and Petitions* (Home Office 1985).

Sir JAMES FAWCETT served as a member of the European Commission of Human Rights for 22 years and as President for 9 years. Professor of International Law at Kings College, London (1976–80) and a former Fellow of All Souls College, Oxford. His books include *Law and Power in International Relations* (Faber and Faber 1982) and *Application of the European Convention on Human Rights* (1968), of which he is preparing a second edition.

EDWARD FITZGERALD is a barrister, who has represented prisoners in prison disciplinary hearings since the *Tarrant* judgement, and has been involved in several High Court cases concerning prisoners and detained mental hospital patients. He has contributed articles on prisoners' rights to newspapers and legal journals and has given evidence to the Prior Committee (concerning the prison disciplinary system) on behalf of the National Council for Civil Liberties.

LARRY GOSTIN and *MARIE STAUNTON*, Ex-General Secretary and Legal Officer respectively of the National Council for Civil Liberties. Marie Staunton is responsible for NCCL's test case strategy for prisoners, and acts for them. Larry Gostin was a Visiting Fellow at the Oxford University Centre for Criminological Research and from 1974 to 1982 the Legal Director of MIND. He is author of *A Human Condition* (2 vols) (MIND 1977); *Mental Health Services: Law and Practice* (Shaw and Sons 1985), and is editor of *Secure Provision: A Review of Special Services for the Mentally Ill and Mentally Handicapped in England and Wales* (Tavistock 1985).

ROY D. KING, Professor of Social Theory and Institutions, University College of North Wales, Bangor. Co-author of *Albany: Birth of a Prison – End of an Era* (Routledge and Kegan Paul

1978); *A Taste of Prison* (Routledge 1976) and *The Future of the Prison System* (Gower 1980). He has recently studied maximum security prisons in the USA and is currently studying security, control and humane containment in the UK prison system.

MIKE MAGUIRE, Research Fellow, Centre for Criminological Research, University of Oxford. Author of *Burglary in a Dwelling: the Offence, the Offender and the Victim* (Heinemann 1982); co-author of *The 'Watchdog' Role of Boards of Visitors* (Home Office 1984) and articles on victims and parole. Currently conducting an evaluation of victim support schemes.

CHARLENE C. MANDELL and *ARTHUR L. MANDELL*, respectively Assistant Director, Correctional Law Project, Faculty of Law and Associate Professor, Faculty of Education at Queen's University, Kingston, Canada. Both are barristers and solicitors. Charlene Mandell provides legal services to inmates of Canadian penitentiaries. She is the author of *National Parole Board Hearings*. Arthur Mandell has acted as consultant to school boards and to the Ministry of Education on disciplinary procedures in Ontario schools.

ROD MORGAN, Senior Lecturer in Sociology, University of Bath. His many publications on prisons policy include (with Roy D. King) *A Taste of Prison* (Routledge and Kegan Paul 1976) and *The Future of the Prison System* (Gower 1980). He was for twelve years a member of the Board of Visitors at Pucklechurch Remand Centre and was a co-founder of the Association of Members of Boards of Visitors (AMBOV), whose Handbook he has edited. His recent research has been on the use and enforcement of fines and he is currently conducting a national survey of post-Scarman police-community liaison committees.

JAN A. NIJBOER and *GERHARD J. PLOEG*, members of the Criminologisch Instituut, University of Groningen, Holland. Since 1976 they have been working in the field of prisoners' rights and, in particular, monitoring on behalf of the Ministry of Justice a new prisoner grievance procedure. Their report, *Klagers Achter Slot en Grendel* ('Complaints Behind Closed Doors') was published in 1983.

PETER M. QUINN is a member of the governor grade of the Prison Service and has served at Hollesley Bay Borstal and Long

Lartin and Durham Prisons. From 1980 to 1984 he was a Tutor at the Prison Service College, Wakefield. He has published articles on judicial review of prison disciplinary hearings.

GENEVRA RICHARDSON, Lecturer in Law, University of East Anglia. She is co-author of *Policing Pollution* (OUP 1983) and has published articles in the areas of public law, regulation and prisoners' rights.

CHRISTOPHER TRAIN is the Director General of the Prison Service for England and Wales.

JON VAGG, Research Fellow, Centre for Criminological Research, University of Oxford. Co-author of *The 'Watchdog' Role of Boards of Visitors* (Home Office 1984). Currently engaged in research on social control and policing in rural and urban areas.

Introduction: accountability and prisons

Jon Vagg, Rod Morgan, and Mike Maguire

I repeat . . . that all power is a trust – that we are accountable for its exercise – that, from the people, and for the people, all springs, and all must exist. Disraeli, *Vivien Grey*, Bk VI Ch. 7

Disraeli's fine rhetoric makes the concept and practice of accountability sound disarmingly simple. Power is seen as a trust held on behalf of 'the people', who must be satisfied by full and regular accounts from the stewards of that power that it is being exercised in a proper manner. But even the most cursory glance at the operation of contemporary state bureaucracies exposes the enormity of the gap between ideal and reality. The last hundred years have seen a major expansion in the scale, range, and complexity of state agencies, evidenced for example by a twenty-fold growth in the size of the United Kingdom civil service between 1870 and 1970. As early as 1929, the Committee on Ministers' powers collected 'extensive evidence revealing the widespread use of quasi-judicial and legislative powers on the part of public agencies' (Collins 1980:466). Furthermore, substantial professional groups have been erected, to whom enormous powers of discretion have been granted and who, in many cases, have become accountable primarily to groups of fellow-professionals rather than directly to Parliament or the public. There are few commentators who would argue that 'the people' are kept sufficiently informed about the activities of modern policy-makers and administrators to make knowledgeable judgements about their use of power, let alone to achieve effective control over its future exercise.

Increasing recognition of these problems has fostered both academic and political interest in the notion of accountability. This book is a contribution to the debate in the context of prisons, an area in which it has not yet been widely explored, but where, it will be argued, the exceptional nature of the powers taken by the state over confined individuals makes effective external scrutiny of their use a matter of particular urgency.

Accountability

Before considering the special circumstances of prisons, a number of general points must be made about the accountability of state agencies. We take it as axiomatic that if basic democratic accountability is to be achieved, the directors of such agencies must be answerable to outside bodies for the running of their departments. This includes, at the very least, providing satisfactory answers to questions about their stewardship of public funds and about their implementation of policies required by the legislature. But genuine accountability should also include a degree of effective external control over the substance of policies produced *within* government departments.

The inspection of financial returns and the determination of future budgets are regarded by Parliament as an important and effective method of ensuring that powers delegated are not powers misused. At the most basic level, there must be a clear assurance that funds are not being misappropriated. Beyond this, public agencies must show that their resources are being used efficiently. However, Garrett (1980) notes that many state departments are called upon to deliver services in which efficiency and economy cannot be measured directly in cost/output terms. They may provide services to which people are (to a more or less precisely specified degree) entitled, or which must be distributed equitably within a fixed budget, or where their provision to one group incurs disbenefits to others. In such cases, accountability acquires social, political, legal, and moral characteristics, raising difficult questions about the appropriate forms of audit and the yardsticks of assessment which should be employed.

More problematic still, the policies for whose implementation administrators may be called to account are often vague and complex in character, capable of many interpretations. There may be widespread disagreement about their overall purposes, or about the practical meaning of key terms within them. For example, people may differ over when certain procedures can be said to be 'fair' or 'safe', under what circumstances a particular set of guidelines applies, or indeed whether whole sets of practices remain within the spirit and letter of the legislation. At the same time, the changing political climate and the activities of pressure-groups may rapidly alter perceptions and create widely conflicting views of what any policy is supposed to be achieving. Some commentators have come to doubt whether, among such confusion, there can be said to be any adequate version of a general 'public interest' or 'national welfare' by which to assess agency performance. Stewart (1975), for example, writes that he has

> 'Come not only to question the agencies' ability to protect the public interest, but to doubt the very existence of an ascertainable national welfare as a meaningful guide to administrative decision.'

Collins (1980:472), too, draws attention to the increasing involvement of government departments in battles between sectional interests, arguing that

> 'agencies, as the institutional embodiment of the state's expanding power, no longer present themselves as neutral administrators of policy above civil society. Rather, they are viewed as supporters of specific entitlement to private interests.'

At least three sets of more practical problems commonly face outside scrutineers attempting to assess an agency's performance. First, the making of sensible judgements about actions taken by professionals often requires a substantial degree of technical knowledge. In such circumstances they may attempt to increase their own knowledge or, more often, will have to depend largely upon evaluations made by the decision-makers' professional peers and colleagues.

Second, the process of calling for accounts often implies a continuing relationship between public agency and 'watchdog' (Hawkins 1984). This may force both sides to consider the effects that certain demands or evaluations may have on their relationship. It may, for example, be judged better to overlook certain issues in the short term for the sake of longer-term co-operation. A particular danger related to this long-term relationship has been noted by Lynxwiler, Shover, and Clelland (1983) among others. Where regulatory bodies are set up, they may find themselves co-opted into the values and goals of the organizations they are required to regulate, thus losing the critical eye of the outside observer. It has also to be recognized that those scrutinizing accounts have to operate in a social and political environment, and must attend to their own credibility and legitimacy within that framework. Calvatia (1983) charts the demise of one regulatory agency which failed to protect itself in this way and lost both political mandate and budget.

Third, effective scrutiny from the outside cannot be achieved unless there is a correspondingly well-organized system of *internal* accountability, with decision-makers at all levels having properly defined goals and responsibilities. All major decisions should thus be clearly attributable. This implies

> 'the delegation to managers of authority over money and manpower; a form of organization in which managers can be made responsible for the activities of sub-units; a strategic planning framework in which the objectives of those managers can be related to corporate objectives; an arrangement of control information so that progress towards that attainment of those objectives can be monitored and a procedural system for securing managerial commitment to unit objectives and for reviewing results.' (Garrett 1980:130)

Accountability *within* government departments is thus a precondition of wider managerial accountability to the outside world.

The articles in this collection discuss, and assess the effectiveness of, a wide variety of modes of accountability, both internal and external. Prison Department staff are required to give accounts, in one form or another, to their own superiors, to other government departments (such as the Treasury), to the legislature (either directly, or through ombudsmen, inspectorates, or commissions), and to the public and press. Finally, they have to take notice of a rather different, but increasingly important, mode of review of administrative decisions, that of actions by individuals in the courts. Attempts are being made in many countries to reestablish the 'rule of law' in various areas of public administration, including within prisons. Courts are now more often asked to rule on the legality (or in the USA, the constitutionality) of particular policies, procedures, or decisions.

The special nature of prisons

The general observations set out above apply to the administration of prisons just as they apply elsewhere in the process of government. However, in this special setting they take on a particular urgency. Prisons are closed and total institutions. Their populations do not constitute a credible interest group; they are not consulted by or represented within management; in the last analysis, the control exercised over them is bluntly coercive; and considerations of control and security (and in the British case, tradition) dictate a great degree of secrecy in their operation. Mundane aspects of life, such as access to lawyers or relatives, communication in general, and a whole range of issues from sanitation to sexual activity, are subject to detailed regulation by prison staff. In addition to, and sometimes instead of, the criminal law, prisoners are subject to institutional disciplinary codes. Punishments such as loss of remission ('good time'), cellular confinement, fines or loss of privileges may be imposed by prison governors or quasi-judicial bodies (such as, in Britain, the Boards of Visitors). All these features of prison life indicate that extensive discretion is exercised over every aspect of inmates' existence. The volume of such decisions, their detailed nature and the extent to which they are taken *in camera*, indicates a need for a correspondingly far-reaching and detailed system of accountability.

Issues of accountability are equally pressing in the broader terms of public policy. Prisons deliver a public service; but how that service may be defined, measured and scrutinized for efficiency and effectiveness, and who should do this work, are complex and open-ended questions. The organizational aims of the prison service have taken a sharp knock in recent years since so many studies have been unable to demonstrate any measurable rehabilitative effect (Brody 1976). This has led to a retrenchment in which the public service delivered is held in many quarters to be little more than the removal from certain citizens of freedoms of movement in society at large and, perhaps, the delivery of a 'just measure of pain' (Ignatieff 1978). Moreover, citizens sentenced to imprisonment are often held to be less eligible for certain services than others in normal society. It is difficult to argue for expenditure on prisons where more deserving individuals – the aged, the sick, schoolchildren – live, convalesce or study in conditions as squalid as many prisons. In short, there are few votes in prison expenditure, few positive ways for the service provided by prisons to be measured, and few ways to demonstrate efficiency or effectiveness other than through an absence of escapes or riots. There is a great deal of scope for the development of new structures within which the prison service can show, in a positive sense, what it is doing; that its activities are morally, socially, legally and politically acceptable; and that it is using its resources efficiently and effectively.

The English prison system

In England and Wales prisons are governed by statute. The Prison Act 1952 vests authority over prisons in the Home Secretary, who in turn is accountable to Parliament (under the Prison (Scotland) Act 1952, Scottish prisons are administered by the Secretary of State for Scotland). Thus, almost uniquely among British public services, prisons are the sole, undivided, administrative and financial responsibility of a central government department. Until 1963, that department was the autonomous Board of Prison Commissioners, but it is now the Prison Department within the Home Office. Local authorities exercise no authority over prisons: the Boards of Visitors – local voluntary 'watchdog' bodies attached to each prison and appointed by the Secretary of State – are the last vestigial link with the magistrates and local authorities who, prior to the Prison Act 1877, administered the local prisons (McConville 1981).

The Prison Act 1952 details, *inter alia,* the Secretary of State's powers and duties: to open, alter or close prisons; to satisfy himself that sufficient accommodation and staff are provided; and to see that rules covering very basic aspects of the treatment of prisoners are complied with. It also provides that the Prison Department shall make an annual report which the Secretary of State is obliged to lay before Parliament. This is the principal official account of the Department's work (see Chapter 15). Scrutiny of the Prison Act, however, provides a poor guide for understanding how prisons and prisoners are managed. In order to uncover routine management policy, one has to penetrate several layers of rules within rules.

The first layer comprises the Prison Rules, which the Secretary of State promulgates by Statutory Instrument under s.47 of the Act. The current Rules date from 1964 (SI No. 388 as amended) and there are separate though similar Rules for Detention Centres (SI 1983, No. 569) and Youth Custody Centres (SI 1983 No. 570). The Prison Rules have something to say on most aspects of prison life but are, as Zellick (1981) has pointed out, diverse in character. They range from diffuse statements of general policy objectives, to definitions of administrative structure and functions, to rules designed to protect individual prisoners. The latter are few in number and mostly concern procedures for discipline and control. The Rules covering conditions and facilities generally provide staff with a wide discretion. Thus, for example, though a convicted prisoner is entitled to send and receive a letter once a week (Rule 34(2)a), it 'may be read or examined' and stopped if 'its contents are objectionable or . . . of inordinate length' (Rule 33(3)). The Rules do not define 'objectionable' or 'inordinate'.

In order to discover how staff are routinely expected to interpret the Rules, one has to turn to prison Standing Orders. However, though copies of Standing Orders have been placed in the libraries of both Houses of Parliament, and have been referred to in the courts, they are not published (an exception is Standing Order 5 governing prisoner communications) and are not generally available to members of the public or to prisoners (Blom-Cooper and Zellick 1982).

Standing Orders are a relatively unchanging body of management rules. They are supplemented by Circular Instructions, a large number of which are issued to governors by Prison Department headquarters each year, and which may or may not be absorbed into amended Standing Orders. Circular Instructions, which are also not generally available, are for the most part concerned with innocuous administrative details. However, they also deal with important and sensitive aspects of management and the treatment of prisoners which have a bearing on broader questions of accountability. For example, the new accounting and management systems described by Train in Chapter 12 can only be fully understood in the light of Circular Instructions. The same is true of the so-called '10/74 procedure' (named after the Circular Instruction which introduced it) by which disruptive prisoners are segregated and transferred between selected prisons (see King Chapter 13). In the final analysis, it can be argued that neither management nor prisoner control processes are accountable if the criteria on which they are based remain shrouded in secrecy.

Purposes of imprisonment

It has been argued (see, for example, King and Morgan 1979) that there is a logical relationship between the absence of minimum standards and prisoner entitlements in the Prison Rules, and the official purposes which govern the system. Rule 1 – 'the purpose of the training and treatment of convicted prisoners shall be to encourage them to lead a good and useful life' – is criticized not merely because it is derived from a discredited rehabilitative ethic, but because, being mythical, it has always been incapable of definition in practice. The objectives of treatment and training, the argument goes, are positivistic in origin and paternalistic in operation, tending to a focus on the perceived needs and deficiencies of prisoners rather than on their rights and responsibilities. The Department has always been scrupulously careful to talk of prisoner privileges rather than rights.

By contrast, the so-called 'justice model' (see also von Hirsch 1976) starts from the proposition that the only defensible aims of imprisonment are punishment and public protection according to judicially determined desert. The punishment is loss of liberty, the duration of the punishment should not be affected by the prisoner's response to his imprisonment (unless he commits a definable disciplinary offence, itself punishable according to due process) and prisoners should retain as many of their civil rights as are consistent with captivity. According to this view, prisoners should, wherever possible, be provided with the minimum facilities assured to other citizens and should be free to use or reject them without prejudicing their release. Finally, it is argued that the prison authorities have a duty to contain prisoners humanely, to assure them of a reasonable quality of life as of right, and to ensure that they do not deteriorate as a consequence of their incarceration (see also Cross 1976).

Of course no prison system, whatever its rules may say, fits neatly into one or the other of these ideal types. And the British prison system, like most others, has incorporated over time ingredients from a variety of penal philosophies: prison administration is a much more pragmatic business than any discussion of abstract models can portray. Thus the most recent official discussion of the aims of imprisonment seems to have arrived at a prescription of what purposes – namely 'positive custody' – should be stated in the Prison Rules, not on the basis of some internally consistent philosophy leading to definable objectives, but rather from the standpoint that morale has to be generated for staff (Home Office 1979: paras 4.25–4.28; King and Morgan 1980). Furthermore, what the Prison Rules say, and the decision as to whether or not they should be amended, owes as much to symbolic politics and budgetary considerations as it does to credible penal justifications.

The importance of standards

The Prison Department has virtually no control over the size and characteristics of the population for which it must cater (currently about 48,000). None the less, it has a responsibility to organize its work with certain priorities in mind. For example, it has a strict duty to prevent escapes, and to maintain control of its establishments. But at the same time, there is considerable flexibility in the methods which may be used to deal with this population in terms of these objectives (for example, in the security categorization of inmates and in the allocation of prisoners to particular parts of the system).

The Department has other mandatory responsibilities, such as the duty to provide educational facilities. But decisions as to the level of service and the specific form it takes are in the main discretionary, and based substantially upon operational exigencies; there are at present no agreed standards by which service provision in these areas may be measured. Even so, it is vitally important that standards be introduced, not just for the protection of prisoners (and staff, for the living conditions for prisoners are the working conditions for staff) but quite simply in order that the terms 'effectiveness' and 'efficiency' should have meaning in prisons.

Gostin and Staunton, in Chapter 5, argue the case for more specific and enforceable standards in the context of what they have described as a 'new legalism' in the process of holding institutions of all kinds to account. Moreover, in Chapter 1, Richardson argues that standards should invest rights in prisoners. The extent of the discretion exercised over them requires that special safeguards against abuse should be provided, and legally-enforceable standards is one avenue for achieving this.

Democratic and legal accountability

Existing systems which might be subsumed under the term 'democratic accountability' are disparate and specialized in function. As mentioned earlier, the Director-General is required to produce an annual report which is laid before Parliament, and may be required to provide evidence to Parliamentary Select Committees which investigate various aspects of government activities on an *ad hoc* basis. The new Prison Inspectorate conducts reviews of establishments and of 'themes' (system-wide functions), having the responsibility

> to inspect and report to the Secretary of State on prison service establishments in England and Wales and, in particular, on
> (a) conditions in those establishments;
> (b) the treatment of prisoners and other inmates and the facilities available to them;
> (c) any other such matters as the Secretary of State may direct.
> (HM Chief Inspector 1982a: 49)

However, as Morgan suggests in Chapter 7, these reviews are selected in consultation with the Department, and thus to an extent reflect the concerns of management.

A broader view of prison conditions may be expressed by the Boards of Visitors. While these bodies are neither elected by nor directly accountable to the community, they are nevertheless intended to be representative of it and were described, rather optimistically, by Home Secretary William Whitelaw in 1980 as a 'window on the world for the prison service'. A large question-mark hanging over them is the future of their disciplinary function, which, it is now widely agreed, seriously compromises their independent position (Martin 1975; JUSTICE 1983; Maguire Chapter 9). The disciplinary side of the Boards' work takes up a great deal of their time: of 70,000 offences against prison discipline in 1982, about 5 per cent were heard by the Boards, and these included the most serious of the offences not brought before criminal courts. This aspect of their role has been significantly affected by two court decisions in particular. In *St Germain* (1979), it was held for the first time that the procedures of Board disciplinary hearings ('adjudications') were subject to judicial review. In *Tarrant* (1984), it was determined that Boards had the discretion to allow prisoners legal representation at such hearings. Fitzgerald (Chapter 2) and Quinn (Chapter 14) discuss legal and managerial issues respectively which arise from the Boards' disciplinary function, the *Tarrant* decision and the particular problems which have followed from it. This whole matter is currently under review by a Departmental Committee headed by Mr Peter Prior, and in Chapter 15 we set out the issues which confront this Committee.

Possibilities also exist for individual prisoners to raise grievances about their treatment. They may complain to the prison governor, the Board of Visitors, the Home Secretary (in writing, known as a 'petition' and usually dealt with by regional or headquarters staff), the Ombudsman, a Member of Parliament, the courts or the European Commission of Human Rights. While some of these bodies are selective in the complaints they will consider, many of the rules governing the sequence in which they must be approached have been relaxed or lifted following domestic and European court decisions. Each of these mechanisms is discussed in this collection of articles.

In the USA, the Eighth and Fourteenth Amendments to the Constitution have enabled prisoners to bring many complaints about prison conditions directly to court. The English courts have been less willing to regard complaints by prisoners as justiciable, a situation not improved by the lack of a written constitution. Indeed, court decisions so far suggest that the Prison Department will have to answer to the courts only where it transgresses one of a limited number of ground-rules concerning issues such as the exercise of quasi-judicial powers by Boards of Visitors and freedom of access to lawyers or the judicial system. Finally, the European Commission and Court of Human Rights have, on the whole, taken a wider view of the extent to which the 'rule of law' (in this case the European Convention on Human Rights) should impinge upon prison life. Their interventions have led to various changes in prison practices in the UK.

Financial and managerial accountability

In terms of financial expenditure, the Prison Department is accountable to the Treasury and to Parliament, the latter utilizing a system of Select Committees to scrutinize annual reports, accounts and estimates, and to examine the financial implications of policy decisions. However, in reality even these committees have found it virtually impossible to penetrate the complexities of the financial situation. The Department for many years employed only a rudimentary audit system which did not, for example, provide breakdowns of the costs of any individual prison (Home Office 1979: 84). In a system which is currently spending over £600 million per annum – a budget which has grown faster than that of any other central government department – it is still impossible to discover such basic information as the costs incurred in escorting prisoners to and from courts (Morgan 1983).

However, a new system of audit has recently been introduced, in which governors for the first time will be given direct responsibility for spending within their own establishments and separate accounts will be kept for each unit under their managerial control. It remains to be seen whether these accounts will be made public, but in any event the new system may enable management to become more cost-effective – if, of course, a workable definition of 'effectiveness' can be reached. A highly significant move in this direction was made in 1984, when the Prison Board produced a 'statement of mission' – or more precisely, two related statements, both of which are reproduced as appendices to the Director-General's contribution to this volume.

Where internal systems of accountability are concerned, it should be noted that management structures have undergone wholesale revision in recent years. A three-tier structure has been created, with four regional offices interposed between the national headquarters and the individual establishments. At the same time, a trend towards the centralization of certain functions has limited the sphere of discretion of 'governing governors'. Increasing specialization, too, has removed some staff such as prison psychologists from some aspects of line management. Their management structures now terminate in specialist directorates within the national headquarters. Within this centralization and specialization some devices for generating internal accountability have been attempted, drawing on the broad principles of 'Management by Objectives'. Current initiatives include the formulation of contractual relationships between prisons and regional headquarters ('accountable regimes') and rolling programmes of small-scale inspections ('operational assessments') carried out by staff unconnected with the particular area being assessed. Last, the Prison Inspectorate was removed from the Department in 1979 and now exists as an agency in its own right, responsible directly to the Home Secretary.

Structure of the book

There has never been a systematic examination of all the mechanisms of accountability applicable to the British prison system. Rather, there have been a fragmented series of debates on particular issues – prisoners' rights, prison conditions (and standards by which to judge them), grievance mechanisms, and management strategies in response to the growing problems in prisons (see also Mott 1985). This book attempts to draw together these hitherto disparate strands of thinking. Furthermore, many of the commentators in these areas have been handicapped by a lack of even the most basic data, for which reason we have taken as one priority the construction of a comprehensive picture of the current situation in each of the four areas outlined above.

Equally important, this text argues that any assessment of the accountability of a public service as complex as the prison system must be based upon a view of the degree to which the jigsaw of the various mechanisms of accountability – be they democratic, legal, financial or managerial – fits together. These cannot be considered in isolation. A feature of all systems is that changes in one part have consequences for what happens elsewhere. So it is with accountability. Democratic accountability is meaningless without management accountability; inspection cannot be penetrating without the existence of standards; for grievance procedures to work the persons handling them must be seen to be independent of management, and so on. Thus in discussing any one procedure, it must always be considered whether adjacent parts of the system reinforce or undermine each other. An example of the necessity for this is given in Chapter 15, where the danger is discussed of improvements in formal disciplinary procedures resulting in an increased resort by staff to 'alternative' administrative controls.

Part 1 of the book deals with the interrelated questions of prisoners' rights and judicial review of (and intervention in) the management of British prisons. Richardson (Chapter 1) puts the case for the development of specific legal rights for prisoners and the remaining chapters outline the success or failure of applicants in persuading the British courts to intervene in internal disciplinary processes (Fitzgerald Chapter 2), in challenging in the courts the Prison Department's use of discretion (Richardson Chapter 3), and in invoking the protection of the European Convention on Human Rights (Fawcett Chapter 4).

The contributors to Part 2 discuss the potential value of articulating or legislating specific standards against which to assess or challenge prison conditions and the treatment of prisoners. Gostin and Staunton put the case for legally enforceable standards and Casale considers the practical problems involved in drafting a code of standards. The other two chapters look at the work of bodies whose function entails the assessment of prison conditions and the treatment of prisoners: the Prison Inspectorate is discussed by Morgan and Boards of Visitors by Vagg. Both writers illustrate the point that effective inspection is crucially dependent upon the existence of agreed standards.

In Part 3, attention is given to the means by which prisoners themselves may make complaints about their treatment. Maguire discusses the role of the Boards of Visitors, Ditchfield and Austin look at internal grievance procedures, and Birkinshaw assesses critically the record of the Parliamentary Commissioner for Administration. All three chapters identify weaknesses in the existing avenues for complaint and thus provide some support for Birkinshaw's recommendation that a special Prisons Ombudsman should be created.

Part 4 is concerned with issues of management, discipline, control and security in prisons. These chapters raise two major questions. First, given the demise of the rehabilitative ideal, what are the future objectives of the Prison Department to be – especially in relation to long-term or 'difficult' groups of prisoners? Second, given the widespread criticism of the formal disciplinary system, backed up by recent court decisions, what is the future for this system?

These questions have exercised two committees, one internal (the Control Review Committee) which reported last year, and one Departmental (the Prior Committee) due to report in 1985. The first contribution here is by the Director-General of the prison service, who has kindly allowed us to publish the text of his important speech to the 1984 Governors' Conference, in which he sets out future management strategy. King then discusses wider aspects of the 'control' question, Quinn considers the changing situation from the point of view of a serving governor, and the editors examine the options open to the Prior Committee.

The final section in the book, Part 5, contains three chapters included for purposes of comparison. Each of the chapters – a study of new grievance procedures in the Netherlands (Nijboer and Ploeg), discussions of legal intervention in prisons in Canada (Mandell and Mandell) and the USA (Morgan and Bronstein) – describes particular mechanisms of accountability which deserve attention outside their own country. While the prison systems of different countries are never entirely comparable, owing to major differences in the social and political framework within which they operate, some useful lessons may be drawn from their experience. In particular, all three chapters further illustrate the point that systems which look attractive from a theoretical point of view often encounter major difficulties in practice.

PART I

PRISONERS' RIGHTS AND THE LAW

1
The case for prisoners' rights

Genevra Richardson

In recent years there has been a rekindling of interest in individual rights, a notion which fell into some disrepute during the ascendancy of utilitarian theories of social justice. This interest has emanated from all points on the political spectrum: individual rights are increasingly being recognized as an essential safeguard against the power of the state whatever its ideological stamp. In step with this more general revival, the specific notion of prisoners' rights is prevalent within the current debate on prison conditions, and many proposals for prison reform rely to some extent on claims to such rights.

Any claim to a right can be merely rhetorical or can refer directly to specific moral or legal entitlements, but, whatever their precise basis, all such claims exploit the powerful political impact of the assertion of a right. For this reason alone the concept of prisoners' rights provides a potentially powerful counter in any discussion of penal policy. Even so, some groups critical of present policies have remained somewhat reluctant to use the language of rights. This is particularly true of the political left, which has traditionally argued that the concept of rights involves an unacceptable form of moralism and that the existence of individual rights derogates from the assertion of collective rights. Carlen (1983), for example, has urged that the language of rights be dropped from penal politics and replaced by the language of powers. However, her criticism of rights seems to centre mainly on those theories of punishment which rely on a right to punish.

She produces no strong arguments against the recognition of rights in the punished individuals, the main concern of this paper, and indeed refers to the need for 'procedural safeguards at all stages' (1983: 211). Nevertheless, Carlen is entirely accurate when she asserts that 'the discourse of rights is still all things to all persons' (1983: 204) and it is thus essential, if the current debate is to develop in a fruitful manner, to examine more closely the notion of basic or human rights in general and prisoners' rights in particular.

An individual asserts a right when he or she makes a claim to performance (action or forbearance) by another. The right is legal when the correlative duty is owed at law, and moral when the duty is morally enforceable. The two are not coterminous but arguably the latter should inform the former. The claim to a 'right' in this sense must be distinguished from the assertion of a mere 'liberty' which implies no correlative duty in another to act or forbear. (An individual claims a liberty to do *X* when there is no obligation on him or her to refrain from *X* nor is there a right in anyone else that he or she shall so refrain: Hohfeld 1919; Hart 1955).

The relative ease with which a 'right' can be defined is to be contrasted with the total lack of agreement both as to the existence of basic, human or moral rights and as to their substance. In a recent attempt to tackle the first issue Gewirth (1984) argues that as a necessary condition of action every human actor has rights to freedom and wellbeing and must accept that all other prospective actors have the same rights. His argument is particularly fascinating since it seeks to establish the existence of basic rights without resort to moral principles, but the criticisms it has attracted illustrate how contentious a topic it remains (Bedau 1984; Pennock and Chapman 1981). Further, a brief glance at the literature reveals that the second issue, that of substance, has proved equally intractable. Commentators in the new-libertarian tradition, such as Nozick (1974), identify only very few basic rights emanating from the right to be free from all forms of coercion or limitation of freedom. A more liberal theory is provided by Dworkin (1977) who attempts to derive the basis of rights simply from an individual's entitlement to equality of concern and respect. Dworkin's emphasis on equality distinguishes him fundamentally from Nozick for whom the supreme value is freedom, with the result that the rights recognized by the two are very different. Finally, Campbell (1983) has recently endeavoured to establish that rights are compatible with socialism. He has developed an 'interest theory' of rights and argues that within a truly socialist state rights ought to be enacted in order to aid the achievement of material justice, the satisfaction of human needs, and the promotion of utility.

While it is evident from the above that opinions vary widely as to the existence and substance of basic rights (bearing out Carlen's assertion), it is equally apparent that most writers who are prepared to recognize the existence of rights are prepared also to recognize their partial loss through punishment. Such 'loss' is recognized by social contract theorists (Rawls 1971: 240–2), is feasible within the purged utilitarian calculations of Dworkin, and is even admitted by Campbell (1983: 79–80). Unfortunately, however, the extent of that loss is never adequately specified and the theories of punishment used to justify it vary enormously.

The problems associated with existence and substance are thus exacerbated when theories of rights become entwined with theories of punishment. In part this additional confusion can be understood as a consequence of the traditional approach to punishment which, according to Garland and Young (1983: 11), 'conspires to present "punishment" as something we can talk of and refer to in the singular, whilst disregarding the plurality and complexity of its empirical supports'. Certainly any suggestion that generalizations about punishment tend to mislead at both a conceptual and an empirical level is borne out by the unproductive nature of the debate concerning the rights of the punished in general. This paper, however, is concerned with the more specific issue of prisoners' rights and here some headway can be made.

The case for prisoners' rights

That rights mean 'all things to all persons' is not for a moment denied. Indeed the statement attests to the *rhetorical* power of 'rights' (Scheingold 1974: 213; Birkinshaw 1981: 156; Hunt 1981), and arguably emphasizes the *political* advantages of joining rather than ignoring the debate (Hunt 1981). The argument here will proceed on the assumption that basic rights exist (Gewirth 1984), that they provide necessary protection for the individual against any state irrespective of ideological hue (Campbell 1983), and that they should be recognized at law. This positive attitude is encouraged by the present subject matter: the case for prisoners' rights is particularly strong.

In the UK imprisonment formally constitutes the law's most severe penalty. Individuals who breach the fundamental tenets of the criminal law are removed from the rest of society, deprived of their freedom of movement, and subjected to numerous further constraints frequently amounting to an alteration in their legally recognized rights and liberties. Certain of these restrictions, relating to freedom of movement for example, flow inevitably from the fact of imprisonment, while others, for example those concerned with communications, are less directly related. Here it will be argued that precisely because prisoners must suffer the loss of certain legal rights they become particularly vulnerable to further loss, and in order to safeguard their basic human rights their remaining legal rights require careful specification and even supplementation.

In principle, any alteration in a prisoner's rights, whether legal or basic (or as some prefer, moral), can be justified only by reference to the recognized aims of imprisonment. Unfortunately, however, this prescription merely begs the question since there is little agreement as to the proper purposes of imprisonment, even if, with varying degrees of reluctance, most commentators accept the need for its continued existence in some form. Indeed it seems likely that, just as has been the case since the nineteenth century, a variety of reasons will continue to be offered for the imposition of imprisonment. Recently, widespread dissatisfaction with the official goals of deterrence, retribution and reformation has led to many reformulations, the most influential of which must be the new retributivism or justice model (von Hirsch 1976). Social protection also, despite the controversy it engenders, is still regarded as a possible justification for detention (Floud and Young 1981). Finally, there is the much criticized yet resilient concept of rehabilitation and training, sometimes merely recognized (Foucault 1977; Cohen 1983; Bottoms 1983), but sometimes cautiously advocated (Walker 1980: ch. 3; Wright 1982: ch. 8)

The confusion and argument surrounding the proper aims of imprisonment are unremarkable. Just as punishment should not be regarded as singular, so the purposes of imprisonment are unlikely to be identical in every case given the variety of offences, offenders and societal attitudes. Nevertheless, despite this inevitable plurality it is possible to argue that any 'acceptable' prison regime must recognize rights in the imprisoned.

To return briefly to the rights/punishment debate, it was suggested above that most theorists are prepared to recognize the *partial* loss of rights through punishment. Such partial loss implies the retention of a residue in the punished individual, the extent of which will depend on the precise view of punishment taken. When applied to imprisonment such an argument suggests that the scope of the rights remaining in the prisoner will depend on the prevailing view of the justification of imprisonment. If, for example, the protection of society is the prime justification then the loss of rights consequent on imprisonment may extend only to those necessary to ensure segregation from the community (Floud and Young 1981). On the other hand, if retribution is the aim the scope of the residue will depend on the nature of the sanction society wishes to impose. Assuming the theoretical basis of any retributive approach ultimately to lie in some form of social contract theory (Plant 1979), then the imprisoned individual must retain some rights unless the hypothetical individuals in their state of initial choice would have removed *all* the rights of those who break the rules. It can be argued that if such total loss were chosen then the selected punishment would be slavery, corporal or even capital punishment. The selection of imprisonment must imply the retention of some rights if only to distinguish it from other yet more intrusive forms of sanction. Similarly, since it is now generally accepted that deterrence can constitute a justifiable aim for imprisonment only when it is limited by the principles of retribution (Packer 1969; Walker 1980), the deterrent use of imprisonment must recognize the retention of rights in the prisoner. Finally, and perhaps most controversially, there is the question of treatment and reformation. One of the most cogent criticisms of this penal objective relates to the denial of the freedom of choice inevitably implied by the more coercive forms of treatment (Plant 1979). Total subjugation of the rights of the punished to the objective of treatment can never be justified.

Thus the recognition of rights in prisoners is essential whatever view of imprisonment prevails. The substance or scope of those rights will, however, vary. Here a minimalist approach will be adopted. It will be assumed that, to whatever end, segregation from the community is the main function of imprisonment. According to such an approach imprisonment justifies only that degree of interference required to achieve separation from the rest of the community: all remaining rights should be safeguarded. Of all the potential prison regimes currently under discussion, 'humane containment', with its advocacy of minimal interference and normalization, is best designed to achieve this particular balance (King and Morgan 1980). Normalization requires that conditions within prison approximate as closely as possible to those outside and would encourage the retention of the rights and duties normally pertaining to free individuals. Further, the notions of certainty, accountability, determinacy and openness, all of which are ideal characteristics of humane containment, support the case for the clear specification of those remaining rights and their recognition at law. If a more punitive approach to imprisonment were to be adopted whereby an individual was sent to prison *for* punishment rather than *as* punishment, then inevitably the residue of rights would be reduced. But, according to the argument in the preceding paragraph, it would still be necessary to safeguard that residue, however small.

Further, it will be argued here that, whatever the precise justification for incarceration, the ideal regime should impose positive obligations on society in addition to the negative notion of minimal interference. This issue is complicated by the experience of treatment and training in this country and elsewhere. Recognizing the dangers of the 'coerced cure', many commentators have viewed with suspicion any regimes which aim to 'rehabilitate' (Kittrie 1971; Morris 1975; Fitzgerald and Sim 1982) and their reservations should be borne in mind in relation to recent Home Office proposals for long-term prisoners (Home Office 1984b). Nevertheless, there is a case for the imposition of positive obligations. Provided the prisoner's participation is voluntary, the provision of satisfying employment and educational and vocational training facilities should be welcomed. Payments could be used to encourage prisoners to take up the facilities so long as participation records were never allowed to affect release dates. Such a scheme should go some way to meeting the Chief Inspector's fears that a voluntary system would be neither 'practical [n]or sensible' (HM Chief Inspector of Prisons 1983a: para. 5.13) and should be regarded as workable by prison staff, while at the same time remaining voluntary in the most crucial respect. Further, certain therapeutic and psychiatric treatment facilities might also be offered on a strictly voluntary basis.

The argument for the provision of these facilities does not rely on any analogy with those available outside prison. It goes further. The above facilities should be available to prisoners and available *as of legal right* precisely because the potential recipients are prisoners. The fact that such rights are not available to the rest of the community is therefore irrelevant (Home Office 1984f). Society has seen fit to deprive prisoners of certain legal rights and thus to increase their dependence. Consequently it has a duty to protect them and to provide them with certain facilities be they employment, educational or medical, or merely the 'physical necessities of life'. In other words, dependence entitles the prisoner to *special rights*. To some extent various elements within prison administration (Home Office 1984a; 1984f) have already accepted the case for the provision of certain facilities, but, as recognized by the Chief Inspector, broadly worded goals are inadequate however laudable in intent (HM Chief Inspector of Prisons 1983a: para. 5.11). The specification of duties with sufficient precision to permit legal enforcement is necessary in order both to meet the requirements of an acceptable prison regime and to have any practical impact in a world of limited resources. Again, as with the extent of the residue of rights, an imprisonment *for* punishment approach would demand fewer such positive rights in the prisoner, but the element of dependence would still necessitate some special protection, for example the provision of food and shelter at the very least.

Finally, it is at this stage essential to justify the emphasis which is being placed on the legal nature of the rights proposed. It is not self-evident that the law is the most appropriate and effective instrument. In the first place, it might be argued that the results of judicial intervention in penal administration have not been altogether encouraging. The US courts appear to have lost their enthusiasm (Aronson 1982) while that of the UK courts has been limited almost entirely to the quasi-judicial aspects of penal decision making (Chapter 3, this volume). Further, the considerable difficulties encountered in securing the implementation of judicial decrees in the US tend to reinforce the view that judges, without comprehensive backup at least, are ill equipped to oversee routine administration (Yale Law Journal 1979; Morgan and Bronstein, this volume). Second, and at a more fundamental level, important questions are now being asked concerning the legitimacy of the courts' role in the control of public authorities in general (Kamenka and Tay 1975; Unger 1976; Prosser 1982; Galligan 1982). It thus becomes important to recognize the limitations and implications of judicial intervention and to specify the extent of the proposed judicial role with some precision.

It was argued above that recognition by the law of the basic rights of prisoners is essential to the existence of an acceptable prison regime. Legal recognition implies the ultimate stamp of formal authority and carries considerable political significance. It need not, however, imply constant resort to legal adjudication. The courts should be used exclusively as a last resort, to supplement rather than supplant more informal control mechanisms. Inevitably reservations will persist concerning the ability of the courts, as presently constituted, adequately to fulfil their proposed role, but such fears can be assuaged to some extent by the enactment of rights in prisoners in a form designed to attract judicial respect. The danger of providing a spurious legitimacy for an unacceptable regime should, in this way, be outweighed by the considerable political value which would attach to the recognition by the courts of rights in prisoners.

In sum, an ideal prison regime should interfere with prisoners' options to the minimum extent necessary to contain them, should carefully specify their remaining rights and liberties and reduce these to law, and should supplement them with additional positive rights. The extent to which the present legal position resembles this ideal is a subject for later articles in this collection. It is, however, appropriate to make some general points by way of introduction.

The present position

Although Lord Wilberforce's statement in *Raymond* v. *Honey* (1982: 759), that a prisoner 'retains all civil rights which are not taken away expressly or by necessary implication', appears to accord with the above prescription, in practice, any resemblance between the position as described by Wilberforce and the ideal is fairly superficial. In the first place, the judiciary possesses extensive discretion due to the considerable uncertainty created by both the elusive legal concept of civil rights and the breadth of the phrase 'by necessary implication'. Even in the USA and under the European Convention on Human Rights, where the basic legal rights are enumerated and where derogation is permitted on specific grounds alone, the real significance of those rights is greatly dependent on the attitude of the adjudicating body (Gobert and Cohen 1981; Beaven 1979). In the absence of any such catalogue of rights the judges in the UK are arguably faced with an even more difficult task and uncertainties inevitably abound (*Malone v. Commissioner of Police of the Metropolis* 1979).

Second, the proposed regime emphasizes a form of rights which the courts are currently reluctant to recognize. Elsewhere I have argued (Richardson 1984) that rights can be usefully, if not categorically, divided into defensive and positive, and special and general. A defensive right to life, for example, implies a correlative duty in others not to kill the right-holder, while a positive right would oblige others to take active steps to keep the right-holder alive (Campbell 1983: ch. 2). Special rights arise out of special transactions or relationships, for example, between individual and state, while general rights are possessed by all (Hart 1955).

The ideal regime, as described above, would both specify the precise restrictions imposed on a prisoner's general and special rights and the exact scope of those that remain, and would vest additional special, often positive, rights in him against the prison administration. In Lord Wilberforce's account of existing law, 'civil rights' include any general legal rights possessed by all citizens and any special legal rights arising between the individual and the state. It fails, however, to mention any additional special rights possessed by prisoners against the authorities. This apparent discrepancy between the ideal and existing law becomes even more evident when recent case law is examined. As will be argued in Chapter 3, current UK law recognizes few special rights in prisoners against the authorities and those that are recognized are seldom very specific: for example, the prisoner's right that the authority take reasonable care to protect him from assault by fellow prisoners. Prisoners are frequently forced to rely instead on the claim to a *general* defensive right and here they meet with little success since the courts are reluctant to uphold a prisoner's *general* rights in the face of strong policy objections from the authorities. For example, a prisoner detained in a control unit in breach of the Prison Rules had no direct remedy for the breach. He had, instead, to claim a general right not to be unlawfully detained, and in that he failed. The authorities had strong policy reasons for wishing to divorce the question of the legality of the detention from the issue of compliance with their obligations under the Prison Rules and the court showed no desire to challenge their arguments.

In light of the above it would appear that a fundamental change in approach to the legal status of prisoners is required. A sentence of imprisonment currently imposes on the authorities a duty to imprison and, by implication, endows them with the necessary powers over the prisoner to enable them to fulfil that duty. It should instead impose not only the duty to deprive the prisoner of freedom of movement but also the duties adequately to house, feed, clothe, to provide work, educational, therapeutic and leisure facilities, etc. These duties should imply correlative special legal rights in the prisoner. In this way the law would protect the basic rights of the prisoner, as redefined by the fact of his imprisonment, and the chosen legal format, by utilizing detailed special rights, would be designed to be taken seriously by the judiciary. The exact substance of the rights will inevitably depend on agreement as to the prime purpose/s of imprisonment, but there can be little doubt that the relevant duties will be quite capable of precise stipulation (King and Morgan 1980; JUSTICE 1983; Casale 1984; and Chapter 6, this volume). The acceptability of imprisonment as a judicial penalty can only be achieved through the proper protection of a prisoner's status.

2
Prison discipline and the courts

Edward Fitzgerald

Since 1899, prisoners have been subject to an internal disciplinary code operated privately, swiftly and often unjustly within the prison walls. This code, contained within the Prison Rules, creates a series of disciplinary offences, prescribes punishments and lays down a rudimentary procedure for trial – according to the gravity of the charge – either by governors or by special tribunals of Boards of Visitors. From 1899 to 1979 this system endured relatively unchanged, apart from Parliament's belated intervention in 1967 to abolish corporal punishment. Government reports (e.g. Home Office 1951; Home Office 1975) recommended relatively minor procedural improvements but repeatedly rejected such 'radical' proposals as the introduction of legal representation for prisoners. The Home Office exercised a somewhat timid supervisory function by remitting some of the more severe penalties imposed on prisoners.

But it is only since the High Courts asserted jurisdiction over BoV adjudicatory hearings in 1979 (the *St Germain* decisions) that the atmosphere has significantly changed. The extent of the change can be gauged by a comparison of the position of a prisoner prior to 1979, and in 1984.

A prisoner in the early 1970s, like his predecessors since 1899, stood at a distance from the adjudicating panel with two prison officers facing him in close proximity (a practice known as 'eyeballing') to protect the Board from any outburst. He faced the Board without any rights except to hear the evidence and put his case. The rules were silent on the burden and standard of proof: he had no recognized right to cross-examine personally or to call his own witnesses; no right to legal representation; and no acknowledged right thereafter to challenge any decision in the courts – even where he had lost hundreds of days of remission and thus effectively been deprived of years of liberty. The system was officially described as 'inquisitorial' rather than 'adversarial', but it would have been more appropriate to use the term 'accusatorial': the psychological reality was that it was not for the prosecution to prove its case but for the prisoner to disprove it. The charge was often phrased in imprecise language, borrowed from military tribunals, which, for example, made it an offence to 'mutiny' or 'in any way offend against good order and discipline'. This left to the prison authorities and disciplinary tribunals a wide discretion as to what they chose to define as such offences.

As a result of *St Germain* and a series of subsequent standard-setting cases, a prisoner facing a Board of Visitors can now expect to be allowed to conduct his defence seated; to be provided with facilities to make notes; and, if the charge is a serious one of 'mutiny' or 'gross personal violence against an officer', he is entitled as of right to legal representation. In all other cases, he is entitled to have an application for representation considered on its merits. He also has the right to call all such witnesses in his defence as can give material evidence – even if the prison authorities must transport them from one end of the country to the other for the hearing. He is entitled to require the prosecution to prove beyond reasonable doubt its case against him. Moreover, he has an established right of review in the High Court where the Board of Visitors errs in law in its interpretation of the Prison Rules, or violates the rules of natural justice in its procedural conduct of the hearing.

From 'court martial' to court

The 1899 Prison Rules introduced the first comprehensive disciplinary code for prisons, and the 'military model' was plainly its blueprint. Efficient, centralized, institutional control called for a militaristic approach to prison discipline, with the governor as the figure of the regimental colonel, beneath him his officers and then the prisoners. Hence the language of martial law, and the governor's role as summary disciplinarian endowed with powers comparable to those of a regimental commanding officer. The Board of Visitors and the Visiting Justices, because of the very severe penalties they could impose (including the cat-o'-nine-tails), because of their function as part of the overall machinery of discipline, and because of their close identification with the institution, occupied a status somewhat analogous to a Court Martial – without the accompanying procedural safeguards. Three factors, conditioning the original rules, created obstacles to reform which would have brought the internal disciplinary system into line with the criminal justice system:

1 The prison disciplinary system, with its special prohibitions and punishments (corporal punishment, forfeiture of privileges), was conceived as a separate system, complete unto itself and immune from judicial intervention.
2 The procedures to be applied were regarded as a matter for these internal tribunals themselves.
3 Since the prohibitions they enforced were regarded as determined by the 'control' requirements of the prison system, comparisons between the interpretation of the Prison Rules and the interpretation of offences in public criminal law could be rejected as inappropriate.

But the prison disciplinary system was to be liberated from its origins by a series of High Court decisions, of which the first was *St Germain*. These decisions recognized at last that what was at stake in disciplinary hearings was the liberty of prisoners, since, as one-third remission increasingly became a *de facto* right in post-war years, the major sanction of forfeiture of remission had become tantamount to a deprivation of liberty. Once this was recognized, the momentum for reforms to bring the internal prison disciplinary system more into line with the criminal justice system became irresistible. A chronological analysis may be used to demonstrate how the transformation came about, since each new decision was to have a 'knock-on' effect.

*The pre-*St Germain *approach*

Two decisions exemplify the 'pre-*St Germain* approach' of both the domestic courts and the European Commission to the prison disciplinary code.

Kiss v. *UK* contains the first analysis of the prison code's prohibitions and sanctions. Kiss was convicted by a Board of Visitors of a charge of making false and malicious allegations against a prison officer, and sentenced to eighty days loss of remission. He complained to the European Commission of Human Rights that the hearing had constituted a violation of Article 6(1) of the European Convention on Human Rights, which guarantees a fair and public hearing of any 'criminal' charge before an impartial tribunal. The Commission rejected his submission that the determination of this disciplinary charge was, in effect, the determination of a 'criminal charge', finding that the nature of the charge made it 'disciplinary' rather than 'criminal' in its purpose and character. More significantly, the Commission found that the nature of the penalty was not such as to bring the hearing into the criminal sphere, because the remission lost was not only of a limited amount but was the loss of a privilege, and did not constitute 'deprivation of liberty'. For these reasons Article 6(1) did not apply.

Fraser v. *Mudge* (1975) was the first case in which the English Courts scrutinized the prison disciplinary code. Fraser claimed to be entitled to legal representation at a prison disciplinary hearing and the Court of Appeal found that there was no such entitlement. In the judgements of Lord Denning MR and Lord Justice Roskill, the same principles were considered to apply to both prison governors' and Boards of Visitors' disciplinary hearings: prison discipline, whether administered by the governor or the Board of Visitors, was indivisible. Viewed as such, the prison disciplinary hearing was regarded as a 'special case', analogous to a summary disciplinary hearing before a commanding officer in the armed forces. The Court thus felt able to distinguish this special type of hearing from other domestic hearings – e.g. *Pett* v. *Greyhound Racing Association (No. 1)* – in which the Court had asserted that a right to legal representation would be appropriate. A key passage of Lord Denning's judgement shows how the military analogy, with particular emphasis on the need for speedy justice, was utilized to mark Board hearings as special:

> 'We all know that, when a man is brought up before his commanding officer for a breach of discipline, whether in the armed forces or in ships at sea, it never has been the practice to allow legal representation. It is of the first importance that the

cases should be decided quickly. If legal representation were allowed, it would involve considerable delay. So also with breaches of prison discipline. They must be heard and decided speedily. Those who hear the cases must of course act fairly. They must let the man know the charge and give him a proper opportunity of presenting his own case. But that can be done and is done without the case being held up for legal representation.'
(*Fraser* v. *Mudge* 1975)

St Germain

After a prisoners' protest at Hull prison in 1976, large numbers of prisoners were charged with serious disciplinary offences and dealt with by Boards of Visitors travelling the country to conduct hearings at prisons to which they were dispersed after the riot. Several were convicted and punished with substantial awards of loss of remission (in one case totalling 720 days). St Germain and others sought judicial review in the Divisional Court on the grounds that the conduct of their hearings had violated the fundamental principles of natural justice (*St Germain* 1978). The Court tried the preliminary issue of whether it had jurisdiction to review prison disciplinary proceedings before Boards of Visitors, deciding that it did not. The reasoning of the Divisional Court was that prison disciplinary hearings, as part of a special category of disciplinary hearings, were exempt from judicial review. It accepted that, on the face of it, Boards of Visitors were discharging a 'judicial' function subject to judicial review by way of *certiorari*, but perpetuated the notion of prison disciplinary hearings as special types of hearing, by introducing a special rule excluding the conduct of disciplinary hearings within closed bodies such as the armed forces, police force, fire brigade and prisons from judicial jurisdiction. Echoes of the military analogy used in the *Fraser* v. *Mudge* judgement were clearly discernible in the following words of Cumming Bruce LJ:

> 'Where breaches of discipline take place, as in a regiment in the army or in a ship in the Royal Navy, it is necessary that the commanding officer take action quickly, firmly and justly, and that the disciplinary sanction that he determines, if any, shall be put into effect at once. . . . The same goes for the kind of disciplinary action taken by the Board of Visitors.'

The Court of Appeal, however, reversed the Divisional Court's decision, marking the end of the immunity of the prison disciplinary code from judicial review. Its decision was that the Courts had jurisdiction to ensure compliance by Boards of Visitors with the fundamental principles of natural justice.

1 It decided that, whilst conducting disciplinary hearings, Boards of Visitors were exercising a judicial function, and must act fairly and independently of the prison administration.
2 It recognized that the right of a prisoner to a full opportunity to present his own case was a right that the Courts could intervene to protect.
3 It laid to rest any lingering reliance on the grounds that remission lost at disciplinary hearings was a privilege rather than a right, recognizing the reality that a prisoner who suffered forfeiture of remission was in fact deprived of liberty he would otherwise enjoy.

The Court of Appeal left undecided the question whether hearings before prison governors, with their more limited powers of punishment, would also be susceptible to judicial review (see below).

Development of procedural rights before Boards of Visitors

Once the Court of Appeal had decided the issue of jurisdiction, the applications in *St Germain* were remitted to the Divisional Court to be decided on their merits (*St Germain* No. 2 1979). The applicants had complained of breaches of the rules of natural justice: specifically, the admission of hearsay evidence against them and the refusal to permit them to call witnesses. Counsel for the Board of Visitors denied that prisoners had any *right* to call witnesses and defended the admissibility of hearsay evidence at Boards of Visitors' hearings. This raised the question of the extent to which the rules of natural justice required the adoption of procedural and evidential rules comparable to those in the criminal courts. The Court declined to assert any general right to call witnesses whatever the circumstances, or to assert any general rule excluding hearsay. But it recognized that in this context fairness would generally require that a prisoner be allowed to call any witness with material evidence to give, and that administrative inconvenience alone could never be a reason for refusal.

With respect to the admissibility of hearsay, it was recognized that, where a prisoner wanted to question a staff witness whose evidence was being given to the Board in the form of a hearsay statement, the prisoner was entitled either to have the witness attend for cross-examination or to have the untested evidence disregarded by the Board. Thus the distinction between criminal procedure and the procedure of Boards of Visitors, who were 'masters of their own procedure', was theoretically retained. But the Court was already moving towards the recognition that 'fairness' in such hearings required a procedure very similar to that at criminal trials.

Between St Germain *and* Tarrant

In the four years between *St Germain* and the next landmark, *Tarrant* (see below), there was progress in the recognition of the special problems of prisoners and the safeguards appropriate to Boards of Visitors' hearings. In *Fox-Taylor* (1982), a conviction was quashed because of a failure by the prison authorities to draw to the attention of a prisoner the existence of a material witness who might have supported his case. In so doing, the court stressed the special problems that faced a prisoner without legal representation. In *Mealy* (1981), two convictions were quashed on the grounds of 'substantial' unfairness on the part of the Chairman, who had in both cases failed to appreciate the nature of the defence the defendant was trying to establish, and therefore arbitrarily prevented him from questioning witnesses (a prison medical officer and a governor) to establish material points. In *McConkey* (1982), a conviction was quashed on the grounds, *inter alia*, that the prisoner had not had explained to him the necessary ingredients of the alleged offence against 'good order and discipline'. Taken together these three High Court decisions furnished evidence that many Boards were not properly discharging their duty to assist prisoners in presenting their own case. Thus the case for a re-examination of the issue of legal representation was established prior to *Tarrant*.

Fraser v. *Mudge* had determined simply that there was no general (or absolute) right to legal representation at Boards of

Visitors' hearings, and consequently it was generally thought that legal representation had no place in disciplinary hearings. The Home Office and the majority of Boards of Visitors confidently relied on *Fraser* v. *Mudge* as a justification for a blanket refusal to consider legal representation at disciplinary hearings.

The background to the successful challenge to the 'no representation' rule in *Tarrant* (see later) was fourfold. First, in the wake of *St Germain*, the analogy with summary military discipline on which *Fraser* v. *Mudge* founded was undermined. It was replaced by an emphasis on the statutory duty to afford a prisoner a 'full opportunity of presenting his case' and a recognition of the serious consequences to prisoners of conviction. Second, when legal questions of interpretation arose, as for example in *McConkey*, the deficiencies of Boards in their inquisitorial functions were highlighted. Third, in the year that *Tarrant* was decided, JUSTICE (1983) emphasized the defects of Boards as adjudicating tribunals and called for the provision of legal representation for serious charges. Finally, the European Commission report in *Campbell and Fell* v. *UK* (1982) qualified the Commission's earlier decision in *Kiss* in that it found that disciplinary hearings of the especially grave offences of 'mutiny' and 'gross personal violence', which are held under the special provisions of Prison Rule 52, would attract Article 6 safeguards because of the severity of the penalties at stake – i.e. unlimited loss of remission. Article 6 safeguards included, of course, the right to legal representation (see also Fawcett Chapter 4).

Tarrant

It was against this background that the *Tarrant* case was heard in 1983. All the applicants had faced serious charges before Boards of Visitors. Tarrant and Leyland had been charged with mutiny, the others with serious charges concerning their part in disorders at Wormwood Scrubs prison. All had faced or received severe penalties for their alleged offences. And all had fallen foul of the 'no representation' rule. Their defences had raised issues of law, such as the proper scope of the offence of 'mutiny', and required the tracing of numerous witnesses dispersed throughout the prison system. The case for assistance from a legal representative was therefore very strong.

It is a tribute to the resources of the common law that the Court was able to find a way round the seeming impasse of the decision in *Fraser* v. *Mudge* and, at the same time, to harmonize its findings with the requirements of the European Convention under Article 6 (as determined by the Commission in *Campbell and Fell*). The Court accepted that *Fraser* v. *Mudge* was binding on it to the extent that there was no general right to legal representation at disciplinary hearings. But it rejected the argument that legal representation was incompatible with the inquisitorial functions of Boards of Visitors and their statutory duty to reach disciplinary decisions without undue delay. It asserted that Boards, as masters of their own procedure, had a *discretion* to grant legal representation and must so exercise it to accord with their duty to ensure that a prisoner had a 'full opportunity of presenting his case'. This implied that in serious cases, where legal issues of interpretation were almost certain to arise and the penalties were severe, the discretion would have to be exercised in the prisoner's favour. (The Court thereby ensured that prisoners would effectively enjoy a 'right' to legal representation in all Rule 52 cases, and English law would therefore conform with Article 6.) This gave rise to more general consideration of the criteria that should govern the granting of legal representation. The basic test laid down by the Court for every case was whether a prisoner would have a full opportunity of presenting his case without the assistance of a legal representative. But Mr Justice Webster laid down four further criteria to be considered in any particular case:

1 The seriousness of the charge and of the potential penalty.
2 The likelihood that points of law would arise.
3 The capacity of a prisoner to present his own case.
4 Procedural difficulties, such as the inability of prisoners to trace and interview witnesses in advance.

These factors were in each case to be weighed against two others, namely the need for reasonable speed in deciding cases and the need for fairness as between prisoner and prisoner, and between prisoner and prison officer.

By highlighting the factors that called for legal representation, Mr Justice Webster laid the foundations for future developments. Boards now tend to grant legal representation where prisoners face serious or multiple charges, particularly where the allegations are of assault or gross personal violence against a prison officer.

This has led prison officers to complain that prisoners are increasingly 'putting them on trial' by way of cross-examination designed to show that a prisoner's assault was a direct response to an assault or provocation by an officer (see, for example, the Prison Officers' Association's evidence to the Prior Committee 1984). Since the Home Office provides a governor's representative to put the case for the prosecution whenever the prisoner is granted legal representation, we are witnessing the overturn of the inquisitorial system and the birth of a new adversarial system.

A further ruling in the *Tarrant* judgement indicates that the standard of proof to be applied should match that used in the public criminal courts. In the course of the judgement, Mr Justice Webster recorded and approved a concession made by counsel for the Board of Visitors while discussing one of the supplementary issues thrown up during the hearing. This was essentially that, at Boards of Visitors' adjudications, the burden of proof was on the prosecution and the standard of proof was that of 'proof beyond reasonable doubt'. This in effect does away with the previous notion that Board hearings are inquiries into 'the truth of the matter', and relegates Boards to the discharge of the more modest function of deciding whether or not the prosecution has, in fact, proved its case. This in turn opens the way to a greater generosity with acquittals – both on technical grounds, and on grounds that the Board simply cannot be sure of the prosecution case.

Post-Tarrant: *the* Smith *case*

The case of *Smith* (1984) typifies one aspect of the new, post-*Tarrant* hearings. Smith was accused of gross personal violence against an officer, an episode which involved several violent confrontations between staff and prisoners at Dartmoor Prison, and ended with Smith being transferred to Exeter prison with a number of injuries. He was represented at the hearing and a governor's representative put the case for the prosecution. At the close of the prosecution case, Smith's representative submitted that there was no case to answer since the medical report submitted had failed to establish evidence sufficient to sustain the charge of gross personal violence. The Board ruled for Smith on this point, but announced its intention to proceed with the hearing as if it were the hearing of a lesser charge of assaulting an officer. This decision to substitute a lesser charge was challenged in the High Court and ruled unlawful on the grounds that (1) the Board itself had no jurisdiction to substitute a lesser charge and (2) the prison authorities, who were responsible for laying charges, could not themselves now lay a lesser charge because the fresh charge would not have been laid 'as soon as possible', as required by Rule 48. This was undoubtedly a highly technical acquittal, and thus serves to illustrate the new emphasis on procedural propriety.

Yet the benefits of the post-*Tarrant* sea-change do not stop here. The prosecution can now be forced to disclose key evidence – especially medical reports in assault cases – in advance. The shackles of chairmen's interference have been removed from cross-examination, which can now be conducted by trained lawyers. More important still, defence lawyers are in a position to track down witnesses, whose version of events has, in some cases, had the effect of demonstrating that the prosecution case cannot be true. The number of acquittals has consequently increased, and we are moving rapidly away from the era in which prisoners boycotted Boards of Visitors' hearings as hopeless charades, or pleaded guilty in order to avoid a flogging (Home Office Report 1951). The criminal justice model has already been proved a far better means of getting at the truth than the inquisitorial model which it has supplanted.

The definition of offences

The defeat of the 'military model' has been similarly dramatic, though not as well publicized, in the interpretation of the *substance* of the prison disciplinary code. The first case to deal with the construction of the substantive code was *McConkey* (1982). McConkey was charged with an offence against good order and discipline in that he was 'present at an illegal drug-smoking party' in another prisoner's cell. The Board convicted him without it being alleged or found that he had in any way participated in the smoking of the drug. In the High Court, counsel for the Board argued that the mere fact of presence at such an occasion was sufficient to constitute an offence. But the Court ruled that it was not. It accepted McConkey's argument that some element of positive participation had to be proved.

The repercussions of this case were very important. The decision put a stop to practices such as charging all the occupants of a cell where obscene graffiti were found on the walls, and new Prison Department circulars have stressed the need to do away with any notions of 'group responsibility'.

More important, the *McConkey* decision marked an emphatic rejection of the military analogy. In military law, the decision as to whether or not a particular course of conduct is an offence against good order and discipline is treated as an issue of fact for the relevant military tribunal to determine: mere presence at a drug-smoking party would certainly constitute such an offence. But in adopting the more liberal approach of the public criminal law, with its stress on individual culpability for any anti-social conduct alleged, Mr Justice McCullough opened the way to a fundamental reappraisal of the way the prison authorities had approached the interpretation of disciplinary offences.

The decision, however, came under challenge in *King* (1984). King had been convicted of 'having an unauthorized article in his cell' contrary to Rule 47(7), on the basis that he had been living with three others when a hypodermic needle was found and that he must have known that it was hidden there. It was not alleged or established that he personally had anything to do with the needle. The governor argued in the Divisional Court that continued presence in a cell, with knowledge that an unauthorized article was there, was sufficient to constitute a disciplinary offence. For King it was argued that this conflicted with the underlying principle established in *McConkey*, in that it allowed conviction of an offence where there was no individual responsibility on the part of the prisoner. Unless a prisoner had a positive duty to inform on his cellmates when they introduced an unauthorized article into his cell, there could be no offence. The Divisional Court rejected King's argument and held that such a duty should be imposed on prisoners: on a strict construction of the rules, a prisoner 'had an unauthorized article in his cell' contrary to the rule if he knew it was there – even if the article was owned by another. It seemed, then, that the Court had undone at a stroke all the progress achieved by *McConkey*, and signalled a return to an approach to the rules dictated by the demands of security and control.

The Court of Appeal, however, resurrected the *McConkey* principle by reversing this aspect of the Divisional Court's decision. It recognized the moral wrongness of an interpretative approach that effectively made it an offence not to inform on one's cellmate. It insisted that the words 'has in his cell an unauthorized article' had to be given their natural meaning of 'possessing' or 'exercising control over' an unauthorized article. And it adopted the approach of the Courts to criminal law offences in so far as it interpreted in those words a requirement of *mens rea* on the part of the prisoner charged with the offence.

The influence of such decisions on life in prisons cannot be underestimated. A frequent complaint by prisoners is that the prison authorities can manipulate the rules to make almost any conduct an offence should they so choose. Recent cases of Boards of Visitors convicting a prisoner of a disciplinary offence for refusing to take his hands out of his pockets and another for wearing a shamrock on St Patrick's Day are classic examples of the consequences of an elastic approach to the substance of the code of disciplinary prohibitions. But the courts' strict approach to the interpretation of the disciplinary code 'as if the offences it created were criminal offences' follows naturally from the fact that conviction of such offences can result in loss of liberty. Thus in *Tarrant*, the Divisional Court applied the common-law definition of 'mutiny' to the offence of mutiny in the prison rules. In *Anderson* (1984) it was recognized that, by analogy with the offence of criminal libel, an offence of 'making a false and malicious allegation' could not be committed by a prisoner 'in the course of communications with his solicitor, or in the course of court proceedings'. More recently in *McGrath* (1984) a conviction for 'refusing to obey a lawful order' was quashed when a prisoner had refused to remove his bed from his cell on the basis that Standing Orders had provided no authorization for the order to take his bed out of his cell. Decisions such as these have at least given prisoners confidence that arbitrary and unpredictable interpretations of the Prison Rules will not be upheld by the courts. The rule of law has at last begun to be established over the exercise of power in prisons.

Jurisdiction over governors' adjudications

One area which the 'rule of law' has not yet penetrated to a satisfactory degree is that of governors' adjudications. This has remained the last bastion of the 'special exclusionary rule' based on the military model.

Whilst the jurisdiction of the courts over Boards of Visitors' adjudications is now well-established, the question of whether the High Court would intervene to review governors' disciplinary hearings was left undecided in *St Germain*, and uncertainty persisted until the somewhat uneasy compromise arrived at in the decision of the Court of Appeal in *King* (1984, see below).

This is a very important issue, for about 96 per cent of the disciplinary charges brought against prisoners are now dealt with by prison governors in summary adjudications. It is possible to argue that to permit the courts to interfere with these decisions would undermine prison discipline and make the lives of governors intolerable. However, the argument for the assertion of judicial jurisdiction over governors' hearings is based on the twin pillars of legal logic and fundamental principle. First, it is illogical to recognize that the Courts have jurisdiction to correct procedural or substantive errors made by the Boards of Visitors, but at the same time to deny the existence of such a jurisdiction to correct the self-same errors when committed by governors operating the same disciplinary code. Second, a more fundamental objection to any jurisdictional distinction between the two types of adjudication stems from the fact that both have the power to impose sanctions which effectively deprive prisoners of their liberty. (Governors can impose up to twenty-eight days loss of remission on one charge and can also give consecutive awards.)

Prior to the Court of Appeal's decision in *St Germain No. 1* (1979), it had been held that there was no viable difference between adjudications by Boards of Visitors and those by governors; indeed, this notion of 'inseparability' was used in *Fraser* v. *Mudge* and in the Divisional Court hearing of *St Germain No. 1* (1979) as an argument for maintaining a judicial 'hands-off' approach to Board hearings. However, the Court of Appeal then seriously undermined the 'inseparability' argument. Lord Justice Megaw founded his judgement on the argument that there was a significant distinction between the two types of hearing, in that Boards were discharging the function of an independent judicial body whereas governors were merely exercising part of their overall disciplinary control. Hence, he concluded, governors should be excluded from judicial review, but Boards of Visitors should not.

Lord Justice Waller inclined to the same view. Only Lord Justice Shaw recognized that there was no valid distinction between the two types of hearing, since both were operating the same code, both were under the same statutory duty to try the case fairly, and it was the function of the courts to ensure that the rights accorded by the Acts and Statutory Instruments were respected by both bodies. The only difference was of *degree* (in that Boards could award up to 180 days loss of remission in normal circumstances, compared with governors' powers of twenty-eight days). Despite this dissenting voice, the overall effect of the judgement and the subsequent concentration of interest upon Board hearings at the expense of governors' adjudications, was to create a gradual acceptance of a distinction, an unfortunate conclusion eventually confirmed five years later in *King* (1984).

In *King*, the Court of Appeal concluded that the applicant had been wrongfully convicted of the offence of 'having an unwarranted article in his cell'. However, it decided that, though the conviction was wrong, the Courts had no jurisdiction to quash a governors' decision and that the only remedy was against the Secretary of State. This is particularly significant because in so doing, the Court (and especially Lord Justice Lawson in his judgement) effectively reasserted the special exclusionary rule for governors' hearings. To understand the extent of the retrogression brought about by this judgement it is necessary to set it against the background of the earlier conflicting judgement of Kerr LJ when the same case was heard in the Divisional Court.

Kerr LJ argued that the time had come for the Courts' well-established jurisdiction over Boards of Visitors' hearings to be extended to governors' disciplinary hearings as well. He reiterated the arguments and conclusion of Shaw LJ in *St Germain* that there was no logical distinction of jurisdictional significance between the two varieties of tribunal. He went on to say that it was clearly necessary to distinguish between a governor's *routine administrative duties* and his *special adjudicatory powers* to try offences and award punishments. In so doing, he recognized that the trend of administrative law has been to found the Courts' jurisdiction on an analysis of the *nature of the power* rather than the *character of the decision-making authority*. The only ground for departing from this principle and declining jurisdiction, he argued, was administrative convenience: namely, the supposed requirements of control in prisons. Kerr LJ was neither impressed by the argument that the

Court's assertion of jurisdiction would undermine discipline, nor prepared to let it prevail over legal logic and the demands of justice. In contrast, Mr Justice Glidewell decided to the contrary precisely on the grounds of administrative convenience and the requirements of prison discipline.

In comparison with Kerr LJ's impressive analysis and principled conclusions, the Court of Appeal's judgement in *King* represents a sorry attempt at compromise between legal logic and administrative convenience. The Court decided – essentially on grounds of expediency, backed up by the military analogy – that governors' disciplinary decisions were not in themselves susceptible to judicial review. But recognizing that it would be intolerable for the Courts to do nothing when a prisoner was wrongly deprived of remission by wrongful conviction, it proposed an alternative remedy that would preserve the inviolability of prison governors themselves from judicial review. Thus it was proposed that a prisoner alleging wrongful conviction by a governor must first challenge the decision by petitioning the Secretary of State; and if the Secretary of State fails to correct the error *the prisoner should seek judicial review of the Secretary of State's, not the governor's, decision*. This restricted method of review has no logical basis, and may in some cases seriously impede the effectiveness of the prisoner's appeal.

Conclusion

The landmark decisions of the Court of Appeal in *St Germain (No. 1)* initiated a process leading to the integration of the prison disciplinary administration into the general body of public law, and brought about a chain reaction whereby the Courts were driven by the momentum of each successive decision to superimpose upon a system derived from a military model the more sophisticated and appropriate standards and principles applied in the public criminal courts. The decision in *King* represents an attempt to stem the tide of change and prevent it from sweeping away not just the Board of Visitors' hearing as it was before 1979, but also the governor's hearing as it has been since 1899. But it is unlikely to achieve the desired effect. For despite the limited mechanism of review proposed, the governor's hearing is now effectively susceptible to judicial review, and the introduction of judicial review to this vast and hitherto untouched area is likely to lead to an improvement in procedural standards and a rethink by the prison authorities as to the wisdom of bringing any of the more controversial lesser charges which tend to increase tension and exacerbate feelings of bitterness in prisoners. There can be no doubt that in the field of disciplinary hearings, the recognition of the prison authorities' accountability to the Courts has improved, and will continue to improve, the lot of prisoners.

3

Judicial intervention in prison life

Genevra Richardson

The present legal relationship between a prisoner and the prison authorities is essentially similar to that which exists between any private individual and a public body with power to affect his or her interests. Thus, as is the case whenever a public authority is party to legal proceedings, the court will be faced with the need to determine the weight to attach to the position of the authority. A public authority, by definition, will be entrusted with the performance of some public function and there is an argument that the performance of that function should not be unduly inhibited by the need to accommodate private interests. On the other hand, since public authorities can exercise immense power over individuals there might be an argument that the interests of the individual require special protection (Harlow 1980; Samuels 1983). In Chapter 1 it was argued that because of the particular vulnerability of a prisoner's position the law should be designed specifically to protect those of his basic rights which are not inevitably removed by the fact of imprisonment and should recognize special rights in addition to those possessed by non-prisoners. The purpose of this chapter is to examine the current judicial attitude to prisoners' claims against the authorities in order to assess the court's potential as a guardian of prison conditions and, particularly, to consider the nature of the balance struck between the requirements of the administration and the individual interest of the prisoners, and to assess the significance attached to the form of the 'right' claimed by the prisoner.

As is the case with any public authority, the law provides two means whereby a prisoner may take action against the prison authorities. If the prison management, without legal authority, inflicts injury on a prisoner which would be actionable if inflicted by one individual on another, the injured prisoner may bring a claim in *private* law against the authority as if it were any other private defendant. In addition a prisoner may challenge the legality of any action taken by the authorities in pursuit of a statutory power or duty, a *public* law claim. Private actions by prisoners against the authorities will be considered first.

Private law

Claims by prisoners alleging that they have suffered injury as the result of the negligence of the prison authorities appear to form the largest category of private law claims. It is well-established that the authorities owe a duty of reasonable care to the prisoners in their custody and in the event of a breach of that duty a prisoner can claim damages for any injury caused (*Ellis* v. *Home Office* 1953; *Christofi* v. *Home Office* 1975). The prisoner thus possesses the same general right as any other individual that no one cause him damage through their negligence, and the authorities, like any other individual, are under a duty not to be negligent. However, in determining both the extent of the duty owed to the prisoner and the existence of the breach, the special relationship between the prisoner and the authorities will be taken into account. In certain respects the nature of this relationship will be interpreted to the advantage of the prisoner. Because of the degree of control exercised by the authorities over the movement of prisoners, the former are regarded as being under a duty to protect one prisoner from the attacks of another (*Ellis*). This duty, for which it is hard to find a precise parallel elsewhere in the common law, arises out of the particular relationship and may be regarded as a special duty giving rise to a special right in the prisoner.

By contrast, the courts have not been so generous when it comes to injuries 'at work'. Outside prisons liability for injuries sustained at work is largely covered by the Factories Act 1961: the employer is placed under a duty to take certain precautions and the employee is entitled to damages in the event of a breach causing him injury. However, the courts have denied that the Factories Act applies to prisons (*Pullen* v. *The Prison Commissioners* 1957) and have further denied the existence of the common law relationship of master and servant (*Davis* v. *The Prison Commissioners* 1963). The prisoner injured in the prison workshops has, therefore, to rely on the general principles of negligence. On the face of it, the law deprives prisoners of special rights which would apply outside prison and does so with little justification since there is no apparent conflict between the purposes of imprisonment and the objectives of either the Factories Act or the common law rules. In practice, of course, a prisoner injured 'at work' may receive ex gratia compensation, and the Home Office has called upon governors to observe not only the provisions of the Health and Safety at Work Act 1974, which it does regard as binding, but also 'any other statutory provisions relevant to . . . the working conditions . . . for prisoners and staff' (Standing Order 15.1). Welcome as such an attitude may be, however, it can provide no real substitute for the legal rights of which the prisoner is deprived.

Even where the courts have recognized special rights and duties, however, judgement for the prisoner is by no means automatic. A breach of the duty leading to damage must be established first. In many of the cases concerning injuries inflicted by other prisoners it is evident that the courts have been unwilling to impose too onerous a burden on the authorities (*Ellis*; *Anderson* v. *Home Office* 1965). The problems of staff resources and administrative convenience are given greater weight than the right of the individual not to be vulnerable to attack. In one case (*Egerton* v. *Home Office* 1978) an ex-Rule 43 sex-offender was beaten up by other prisoners. The attack took place when sixty prisoners were being supervised by about five officers, none of whom knew the plaintiff's history. The court held that, although the officers should have been told of the plaintiff's history, there was no breach of duty since the spontaneous attack could not reasonably have been anticipated. In the one case where the authorities were held liable for an attack by other prisoners it is interesting to note that the finding was made by a jury (*D'Arcy* v. *The Prison Commissioners* 1955).

Occasionally the private actions of prisoners bring the courts into direct contact with currently controversial issues within prison administration. *Freeman* v. *Home Office* (1984), a case ultimately brought in trespass rather than negligence, raised the whole question of proper provision of medical treatment within prison. Over the last few years concern has been mounting over the standard of health care in prisons (Cohen and Taylor 1978: 59; Fitzgerald and Sim 1982: 82, 117). The debate has been embittered by allegations concerning the forcible administration of drugs to prisoners, but strong arguments have emerged for the replacement of the prison medical service by the National Health Service (Cohen and Taylor 1978: 63–4; for an alternative see Brazier 1982).

Freeman alleged that he had been given drugs against his will and claimed damages against the Home Office in trespass. His evidence that he had been physically held down and injected was not accepted, but he went on to argue, among other things, that even if he had 'consented' that consent was inadequate because as a prisoner he was unable in law to 'consent' to treatment by a member of the prison medical staff due to the relationship of control that existed between them. The court, however, was unimpressed. It recognized the risks inherent in the prison setting, but held that, although the courts should be aware of those risks when assessing the validity of any 'consent', the nature of the relationship would not automatically disable the prisoner from giving true consent.

Given Freeman's apparent lack of credibility coupled with the law's attitude to the liability of doctors in general (*Sidaway* v. *Bethlem Royal Hospital* 1985) the eventual outcome of the case is perhaps unsurprising. It is, however, worth noting that the court was much impressed by the difficulties that would flow from any indication that lawful consent was impossible under the present system and that it was unwilling to develop principles to protect prisoners from the special pressures of prison life despite the example of the Mental Health Act 1983. It undertook merely to be 'alive to the risk' and the prison medical service emerged relatively unscathed.

All the remaining private law claims raise a single central issue which underlies many prisoners' actions in both private and public law: the legal status of the Prison Rules (SI 1964 No. 388 as amended). Duties imposed by statute, including delegated legislation, can, if breached, give rise to rights in the affected individual: he or she may bring an action in the private law of tort for breach of statutory duty and claim damages for injuries arising from a failure to meet the duty. The Factories Act, for example, provides employees with such special rights against their employers. In any context the court's decision whether to recognize such rights will inevitably involve a question of statutory interpretation and will depend on the judge's view of the intentions of the legislature. As regards the Prison Rules, a piece of delegated legislation, it is clear that policy arguments have played a significant part in the court's attitude: 'it would be fatal to all discipline in prisons if governors and wardens had to perform their duties always with the fear of an action before their eyes if they in any way deviated from the rules' (Lord Goddard, *Arbon* v. *Anderson* 1943: 255). Accordingly, the courts have so far denied that the Prison Rules vest prisoners with any special rights. An action for breach of statutory duty is not available in the event of the authority's non-compliance with the Prison Rules (Tettenborn 1980; Zellick 1981, 1982).

The practical impact of this judicial attitude has been extremely significant. The Prison Rules constitute the most detailed publically available statement of the powers and duties of the prison authorities, yet prisoners have been effectively deprived of any direct private law means of ensuring the authorities' compliance. For example, a prisoner who believed that the control unit in which he had been detained had been set up and operated in breach of the Prison Rules could not claim directly for breach of statutory duty, but had instead to allege false imprisonment. In the event, even that device failed (*Williams* v. *Home Office* (No. 2) 1981). The court held that the detention of a convicted prisoner in prison is justified in law by the sentence of the court and by section 12(1) of the Prison Act 1952 and, further, that that detention cannot become unlawful (i.e. false imprisonment) merely because of the conditions in which it is served (i.e. in a control unit rather than an ordinary prison). The court did, however, agree that the control unit had been operated in breach of the Prison Rules. But it followed from the court's own reasoning that such a breach could not affect the legality of Williams' confinement in the unit.

The rather timorous approach to the Prison Rules apparent in *Williams* is typical of that commonly displayed by the courts but should be contrasted to the much more robust attitude adopted by the House of Lords in *Raymond* v. *Honey* (1982). In that case, there was no question of breach of statutory duty.

Rather the House of Lords confirmed that the governor of Albany prison was in contempt when he prevented Raymond, a prisoner, from lodging an application with the High Court. With regard to the Prison Rules the case is significant in that the Lords were prepared to subject the Rules to the same constitutional principles as apply to other pieces of delegated legislation. Specifically, the court held that since the Prison Act 1952 does not expressly authorize the removal of unimpeded access to the court, any attempt to impede such access through the Prison Rules would be *ultra vires*. This conclusion, although not startling in itself, does illustrate a willingness in the highest appellate court to challenge the Home Office's interpretation of the Prison Rules. It is, therefore, particularly unfortunate that the substantive issues in *Williams* never reached appeal. Admittedly there is nothing in the more recent case of *O'Reilly* v. *Mackman* (1982) to suggest that their lordships might be prepared to overturn judicial orthodoxy regarding the general status of the Prison Rules, but the issue is crucial and direct consideration of it by the House of Lords is long overdue.

It is evident from the above cases that only very rarely have the courts been prepared to hold that the special relationship between the prisoner and the authorities imposes additional obligations on the latter in private law. Consequently, the majority of private law claims involve the assertion by the prisoner of a general right against the authorities, e.g. the right that no one injure him through their negligence. In particular, the insistence of the courts that the Prison Rules create no special rights in prisoners effectively forces prisoners to resort to the assertion of general rights. Thus Williams, deprived of any special right to damages for breach of the Rules, had instead to claim a general right that the authorities refrain from unlawfully imprisoning him. As we have seen, his claim failed. Pullen, placed in a similar position by the court's refusal to apply the provisions of the Factory Act providing special rights, also failed in his attempt to establish an alternative general right.

It is further evident from the cases that even when a special right is recognized, as with the right to reasonable protection from attack by other prisoners, it is extremely hard to establish a breach of the corresponding duty on the part of the prison authorities due to the lack of specificity in the special right.

In one case, however, the prisoner did succeed in establishing a general right: Raymond successfully claimed a general right that no one impede his access to the court. His was undoubtedly an important victory which has spawned further successes on the part of prisoners. However, the circumstances of the case could be said to have invited judicial intervention. A major constitutional principle was at stake and the courts' own independence was threatened. It would, therefore, be unwise to regard *Raymond* v. *Honey* as sufficient evidence on its own of a new enthusiasm on the part of the senior judiciary for the concept of prisoners' rights.

In sum, the public interest in the smooth running of the prison system is commonly accorded greater weight than the interests of individual inmates and the absence of well-defined special rights in prisoners serves merely to reinforce this ordering of priorities. There is a marked reluctance to recognize rights in prisoners in any form which would enhance the court's potential as an overseer of prison conditions.

Public law

An individual who feels aggrieved by the behaviour of a public authority, but has suffered no injury to a private right, is still able to test the validity of the authority's actions in public law by way of judicial review. This method of challenge is frequently all that is available to a prisoner due to the court's refusal to regard the Prison Rules as a source of special rights in private law (*O'Reilly* v. *Mackman* 1982; Birkinshaw 1983). The procedure for judicial review does, however, entail certain disadvantages for the applicant, including a time limit of three months (Supreme Court Act 1981, s. 31), which can make the public/private law distinction crucial. According to Lord Diplock (*O'Reilly* v. *Mackman*) these restrictions are essential in order to protect public authorities, and certainly their presence indicates a sympathy in the law for the plight of public authorities.

Setting aside the procedural implications, however, it is necessary to consider how the courts have dealt with the substance of the public law claims brought by prisoners: how willing have the courts been to adjudicate upon the conditions within prisons? How have they resolved conflicts between the interests of prisoners and the requirements of the administration? To what extent have they recognized rights in prisoners?

From the reported cases it is evident that certain aspects of prison life have attracted judicial intervention more readily than others. Since St Germain's success in 1979 (*St Germain* (No. 2) 1979) the courts have been quite prepared to oversee the disciplinary function of Boards of Visitors by reviewing the legality of their determinations. Boards of Visitors have been held to be bound by the rules of natural justice (*St Germain* (No. 2) 1979), they have been empowered to allow prisoners legal representation and in certain circumstances will be required to do so (*Tarrant* 1984) and their interpretation of the Prison Rules has been corrected (*McConkey* 1982; *Smith* 1984). The many issues raised by the whole question of disciplinary hearings have been dealt with in detail in Chapter 2. Nevertheless, it is necessary at this stage to discuss some general points.

In the first place, it is useful to examine the nature of the rights at issue. In the above cases prisoners successfully claimed special rights against their Boards of Visitors in public law and had their disciplinary awards declared invalid as a result of the Boards' failure to meet the duties imposed by those rights. In *St Germain* and *Tarrant* the right imposed a duty to comply with certain procedural requirements, while in *McConkey* and *Smith* the prisoners claimed the right not to be punished save in accordance with the strict interpretation of the Prison Rules.

In contrast to this evident willingness to review the legality of the decisions of Boards of Visitors and to recognize rights in prisoners *vis-à-vis* the Boards, it is extremely interesting to note the court's current attitude both to disciplinary hearings before governors and to decisions of the parole board. As described in Chapter 2, the Court of Appeal has refused directly to review disciplinary hearings before governors even when loss of remission is involved (*King* 1984). In law it is virtually impossible to distinguish governors' hearings from those of Boards of Visitors, as Browne-Wilkinson LJ in the Court of Appeal recognized, and indeed the actual error made by the governor in *King* was of a type which would normally render the decision of a public authority completely invalid.

In *King*, therefore, the court recognized the illegality but refused to intervene, declaring that the proper course was for the prisoner to petition the Home Secretary and then, if necessary, challenge the legality of the Home Secretary's ruling. With regard to parole decisions the courts have denied the presence of any illegality. In *Payne* v. *Lord Harris of Greenwich* (1981) a prisoner sought declarations against the chairman of the parole board and of the local review committee, and against the Home Secretary that their decision to refuse to release him on licence was reached in breach of natural justice and, specifically, that he was entitled to be given reasons for the eventual refusal. The Court of Appeal unanimously rejected Payne's arguments. More recently, the Appeal Court has refused to declare that a life sentence prisoner released on licence is entitled under s.62(3) of the Criminal Justice Act 1967 to be told the reasons for his recall in any specific form, nor, according to the Divisional Court, is he entitled to an oral hearing before the parole board (*Gunnell* 1984). Both *Payne* and *Gunnell* involved the interpretation of the statutory requirements relating to the grant and revocation of parole but, arguably, there is ample authority in the common law to have enabled the courts to supplement the statutory procedures had they wished to do so (Richardson 1984). In the event, both courts chose to judge the standard of legality by the statute alone.

On an analytical level, *Payne* and *Gunnell* are similar to *St Germain* and *Tarrant*. In relation to both remission and parole the authorities have, in certain circumstances, the power to release a prisoner and, in respect of parole, the prisoner can obtain an express right to be considered for release by the parole board (SI 1967 No 1462 Rules 5 and 6(1)). However, whereas in the case of remission the courts are prepared to impose certain procedural requirements on the body empowered to delay release (the Boards of Visitors), they have refused to so supplement the statutory obligations of the parole board. Prisoners apparently possess special rights before Boards of Visitors which they do not enjoy *vis-à-vis* the parole board.

In the absence of any significant analytical distinction between remission and parole on the one hand and between Boards of Visitors' and governors' hearings on the other, it becomes necessary to look elsewhere for the reasons for the courts' attitude. Indeed it is perfectly clear from the judgements that the decision not to intervene in *King*, despite undoubted illegality, and the failure to find illegality in *Payne* were both strongly influenced by the courts' attitude towards the policy implications. In relation to the duty to give reasons in *Payne*, Lord Denning asserted: 'in the end I think the problem comes down to this: what does public policy demand as best to be done? To give reasons or withhold them?' and concluded that 'in the interests of society at large' it is best to withhold them (*Payne* 1981: 846). Similarly, in *King* the Court of Appeal was conscious of the governor's essentially managerial role within a prison and was anxious not to undermine his authority by allowing judicial review of his disciplinary determinations: all prisons 'are likely to have [prisoners] who delude themselves that they are the victims of injustice. To allow such men to have access to the High Court whenever they thought that the Governor abused his powers, failed to give them a fair hearing or misconstrued the prison rules, would undermine and weaken his authority and make management very difficult indeed' (*King* 1984: 902). The public law (it seems) must not be allowed to encroach too far on the management of prisons. The public interest in the smooth running of the system apparently outweighs the prisoner's individual interest in speedily ensuring the lawful determination of a disciplinary charge against him.

Finally, it is possible to draw certain conclusions from the variations in judicial attitude. The courts evidently feel that the functions performed by the various bodies differ significantly. Boards of Visitors, when determining disciplinary charges, are seen as quasi-judicial bodies, whereas the governor is a predominantly managerial figure and the parole board is a panel of experts performing an administrative task. This classification of functions into quasi-judicial and administrative was discredited in the 1960s (*Ridge* v. *Baldwin* 1964) but is still occasionally revived when courts need convenient labels with which to justify their action or lack of it: a function is quasi-judicial if intervention is favoured, administrative if not. It is a distinction which illustrates the courts' underlying view of the purpose of public law. The more judicial and thus familiar the role of the authority, the more applicable the courts feel their intervention to be (and presumably the more deserving of protection as legal rights are the interests of affected individuals). Substantial areas of 'administrative' decision-making within prisons are thus effectively removed from judicial scrutiny and even though they may affect the liberty of the subject (parole and remission) they do not apparently concern legally recognized rights.

Apart from the introduction of judicial review to Boards of Visitors' hearings, judicial activity has had most practical effect in the area of prisoners' correspondence and access to lawyers, both issues which are crucial to the efficiency of the courts as enforcers of standards within prisons. Admittedly, the incentives have come mainly from Strasbourg, but the British courts have not been silent.

As a result of pressure from Strasbourg (see Fawcett Chapter 4) the Home Office introduced a so-called 'simultaneous ventilation rule' to replace the old 'prior ventilation rule' which used to govern correspondence between prisoners and their lawyers. The new rule prohibited visits from and letters to lawyers containing complaints about prison treatment which the prisoner had not mentioned internally (Standing Order 5A(34) and 5B(34)(j)). In *Anderson* (1984) the validity of the rule was challenged.

Anderson wanted to pursue a private law action for assault against the authorities but his solicitor was prevented from visiting him on the grounds that he had initiated no internal complaint. The court rejected the Home Office argument that it was 'fundamental to the good order and discipline of a prison that complaints about prison treatment are communicated to the Governor as soon as they arise' and held that the simultaneous ventilation rule constituted an impediment to the right of access to the courts. In an exhibition of unusual enthusiasm for the rights of prisoners Goff LJ allowed Anderson's general rights to prevail over arguments of administrative convenience: 'there is no room for the type of balancing operation proposed by counsel for the respondents. If any restriction . . . constitutes an impediment to the right of access to the courts, it is on the authority of [*Raymond* v. *Honey*] unauthorized by the Prison Rules 1964 or indeed by s.47(1) of the Prison Act 1952' (*Anderson* 1984: 928).

Thus, as a result of judicial pressure, both European and domestic, prisoners have been granted much freer access to lawyers, and may certainly feel encouraged by the uncompromising stance taken by the court on the policy arguments put forward by the Home Office in *Anderson*. However, although Anderson and Raymond took different routes to the courts, the substantive points raised were similar. *Anderson* is in effect son of *Raymond* and the same reservations as to the wisdom of regarding *Raymond* as illustrative of a new judicial willingness to intervene apply. Both cases presented the courts with a direct threat to their independence and, arguably, were thus more likely than most prisoners' claims to attract judicial sympathy.

When the official decision under challenge is in no sense judicial nor directly threatening to principles jealously protected by the judiciary, prisoners have met with less success, as has been seen in relation to the parole board and governors' hearings. Another example of judicial shyness is provided by *McAvoy* (1984). McAvoy was being held on remand in London to face trial for his alleged part in a £26 million gold bullion robbery. In June 1984 he was transferred without warning to Winchester prison. As a result his invalid parents, solicitor and counsel all found it extremely difficult to visit him due to the distance and the poor visiting facilities in Winchester. McAvoy claimed that the transfer was unlawful since the Secretary of State had failed to give due weight to his general 'rights' to freedom of association and to a fair trial, as reflected in the Prison Rules concerning lay and legal visits (Rules 34(i) and 37(i)). The Secretary of State, for his part, claimed that he was acting under powers granted by the Prison Act, section 12(2), the exercise of which was not subject to review by the courts. Webster J rejected this latter submission: transfer decisions are reviewable and the obligations contained in the Prison Rules must be taken into account. However, if, as in McAvoy's case, 'operational and security' reasons are claimed for the transfer, then the court should not look behind those reasons which will almost invariably outweigh the prisoner's right to visits, lay or legal.

This case is interesting since it indicates a willingness to review the legality of an administrative/managerial decision. More specifically, by returning to the primary source of the power in question – the Prison Act – and inquiring whether it had been exercised with sufficient regard to the obligations contained in the Prison Rules, the court ostensibly provided for the indirect enforcement of the Prison Rules. However, the right recognized in the prisoner was merely to have the authority's obligation to allow him to receive certain visits taken into account. The possible alternative of a justifiable right to receive visits was not pursued, and in the event the court bowed before the Home Secretary's evocation of 'operational and security reasons'. The Secretary of State had apparently fulfilled his obligations by giving *thought* to the question of visits and *priority* to security. The dispute, of course, brings into focus the whole dilemma of conflicting rights. It is not suggested here that a prisoner should possess an absolute right to visits, overriding all security considerations: the submission is rather that the court's approach was weighted too heavily in favour of security and 'operational' factors, especially in light of the court's apparent reluctance to examine the Home Secretary's claims. The right in fact recognized in the prisoner was insufficiently rigorous in form to win the prisoner's interests much priority.

A final example of judicial reluctance to intervene is provided by the House of Lord's recent refusal to upset the Home Secretary's new parole policy (*Findlay* 1984). At the Conservative Party Conference in October 1983 the Home Secretary announced that he intended to exercise his discretion under the Criminal Justice Act 1967 in order to ensure that all prisoners serving over five years for violence or drug trafficking would not be released on licence until a few months before their remission date unless the circumstances are 'genuinely exceptional', and further that certain categories of murderer would normally serve at least twenty years. (For a discussion of release procedures for lifers see Maguire, Pinter and Collis 1984.)

Two fixed-term prisoners and two lifers directly affected by this change of policy sought to challenge its legality. They contended that the Home Secretary's initial failure to consult the parole board was fatal to the legality of his subsequent policy and that the policy itself was unlawful since it was contrary to the implied statutory requirement of individual consideration in each case free from preordained policies. Although one High Court judge and one Appeal Court judge had found for the prisoners, the House of Lords unanimously rejected their claims. Lord Scarman declared that there was no implied statutory duty on the Home Secretary to consult the parole board, nor was it 'unreasonable' for the Home Secretary initially to devise his policy without regard to the views of the board. He further concluded that the Home Secretary was free to deny parole to certain categories of offender if he felt that deterrence, retribution, and public confidence so demanded and provided each case was examined for the presence of any exceptional circumstances.

It is not appropriate here to pursue all the legal implications of such a judgement, suffice it to say that their Lordships chose a most moderate path through the notoriously variable principles governing the judicial review of administrative/executive discretion (Richardson 1985). More significant for present purposes is the light thrown by the case on the nature of parole. The new policy has greatly emphasized the executive element within the system and consequently in relation to certain categories of prisoner, has reduced the parole board's role to the search for 'exceptional circumstances'. Further, according to Forbes J, it has 'impinge[d] on and distort[ed] the judicial function of consistent sentencing'. The Home Secretary has effectively abolished parole for certain classes of prisoner and, while a significant body of opinion might favour the abolition of the present parole system, selective abolition by executive announcement is hardly the solution most critics would advocate.

Finally, individual prisoners still retain their statutory right to consideration for release, but it is a right to consideration 'in the light of whatever policy the Secretary of State sees fit to adopt' (*Findlay* 1984: 830). Thus, if the Home Secretary considers that public confidence demands the denial of parole to certain categories of offender, then the prisoner's right is reduced to the search for exceptional circumstances, and such circumstances can be most elusive. Indeed the court refused to regard the circumstances of the two lifers in *Findlay* as exceptional. Both had been transferred to open prisons prior to October 1983 in the tacit expectation of impending release but had been returned to closed conditions immediately prior to the Home Secretary's announcement. They cannot now expect release before 1989 and 1993 respectively at the earliest.

Conclusions

In Chapter 1, it was claimed that the recognition of additional rights in prisoners was essential to the existence of an acceptable prison regime and it was suggested that the courts could provide a vital final forum for the adjudication of disputes arising over prison conditions. At first glance, however, the recent case law does little to encourage confidence in the court's enthusiasm for such a task. The practical interpretation of Lord Wilberforce's brave statement can offer the prisoner little satisfaction. Private law has been slow to recognize special rights in prisoners and, even when it has appeared to do so (as in *Egerton*, concerning inter-prisoner violence), the right has been so conditional as to be of little practical value. Similarly, in the field of public law the arguments of administrative necessity have commonly outweighed the interests of the individual prisoner (*Payne*, *King*, *McAvoy* and *Gunnell*). A prisoner's general rights have prevailed only when they have related to issues of particular interest to the judiciary (*Anderson*), while effective special rights have been recognized only where the challenged decision is seen as quasi-judicial and the courts are able to apply a body of familiar principle (*St Germain* and *Tarrant*).

Such conclusions, however, should not be allowed to destroy the case for judicial intervention. As argued in Chapter 1, judicial enthusiasm for the task of overseeing prison conditions would be increased by the legislative recognition of specific rights in prisoners in a form designed to be taken seriously by the judges. Recent case law would suggest that prisoners will meet with most success when they can establish specific special rights, as in relation to claims to natural justice before Boards of Visitors. It can thus be argued that the formal recognition of similar rights in prisoners in other contexts would significantly influence judicial attitudes.

The recognition of enforceable special rights in prisoners arising from the Prison Rules would be a useful first step but, as has been argued elsewhere (Zellick 1981), the Rules are not drafted in a particularly suitable form. More specificity is needed. The case of *McAvoy* can be used to illustrate the argument. In that case the existence of a justiciable right to lay and legal visits under the Prison Rules was not pursued, but, even if recognized, such a right would not have been absolute since the wording of the Rules vests the authorities with extensive unstructured discretion. Indeed, under the present law, the right to have visits considered is perhaps all the prisoner could expect, and we have seen how impotent such a right can be in practice. An absolute right to visits, however, would not necessarily be the answer, as it could give rise to legitimate resource and/or security problems. Instead, a solution might be found by imposing an enforceable duty on the authorities both to provide space and time for visits, and to house a remand prisoner within convenient distance of his lawyer except in specified circumstances which can readily be verified by a court, *in camera* if necessary. By refining the specificity of the rights and duties it is possible to define away most conflict (Cottingham 1984) and to provide clear principles to structure the residual discretion. Prisoners should possess special rights *vis-à-vis* the prison authorities in a sufficiently detailed form to promote effective supervision by the courts.

4

Applications of the European Convention on Human Rights

Sir James Fawcett

The European Convention on Human Rights was inspired in the Council of Europe by the belief that there was in its member countries a sufficiently 'common heritage of political traditions, ideals, freedom, and the rule of law' to allow the Governments of European countries 'to take the first steps for the collective enforcement of certain of the Rights stated in the Universal Declaration'.[1] The Convention was drafted in 1949–50, and came into force on September 3, 1953, between eight member countries. All twenty-one members of the Council of Europe are now parties to it.[2]

The Convention is composed of statements of the rights and freedoms which the contracting parties 'shall secure to everyone within their jurisdiction' (Article 2) and of provisions establishing the structure and competence of the European Commission of Human Rights and the European Court of Human Rights, 'to ensure the observance of the engagements undertaken' by the contracting parties under the Convention (Article 19). Thirteen of the Convention countries have incorporated the Convention in their internal law,[3] which means that its provisions can be invoked and directly enforced in their courts. In several countries, too, the Convention has constitutional status ranking as 'higher law', in relation to subsequent (and sometimes to all) statutes.[4] The United Kingdom, however, has not yet taken any of these steps.

Procedures

The machinery of accountability under the Convention consists of interstate applications and individual petitions. Any party to the Convention may refer to the Commission[5] any alleged breach of provisions of the Convention by another party, but not surprisingly such applications by governments are infrequent.[6] Individual petitions may be brought by any person, group of individuals, or non-governmental organization against any party to the Convention that has recognized the right of individual petition (this right is currently recognized by all the Convention countries except Malta, Greece, Cyprus and Turkey). Such an application may be brought only by a victim of an alleged breach of the Convention – no *actio popularis* is possible as under the interstate procedure – and only after all domestic remedies have been exhausted. It must also be brought within six months of any final domestic decision. Domestic remedies will be discussed further below.

The Commission has the first task of deciding whether an application is admissible. In particular, it must not be anonymous, there must be clear evidence of the exhaustion of any domestic remedies that are available and effective, and the complaint must be against the act or conduct of some public authority, whether central or local, administrative or judicial. Further the application must relate to some provision of the Convention, and must not be 'manifestly ill-founded', that is, the facts presented must show *prima facie* that there is a breach of the Convention, and there must be no 'abuse of the right of petition' (Article 27). Over the last few years, the Commission has been opening approximately 2,500–3,000 provisional files annually in response to applications or inquiries, and has officially registered annually 350–500 applications. A certain backlog has developed, and at the end of 1983 there were 780 registered applications pending before the Commission (Council of Europe 1984). Well over 90 per cent of registered applications are eventually declared inadmissible – a figure understandable in a system of free application.

Applications from UK citizens have always provided a significant proportion of the total. For example, in 1983, 785 (25 per cent) of the 3,150 provisional files opened and 152 (30 per cent) of the 499 applications registered were from this source. Moreover, prisoners or other persons held in detention have always been one of the major groups using the system. The table below shows the percentage of registered applications emanating from people in detention for selected years between 1955 and 1983. It can be seen that from a peak during the 1960s both the number and proportion of such applications has fallen substantially (particularly over the last five years), but that detention still forms an important area of the Commission's work.

Registered applications: selected years, 1955–83

year	*number of applications registered*	*applicants in detention: number*	*%*
1955	138	24	17
1958	96	22	24
1961	344	114	33
1964	293	137	47
1967	445	219	49
1970	379	133	35
1973	442	202	46
1976	427	197	46
1979	378	90	24
1980	390	87	22
1981	404	84	21
1982	590	91	15
1983	499	60	12

Source: European Commission of Human Rights (1983).

The task of the Commission on admitted applications is to investigate them and to try to reach a settlement. The investigation can be prolonged; essential information on the facts, the applicable law, and administrative practice is obtained from the applicant and the Government concerned, and their respective arguments about the relevant Convention provisions are presented, often in a hearing in which both the applicant and Government representatives[7] participate. The applicant can be legally represented throughout the application and may obtain legal aid from the Council of Europe. After deliberations, the Commission arrives at a provisional opinion as to whether or not there has been any breach of the Convention shown in the application, and this opinion is communicated to both sides for the purpose of bringing about a friendly settlement, if possible. Such a settlement rests essentially on exchanges between applicant and Government, and the Commission will approve it provided there is no inconsistency with the Convention: for example, a Government could not preserve a bad administrative practice, contrary to the Convention, by simply buying off a particular applicant with compensation. It should also be stressed that the members of the Commission are not Government representatives, and all its proceedings are confidential, a principle giving considerable freedom of action, including disclosure of information, to both applicant and Government.

If there is no settlement, the Commission takes a final decision by majority vote on breach or no breach of the Convention, and sends a full report of the facts, the procedure followed, and its final *opinion*, to the Committee of Ministers of the Council of Europe, it being the latter's task under the Convention to decide by a two-thirds majority whether there has been a breach of the Convention. The usual practice has been to go along with the Commission report.

Within three months of submission of the Commission report to the Committee of Ministers the case may be referred by either the Commission or the Government concerned to the European Court of Human Rights: no individual can bring a case before the Court, and, if a case is brought, the applicant participates in the proceedings under the wing of the Commission. The Court is composed of one judge from each Convention country, and its jurisdiction is recognized under the Convention by all, except Malta and Turkey. The parties to the Convention 'undertake to abide by the decision of the Court in any case to which they are parties' (Article 53), but its judgements are not enforceable in the same sense as those of the European Court of Justice.[8] Court cases are relatively few in number. By the end of 1983, 72 cases had been sent to the Court, of which about 15 involved imprisonment or its conditions. Four of the latter emanated from the United Kingdom.

Prisons and the Convention

The Convention contains a number of Articles relevant to imprisonment, and various principles have been developed over the years. We may now examine these and illustrate them by reviewing some characteristic applications brought under the Convention. They will be discussed under the broad categories of (1) grounds for detention and (2) conditions of imprisonment.

1 GROUNDS FOR DETENTION

Two general principles governing the grounds for detention are set out in Article 5 of the Convention:

> 'No one shall be deprived of his liberty save . . . in accordance with a procedure prescribed by law';

and

> 'Everyone who is deprived of his liberty by arrest or detention shall be entitled to take proceedings by which the lawfulness of his detention shall be decided speedily by a court and his release ordered if his detention is unlawful.'

Most applications involving detention raise the issue of its lawfulness. An application against the United Kingdom involving detention in a secure mental hospital in England[9] provides a useful illustration of the greater scope in practice which exists in the European Court in comparison with the British courts, for successful challenges to administrative authority and for the determination of lawfulness of detention. The applicant, X, had been detained initially in Broadmoor Hospital under s.65 of the Mental Health Act (1959)[10] after pleading guilty to a charge of wounding with intent. This legislation allowed a court, on the evidence of two medical practitioners that the accused was suffering from 'mental illness, psychopathic disorder, subnormality or severe subnormality' and in the belief that he or she posed a significant danger to the public, to impose a 'restriction order'. Patients so detained had the right to a hearing before a Mental Health Review Tribunal,[11] but conditional or absolute release could be granted only on the order of the Home Secretary. X was eventually granted conditional release, but three years later was arrested and taken back to Broadmoor by the order of the Home Secretary on the recommendation of a probation officer. On his application to a divisional court for a writ of *habeas corpus*, it was pointed out on his behalf that he had been in regular employment and had committed no criminal offence since his release. Further, letters were presented to the court from three of his workmates saying that they found nothing unusual in his behaviour. However, the court was informed in a letter from the Home Office that his 'condition was giving cause for concern'. This was not explained and the probation service declined to give any information, but the responsible medical officer at Broadmoor was of the opinion on his readmission that he should be retained for treatment. The divisional court rejected his application without stating full reasons, merely noting that it was the probation officer who was responsible for the applicant and for recommending any required action. An application was then submitted to the European Commission and a case was eventually brought before the European Court.

This case first of all demonstrates that, as is generally accepted from the case law, the domestic remedy of *habeas corpus* is not wholly secure. Under the Habeas Corpus Act (1816), the courts may inquire into the 'truth of the facts' stated in the official return to the application for the writ. But if the adminstration can, as here, demonstrate its statutory authority for recalling a person into detention, and that the recall was executed in the terms of the statute, the courts will not look into the grounds of the decision. The burden is on the detainee to show that the detention is for a wrong purpose, or is capricious or wholly unreasonable in the circumstances.[12] Section 65 of the Mental Health Act (1959) gave exclusive control of a detainee to the Home Secretary as far as continuing detention or conditional or absolute release were concerned. The Home Office was thus able to demonstrate statutory authority for the action.

However, it is plain that, as the European Court of Human Rights unanimously found, the system did not meet the requirements of Article 5(4) of the Convention. The Court said of Article 5(4) that it:

> 'does not embody a right to judicial control of such scope as to empower the court, on all aspects of the case, to substitute its own discretion for that of the decision-making authority. The review should, however, be wide enough to bear on those conditions which, according to the Convention, are essential for the "lawful" detention of a person on the ground of unsoundness of mind, especially as the reasons capable of initially justifying such a detention may cease to exist. . . . This means that in the instant case, Article 5(4) required an appropriate procedure allowing a court to examine whether the patient's disorder still persisted and whether the Home Secretary was entitled to think that a continuation of the compulsory confinement was necessary in the interests of public safety.'[13]

The notion of a court in Article 5(4) includes any body which is independent of the authority whose action is to be controlled, uses at least a quasi-judicial procedure, and is competent to determine the lawfulness of the action in question. A Mental Health Review Tribunal met two of these conditions, but not the last.[14] Moreover, in the *habeas corpus* proceedings brought by the applicant neither the Home Office nor the Probation Service had been compelled to state what aspect of his condition was 'giving cause for concern', the reason advanced for his recall into detention. It was not possible then for the court to determine the 'lawfulness' of the recall, which, in the sense of Article 5(4), had to depend at least on the actual condition of the applicant, and evidence that the recall was necessary in the public interest.

Largely as a result of this case, important new legislation governing the detention and release of mental patients was introduced in the UK. The Mental Health Act (1983) has transferred to the Mental Health Review Tribunals the substantive decisions on 'restriction' and recall into restriction; and their composition and methods of work indicate that they rank as courts under Article 5(4). Its conditions appear now to be met.

Where ordinary forms of imprisonment are concerned, the *length of sentence* imposed for particular offences varies widely between jurisdictions, and it is not surprising that neither the Convention nor the Standard Minimum Rules have attempted to formulate any specific rules about it. *Detention on remand*, however, is covered by the Convention in that Article 5(1) permits:

> '(c) the lawful arrest or detention of a person effected for the purpose of bringing him before the competent legal authority on reasonable suspicion of having committed an offence or when it is reasonably considered necessary to prevent his committing an offence or fleeing having done so.'

And Article 5(3) provides that:

> 'Everyone arrested or detained in accordance with the provisions of paragraph 1(c) of this Article shall be brought promptly before a judge or other officer authorised by law to exercise judicial power and shall be entitled to trial within a reasonable time or to release pending trial. Release may be conditioned by guarantees to appear for trial.'

What is a 'reasonable' time of detention on remand will depend, in particular, on the scale of sentence to be expected, the conduct of the case by the judicial authorities, and the conduct of the detainee. The number and the geographical dispersal of the offences involved in the case may call for long inquiry if the detainee is charged with a number of related offences, but it may sometimes be asked whether it is necessary to prosecute them all. It must also not be overlooked that the presumption of innocence, expressed in Article 6(2) of the Convention, remains the prior rule governing detention on remand. Nevertheless, the Commission has been cautious on the subject of remand time. For example, an applicant against Switzerland (*Schertenleib: 8339/78*) complained of detention on remand lasting for thirty months. He was charged with financial fraud involving operations in Switzerland, the USA and the Bahamas, which called for extensive investigation. He made eleven applications for release, and brought six complaints, taking them to appeal, against the conduct of the judges. In this case, the Commission found on balance no breach of Article 5(3).

2 CONDITIONS OF IMPRISONMENT

The Convention itself has no general provisions expressly governing the conditions of imprisonment, although Article 10(3) of the Civil and Political Rights Covenant, which the UK has ratified, does specify that:

> 'The penitentiary system shall comprise treatment of prisoners the essential aim of which shall be their reformation and social rehabilitation. Juvenile offenders shall be segregated from adults and be accorded treatment appropriate to their age and legal status.'

More importantly, in 1973 the Council of Europe adopted Standard Minimum Rules for the Treatment of Prisoners.[15] The resolution begins:

> 'The following rules are not intended to describe in detail a model system of penal institutions. They seek only, on the basis of the general consensus of contemporary thought and the essential elements of the most adequate systems of today, to set out what is generally accepted as being good principle and practice in the treatment of prisoners and the management of institutions.'

These rules are not then binding in law, either internationally or in national systems, but they are intended to serve as guidelines in practice both for the Convention organs and national administrations and courts. The Council of Europe recommends that 'governments of member states be guided in their internal legislation and practice by the principles set out . . . with a view to their progressive implementation'. These and other provisions will now be considered in so far as they apply to: inhuman or degrading treatment; contacts with family and correspondence; and prison work.

The Convention rule (Article 3) covering *inhuman treatment*, which states that 'no one shall be subjected to torture or to inhuman or degrading treatment or punishment', is *absolute*, in that there can be no derogation from it in any circumstances, even 'in time of war or public emergency threatening the life of the nation' (Article 15). Nevertheless, what constitutes torture or inhuman treatment remains an issue of fact and not of definition; further, the *purpose* of a particular treatment may come into account. While the terms are the same in the various instruments, the Standard Minimum Rules are more specific:

> '31. Corporal punishment, punishment by placing in a dark cell and all cruel, inhuman or degrading punishment shall be completely prohibited as punishment for disciplinary offences.'

Various working descriptions have come into general use: in particular, inhuman treatment is what causes severe physical or mental suffering, immediate or prolonged, resulting from negligence or indifference or some purpose, the last constituting torture. Torture is inhuman treatment 'intentionally inflicted . . . for such purposes as obtaining information or confession . . . intimidation or coercion',[16] or as punishment.

Among the numerous complaints that have been brought under Article 3 of the Convention, the use of the so-called 'five techniques' in Northern Ireland is chosen for description here, because it reveals some of the difficulties of setting limits to the ill-treatment of detainees.

The applicants in *Ireland* v. *UK* had been taken into custody in barracks or other military centres for the purpose of interrogation. They were subjected to:

Wall-standing: being forced to stand spread-eagled against a wall for some hours, and 'on the toes with the weight of the body mainly on the fingers'.[17]

Hooding: putting a bag over the head during the detention, except under interrogation.

Deprivation of sleep.

Subjection to noise: continuous loud and hissing noise produced by a machine.

Deprivation of food and drink: reduced diet during the detention.

The Commission, while doubting whether any one of these techniques alone could be of the severity required to show a breach of Article 3, found their combined uses and purpose to constitute torture and ill-treatment of the individuals:

> '. . . the five techniques applied together were designed to put severe mental and physical stress, causing severe suffering, on a person in order to obtain information from him.'

Such 'disorientation' or 'sensory deprivation' techniques were, in its view, a 'modern system of torture'.[18] The Court, on the other hand, considered that torture is characterized, not by its purpose, but by 'the intensity of the suffering inflicted'. It concluded that the five techniques, used against an individual in combination, constituted 'inhuman treatment' but not torture.

While the difference of approach between the Commission and the Court may seem artificial, the factor of purpose in inhuman treatment can be important. It should be remembered that the Parker Committee Report (Home Office 1972) had reached the superficially appealing, but dangerous, conclusion that what is inhuman treatment should be judged:

> '. . . in the light of the circumstances (in Northern Ireland) in which the techniques were applied, for example, that the operation was taking place in the course of urban guerrilla warfare in which completely innocent lives are at risk; that there is a degree of urgency; and that the security and safety of the interrogation centre, of its staff and of its detainees are important considerations.'[19]

As a result of the Court's findings, the UK Government not only paid compensation to detainees, who were victims under Article 3, but introduced a number of administrative measures which would eliminate in particular the use of the 'five techniques'.

Other important findings by the Convention organs of inhuman and degrading treatment have included the infliction of severe physical pain by bastinado in prison in Greece in 1968, and by corporal punishment of a juvenile, ordered by a court, in the Isle of Man in 1972. In both countries the offending practice was discontinued. However, in the Isle of Man there was merely a change in practice, not in law, while the UK government subsequently terminated the right of individual petition (under Article 25 of the Convention) in the island.

It is worth briefly mentioning at this point provisions covering the *deprivation of life*, which is permitted by the Convention. These are irrelevant in most Convention countries owing to the widespread abolition of capital punishment.[20] However, an odd provision in the clause is that the deprivation of life is not in contravention of the Article when:

> 'a. . . . it results from the use of force which is no more than absolutely necessary:
> b. in order to effect a lawful arrest or to prevent the escape of a person lawfully detained.'

It is to be hoped that, if the Convention is to be revised, this absurd and impracticable proposition is removed. It is absurd because it contradicts in any common sense another purpose of the Convention – namely, to prohibit absolutely the degrading treatment of a prisoner – but allows him to be killed if he tries to escape. It is impracticable because no domestic law could incorporate such a rule: is what is 'absolutely necessary' to be left to the decision of the killer?

The element of protection of a prisoner enters also into the issues of *solitary confinement*, the *forced administration of medicine*, and *forcible feeding*, and certain practical and moral problems can arise here. Solitary confinement, while usually a disciplinary measure, may also be needed to protect prisoners – for example, the Baader–Meinhof group in the Federal Republic of Germany – from the hostility of their fellow-prisoners. Forcible feeding might be said to be degrading treatment, or an interference upon private life (by a breaking of the will) or upon freedom of choice, but can also be used to save life. Does every Convention freedom necessarily entail a right not to exercise it: hunger strike, euthanasia, closed shop? The Commission has said that at least the forced administration of medicine to a detainee is not contrary to the Convention.

Correspondence and *family contacts* are related issues. Article 8(1) of the Convention states that:

> 'Everyone has the right to respect for his private and family life, his home and his correspondence.'

And Article 8(2) that:

> 'There shall be no interference by a public authority with the exercise of this right except such as is in accordance with the law and is necessary in a democratic society in the interests of national security, public safety or the economic well-being of the country, for the prevention of disorder or crime, for the protection of health or morals, or for the protection of the rights and freedoms of others.'

The Standard Minimum Rules also provide that:

> 'Prisoners shall be allowed under necessary supervision to communicate with their family and reputable friends at regular intervals, both by correspondence and receiving visits.'

Restrictions on correspondence have led to many applications to the Commission, and the whole issue was sent finally to the Court, which examined a large number of illustrative letters. In its judgement (*Silver and Others* v. *UK*, 1983)[21] it recognized that owing to the sheer volume of letters subject to control by prison authorities – estimated at around ten million a year in all the UK prisons – it was impossible to make detailed and general rules. The judgement limited itself to an assessment of the handling of the illustrative letters shown to it, and it found in a number of cases restrictions of correspondence which failed to meet the requirements of Article 8(2). Among these were cases relevant to the important question of prisoners' rights of access to lawyers and the courts. This will be discussed separately later.

How far the control of prisoners' letters, outgoing and incoming, should be carried will be often a matter of opinion. The Convention allows the restriction of correspondence if this is necessary for public security, the prevention of crime, and the protection of order in the prison. But whether the prison authorities should undertake to stop correspondence which may be libellous or obscene, thus becoming potentially subject to the 'protection of health or morals' stipulation in Article 8(2), is less certain. The spread of information and ideas may also come into account. Should Marxist or National Front propaganda be stopped in correspondence? The European Court of Human Rights, without entering into these last issues, laid down two general principles for the control of prisoners' correspondence: first, the measures of control must be contained in formal directives, available to and understood by prisoners – the principles of 'accessibility and foreseeability' named by the Court; second, a petition to the Home Secretary would rank as an effective remedy if it complained of non-compliance by a prison authority with such an administrative directive.

The position of the Convention in the UK

We may now consider what obstacles there are to the application of the Convention to prisoners in the UK. In assessing its impact in this country, we must repeat that the Convention is not incorporated in our domestic law. But, without entering into the controversy about whether we should have a new Bill of Rights (the old Bill gets little mention) which could incorporate the Convention in whole or in part, it can at least be said that the UK has always cooperated fully in the processes of the Commission and Court, and that it considers itself bound in social policy and legal practice to observe the provisions of the Convention, subject of course to their interpretation. It treats the opinions of the Commission as authoritative and has undertaken, as required by the Convention, to give effect to the judgements of the Court.

But this points up the distinction between what is and what is not justiciable. Much of the Convention deals with the non-justiciable; for example, the correspondence and family contacts of detainees are matters of social policy, for which the Convention offers a framework in Article 8, but cannot provide effective rules. So the opinions of the Commission on matters of social policy can have greater influence and effect than judicial decisions. As previously stated, the practice of corporal punishment of juveniles in the Isle of Man, condemned by the Court, was not changed in law, but in practice.

A second problem is that there are for detainees general obstacles to the invocation of the Convention, arising by 'necessary implication' – to quote Lord Wilberforce – from the status of imprisonment. Until relatively recently, access to justice has been a major problem for prisoners, particularly in terms of correspondence and access to legal advice. Moreover, prisoners making a complaint against a prison officer or the prison authorities still have to go through the lengthy 'internal ventilation' process before an application can be registered under the Convention, and with the additional time required for processing through the Commission and Court, it can be many years before a resolution is reached.

The first important landmark over access to lawyers was the *Golder* (1975) case. Golder, serving sentence in Parkhurst Prison, was accused by a prison officer of having assaulted him during a disturbance in the prison. Golder was not allowed to consult a solicitor for the purpose of bringing a civil action for defamation against the prison officer. Both the Commission and the Court held this to be a denial of access to the courts, under Article 6(1), and an unjustified interference with correspondence, under Article 8.

Following this decision, the UK government issued new instructions to prison authorities to allow any communication by a prisoner to a solicitor about proposed civil proceedings, and the institution of such proceedings. However, if the proposed proceedings were against the Home Office, and arose out of or were connected with the imprisonment of the applicant, no such communications would be allowed until any complaints involved had been ventilated through prison channels. This was called the 'internal ventilation' rule.

Subsequently, in the case of *Silver* (1983), it was held that the stopping of letters addressed to legal representatives was not justified under Article 8(2). The Commission had earlier noted relative to this case that:

> 'it is fundamental in a democratic society that people may seek responsible legal advice on any subject in order to protect or enforce their rights, or simply to be reasonably well-informed.'
>
> (*Silver*, Report: para. 312)

A broad range of issues, including that of correspondence, was considered in the case of *Campbell and Fell* (1984). These two prisoners, serving sentence in Albany Prison, engaged with four other prisoners in a 'sit-down' protest in a corridor of the prison; in an ensuing struggle with prison officers, both applicants sustained injuries. Examination of Campbell by an outside doctor was refused. Charged with mutiny and gross personal violence to a prison officer, they were subjected, after proceedings before the Board of Visitors, to loss of remission of sentence (570 days in Campbell's case, 590 in that of Fell) and to a number of days of cellular confinement.

Both applicants alleged that they had several times been refused permission by the prison authorities to seek legal advice in connection with claims for compensation for the injuries sustained in the incident. Fell also alleged that he had later been refused permission to consult his solicitors out of the hearing of prison officers. The Court, sitting as a Chamber of seven, came to the unanimous conclusion that, as regards both claims, there had been breaches of Articles 6(1) and 8. Fell further alleged that the prison authorities had refused him permission to correspond with certain individuals on the grounds that they were not relatives or existing friends, and here the Court unanimously agreed that there had been a breach of Article 8.

The case was also important as a test of the fitness of Boards of Visitors to conduct disciplinary hearings. Campbell alleged that he had been convicted of disciplinary charges which amounted in substance to criminal charges which should have been heard in a court of law; that the Board was neither independent nor impartial; that the hearing was not held in public and the decision not publicly announced; that he had not been allowed legal assistance or representation; and that he had not had a fair hearing.

The Court decided that there had been no violations of the Convention on the general issues of independence, impartiality and fairness, nor where the application regarding a public hearing was concerned. The determination of what is a 'criminal charge', as distinct from disciplinary measures, was set by the Court, following an earlier decision (*Kiss* v. *UK*), to rest on three factors:

1 whether the provisions defining the offence are part of the domestic criminal law, or disciplinary rules, or both;
2 the 'very nature of the offence';
3 the degree of severity of the penalty to be imposed.

The combination of these criteria takes account of the fact that it would be obviously impracticable to maintain that every prison incident falling under the criminal law requires a determination by the criminal courts. On the related issue of the status of a Board of Visitors, as an 'independent and impartial tribunal' under Article 6(1), the Court invoked the decision of the Court of Appeal in *St Germain* (*No. 1*) (1979),[22] and observed that the term 'tribunal' in Article 6(1) is 'not necessarily to be understood as signifying a court of law of the classic kind, integrated within the standard judicial machinery of the country'.

However, it held by five votes to two that there had been a violation of Article 6(1) in that the Board had not made its decision public, and by a similar margin that Campbell's inability to obtain legal assistance or representation constituted a violation of Article 6(3).

The Court's decisions in this case were important in their own right, but were to some extent made redundant by changes in practice in anticipation of this and the *Silver* judgement, and by the consequences of cases in the domestic courts which predated it (see also Fitzgerald, Quinn, Richardson this volume). Pressure from the Commission had as early as December 1981 led the Home Office to issue new Standing Orders with respect to correspondence. Under these, a prisoner was allowed to correspond with any person or organization, provided that the regulations on the contents of correspondence were observed; and legal advice could be obtained concerning civil proceedings, including those relating to prison treatment, as soon as the prisoner had raised any complaint about such treatment through the internal channels. The prisoner was then no longer required to await the outcome of the internal inquiry. This was called the 'simultaneous ventilation' rule. In fact, even this rule has since been found by a domestic court to constitute an unacceptable impediment to access to justice (*Anderson* 1984 – see Richardson Chapter 3).

It should also be noted that the issue of legal representation at Boards of Visitors' hearings had already been affected by another domestic case, that of *Tarrant* (1983 – see Fitzgerald Chapter 2).

The *Campbell and Fell* case highlights what is probably the most trenchant criticism of the Commission and Court apparatus – namely, that of inordinate delays before decisions are reached. It is true that this is due in great part to the increasing burden of work carried out by what is a part-time body. However, the incident out of which *Campbell and Fell* arose took place in September 1976; the applications were introduced to the Commission in March 1977; the Commission's report was adopted in May 1982; and the Court's judgement was published in June 1984.

The above problem might eventually be solved through a restructuring of the apparatus and by increases in resources. Problems relating to the implementation of decisions in the UK would greatly be aided if that country incorporated the Convention in its internal law. However, a deeper problem will almost certainly always remain. This is that imprisonment and human rights are naturally in conflict, and there are many dilemmas in resolving the conflict. Lord Wilberforce has observed:[23]

> '... a convicted prisoner, in spite of his imprisonment retains all civil rights, which are not taken away expressly or by implication.'

This may be using the term 'civil rights' to describe the limited number of rights that cannot in any circumstance be denied: for example, the prohibition of torture or inhuman treatment, or the right to a fair hearing in the courts. But there are few rights that are, as they are sometimes called, fundamental or inalienable. The structure and application of the Convention, as well as of national constitutions, show that almost all rights and freedoms have to be qualified or restricted either in the public interest, or to make their exercise equal for all.

Notes

1 Preamble to the Convention.
2 Austria, Belgium, Cyprus, Denmark, Federal Republic of Germany, France, Greece, Iceland, Ireland, Italy, Liechtenstein, Luxembourg, Malta, Netherlands, Norway, Portugal, Spain, Sweden, Switzerland, Turkey, United Kingdom.
3 Austria, Belgium, Cyprus, Federal Republic of Germany, France, Greece, Italy, Luxembourg, Netherlands, Portugal, Spain, Switzerland, Turkey.
4 Austria, Belgium, Cyprus, France, Greece, Netherlands.
5 Composed of 21 members, one from each Convention country, serving as individuals and not as Government representatives.
6 Ten applications in thirty years, including three against the United Kingdom: from Greece in 1956 and 1957, in respect of the administration of Cyprus; and from Ireland in 1971 in respect of Northern Ireland.
7 In a recent case a team, including the Attorney General, represented the UK Government.

8 The judicial body of the European Communities.

9 *X* v. *UK* (6998/75: 8 Decisions and Reports 106).

10 Now replaced by Mental Health (Amendment) Act 1982, and Mental Health Act (1983) Section V.

11 Established under s.3 of the 1959 Act and composed of a lawyer, a psychiatrist, and a third member suitably qualified. Requests may be made one year after the date of the hospital order, one year after that, and then every two years.

12 See, for example, *Zamir* v. *Secretary of State (1980) 2 All ER 768.*

13 Judgement No. 46 (5.11.1981) 58.

14 It is interesting to compare the system in Belgium, in which a convicted person ordered by the court to be placed in psychiatric detention, is then under the charge of a Commission de Defense Sociale (Social Defence Committee). Each of these committees is composed of three members – a presiding magistrate, a member of the Bar, and a practising doctor. Its proceedings take place *in camera* in which the detainee is heard, and in which he must be assisted by a lawyer, who may consult the case-file. The Committee decides whether, or for what periods, the detention is to continue. It then meets the conditions described above, as the Commission found in an application to it by a detainee.

15 Committee of Ministers Resolution 73/5. It was adopted on 13.1.1973.

16 Draft Convention on Torture and other Inhuman Treatment (7.1981).

17 Continuous standing ranged from periods of 9 to 16 hours.

18 It referred to the UN General Assembly Resolution 3452-XXX (9.12.1975) which declared that: 'Torture constitutes an aggravated and deliberate form of cruel, inhuman or degrading treatment or punishment.'

19 Cf. Trinquier, *Modern Warfare* (1961): The 'irregular fighter': '. . . must be made to realise that when he is captured he cannot be treated as an ordinary criminal, nor like a prisoner taken on the battlefield. . . . No lawyer is present for such an interrogation. If the prisoner gives the information requested, the examination is quickly terminated: if not, specialists must force his secret from him. Then, as a soldier, he must face the suffering and perhaps the death he has heretofore managed to avoid. The terrorist must accept this as a condition of his trade.'

The UN Code of Conduct for Law Enforcement Officials (1979) Article 5 would forbid this.

20 The death penalty has been retained in law (but has fallen into disuse) for certain offences in Belgium, Cyprus, Ireland and Liechtenstein, and for certain military offences, committed in wartime, in Italy, Spain, Switzerland and the United Kingdom. Only Malta and Spain retain it for 'ordinary' offences of murder.

21 Judgement No. 61 (25.3.1983).

22 The Court of Appeal said that when a Board of Visitors is adjudicating charges against discipline, under the Prison Act (1952) and the rules made under it, it is performing a 'distinct and independent function'; it has a duty to act judicially, and its decisions, though administratively enforceable, are subject to appeal to the courts for *certiorari*.

23 *Raymond* v. *Honey (1982) 1 All ER 756.*

PART 2

WORKING TO A STANDARD

5

The case for prison standards: conditions of confinement, segregation, and medical treatment

Larry Gostin and Marie Staunton

This chapter provides an overview of the concerns of civil liberties and prison reform groups about the absence of positive rights for prisoners, particularly in relation to conditions of confinement. Our working assumption is that the punishment intended by a prison sentence is simply deprivation of liberty. Minimally, society is entitled to expect that deprivation of liberty does not cause the individual any lasting harm of a physical or psychological kind. We shall argue that the most effective way to enable the development of a positive right, which we call *protection from harm*, is through the establishment of minimum standards of confinement and treatment, debated and agreed by Parliament and open to review by the courts.

In the first half of the paper, we highlight a number of areas in which the development of a set of agreed standards is a matter of some urgency. After a few illustrations of the unsatisfactory nature of conditions of confinement in general, we argue that groups concerned with prisoners' rights should pay particular attention to two specific areas: segregation and medical treatment – the latter with particular regard to the treatment of mentally disordered offenders. We then outline ways in which standards could be introduced and how they could be monitored so that any violations are remedied.

General conditions of confinement

In this section we present a few sources of evidence which indicate that the punishment currently experienced by prisoners is much more than simple deprivation of liberty. In some cases, physical and mental harm may be suffered because of the conditions of confinement.

Criticism of the conditions under which prisoners are held have come not only from voluntary organizations advocating prison reform but also from those administering and inspecting prisons. For example, there is widespread acceptance that conditions in local prisons in London are intolerable. In a reply to Jo Richardson MP in August 1983, the Home Office stated:

> 'It is very much regretted that our Victorian local prisons in London (which were originally designed to take a much lower number of prisoners than they hold today) are overcrowded to the point where there is difficulty in providing all the amenities we would wish to be available.'

A Report of HM Chief Inspector of Prisons (1983e) put the same point more forcefully:

> 'Although Wormwood Scrubs is less overcrowded than other prisons which we have seen recently we nevertheless consider that it is such that, other than in D Hall, prisoners are not being held in conditions which ensure respect for human dignity.'

A month earlier, in January 1983, the Governor of that prison had resigned, graphically describing conditions there as 'a penal dustbin full of overcrowded cattle pens'.

While the physical conditions in which convicted and unconvicted prisoners are held have been widely condemned, the courts have failed effectively to provide a remedy. The case of the Nahar brothers (1983) illustrates this well, as it involves conditions of confinement – in police cells – worse even than those existing in any British prison. If the courts are unable to remedy such an extreme situation, there is little hope that they will act effectively on general prison conditions. The Nahar brothers were remanded in custody in Camberwell police cells and applied to the Divisional Court for *habeas corpus* on the basis that the conditions under which they were held were inhuman and degrading and therefore that their detention was unlawful.

> 'The two applicants were in a cell six feet by eight feet. The cell had no windows, the applicants were permitted no exercise outside their cells in the cell area. The cell was lit by one weak light bulb and ventilation was provided by two ventilators near the ground.'
> (*Nahar* 1983)

The court held that although there must be some minimum standard which could render detention unlawful, neither the Imprisonment (Temporary Provisions) Act (1980) which provided for remands in police cells, nor the European Convention on Human Rights assisted in defining that standand. The applications were refused without the court itself suggesting any appropriate standard.

The effects of inadequate treatment and conditions may go far beyond physical discomfort. The repeated transfer of remand prisoners is an effective denial of the few rights which the Prison Rules and Circular Instructions specifically allow them because of their unconvicted status – to have their own food and clothes and access to their own doctors. In 1983, Mr T was transferred twenty times to a variety of prisons and police cells between the New Forest and Leamington Spa. He was in effect denied his visiting rights during that period: his wife had great difficulty in both tracking him down and in travelling to different parts of the country to visit him (NCCL casefile).

Every year the National Council for Civil Liberties' team of legal volunteers answers about 2,000 letters from prisoners. Complaints refer *inter alia* to damp, cold, lice, poor toilet facilities, overcrowding, lack of exercise, and difficulty in seeing a doctor or obtaining appropriate medical treatment. It is clear from this list that the physical conditions of imprisonment are only one aspect of the privation of prison life as perceived by prisoners. The lack of visits, inability to establish any privacy or territory of their own, lack of access to education, the perceived unfairness of loss of privileges or the operation of Rule 43 (see below) not only make conditions more difficult to bear but may lead to destructive behaviour. Similarly, sudden changes of policy, such as the recent change in regulations governing parole eligibility – set out in the Home Secretary's speech at the Conservative Party conference in October 1983 (Home Office 1984g; and see Maguire *et al.* 1984) – not only lead to many requests for NCCL help by prisoners and their families but also to an increase in the tension in prisons. And the frequent movements between cells or between prisons can have a deleterious effect upon a prisoner's mental state, as illustrated by this account of imprisonment in 1983:

> 'My mental state was very bad. Once you are settled you go to a cell and if you know you have to stay there you can make it as comfortable as possible, try to keep it clean, wash the walls because in some of the cells walls are impossible to look at, get your own plate, fork, knife – they are yours, they are clean. You even keep some bread and butter inside so if you are starving in the evening, a slice of bread and butter can calm your stomach. But when you are moving like that you are always in a new place, you never know where you are going.'
> (Mr M, NCCL casefile 1984)

Segregation

The segregation of prisoners is one of the forms of confinement where the risk of harm to the prisoner is most obvious. In its most extreme form, the conditions of confinement restrict normal environmental stimulation including association (see *Williams* v. *Home Office* (*No. 2*) 1981). Since any segregation is unavoidably restrictive to some extent, its use must be clearly justified and subject to independent examination. As will be argued later, where segregation is justified, there are strong grounds for insisting upon an enforceable set of minimum standards relating to sanitation, amenities, association and, where necessary, care and treatment. This would ensure the maintenance of the prisoner's physical and mental health as well as his self-respect and dignity.

1 EFFECTS OF SEGREGATION

There have been a number of studies of the effects of environmental deprivation on individuals (for a review, see Irving and Hilgendorf 1980). The only safe conclusion from these studies is that individuals respond differently to the effects of such deprivation and that there are no reliable indicators as to how any individual will repond. There are, however, high risk groups. For example, mentally ill or mentally handicapped prisoners tend to respond particularly badly to solitary confinement, which can exacerbate their behavioural problems. 'Sensation seekers' too – a category clearly inclusive of many prisoners who may be seen as a threat to good order and discipline – have been shown to suffer severe effects from periods of quite limited forms of restricted environmental stimulation, in some cases after only twenty-four hours. Other effects of solitary confinement may include increased aggression (physical and mental), self-punishment including self-mutilation (particularly noticeable in women prisoners suffering from mental stress), withdrawal, impaired mental functioning, disorientation, anxiety, reduced visual, auditory and kynesthetic sensations, fantasies and delusions, alternations in body image and conceptual disorganization. Many of these simulate the symptoms of psychosis.

2 VOLUNTARY RULE 43

There are a sizeable number of prisoners who choose to serve part of their sentence under Rule 43, which provides that:

> 'Where it appears desirable, for the maintenance of good order and discipline or in his own interests, that a prisoner should not associate with other prisoners . . . the governor may arrange for the prisoner's removal from association.' (Rule 43(1))

Prisoners may ask for segregation for their own protection or for many other reasons. They may, for example, be sex offenders or 'informers' – such inmates are often regarded by other prisoners with a considerable degree of antipathy, and indeed each category may regard the other as undesirable company. Or they may have incurred 'debts' of tobacco or personal services in the course of unofficial loans or gambling which they are unable or unwilling to pay.

'Going on the Rule' does not entail severe deprivation of the kind illustrated by the *Williams* case. However, the regime is usually a good deal more spartan than others in the prison, association is limited, and some cases of segregation have lasted for very long periods. In as much as prisoners ask for Rule 43 segregation out of fear for their safety, their choice cannot be said to be freely made, nor does it show a desire for solitary confinement *per se*. Some establishments, such as Maidstone prison, enable some Rule 43 prisoners to live in as normal a regime as possible in a self-contained wing. This opportunity should be available as a realistic option to *any* Rule 43 prisoner: moving to such a unit should not entail loss of proximity to family, and the units themselves should operate regimes whose standards are equivalent to those of the prisons in which they are situated. It is unjustifiable that a prisoner whose physical safety cannot be secured in normal prison conditions should have to face the sole alternative of having his mental well-being put at serious risk in solitary confinement.

3 INVOLUNTARY RULE 43 AND RULE 48

Rule 43 does not, of course, require a prisoner's consent to segregated without consent pending adjudication. Segregation of inmate is to be charged with a disciplinary offence, he may be segregated without consent pending adjudication. Segregation of a prisoner without his consent can be justified only where he is likely to cause imminent harm to others. Clearly in urgent situations where immediate action is needed to prevent a prisoner from causing a danger, it is reasonable for the decision to segregate to be taken by the governor, as at present. Any period of segregation of a total of more than twenty-four hours should be confirmed after examination of the evidence by an independent authority – i.e. an authority which is independent of the prison and the Prison Department. This is intended to occur in Rule 43 cases at present; however, the reviews currently undertaken by Boards of Visitors have been inadequate (see, for example, Maguire and Vagg 1984). Rule 48, moreover, does not require any authorization or ratification by an independent body. Below we propose other methods of accountability.

Clearly, some extreme cases – such as prisoners who have already killed other prisoners – do and will raise problems with respect to the very great length of time for which they are segregated. Realistically, such prisoners may never return to the ordinary prison regime, not least because other prisoners would not tolerate them. In such cases, even though regular review of their segregation may in practice never reach the point at which removal from segregation becomes an option, it must ensure that the prisoner is not deteriorating mentally or physically, and that the quality of 'regime services' provided to him are comparable with those of the prison system in general – even if special arrangements for this have to be made.

4 SEGREGATION AS A PUNISHMENT

While segregation may be necessary as a temporary measure to prevent imminent harm, *extended* periods of segregation as a disciplinary (i.e. punitive) measure cannot be justified. However, the Prison Department appears to condone the use of segregation for precisely this purpose, even where no specified offence has been committed. An illustration of this is provided by the case of a prisoner acquitted by the Albany Board of Visitors on 4 July 1984 of two charges of assaulting an officer and incitement to acts of indiscipline (Prison Rule 47(20)). He had been in solitary confinement for over two months on Rule 48(2) awaiting a hearing. After the acquittal he was taken to HMP Parkhurst on Rule 43. There were no intervening incidents or charges and he was still on Rule 43 in October 1984 (NCCL casefile). If prisoners are to be deprived of association this should be done by due process. Thus, a clear offence must be stated and the justification must be tested using a judicial process.

5 'GHOSTING'

'Ghosting' is used to describe the transfer of prisoners from one place to another without notice. It is frequently coupled with removal from association. 'Ghosting' is often used as a control measure to remove a prisoner suspected of being disruptive from continued association or to break up a group of prisoners. Such transfers are authorized under Circular Instruction 10/74 as amended in April 1984. As has been noted elsewhere (King; Morgan, Maguire, and Vagg this volume), the use of Circular Instruction 10/74 has become an alternative disciplinary system which is unaccountable, and therefore undesirable. In line with our proposals on Rule 43 we suggest that the authorities must have a clear justification for unrequested transfers, and that there must be independent review and periodic assessment. It must be rare indeed where there is no alternative to an immediate transfer; a period to allow representations and independent decision making should always be possible.

Medical treatment

1 STANDARD OF SERVICES

The Prison Medical Service (PMS) is not part of the National Health Service (NHS), and there has been persistent criticism of the quality of care in the PMS since the report of the Gwynn Committee (Home Office 1964). Gwynn referred to the difficulty of attracting medical and nursing staff of sufficient calibre and qualifications. The Royal College of Psychiatrists (1979) went further; it proposed the abolition of the PMS and argued that medical services to prisoners should be provided wholly by the NHS. The May Committee (Home Office 1979) did not consider that the Royal College proposal was within its remit but remarked on the highly inhumane care and treatment of mentally disordered prisoners in the PMS. Gunn (1985) lists five fundamental problems with the PMS: recruitment and training; compulsory treatment; the production of court records; ethical problems, and numbers of prisoners. Below, we deal solely with the questions of treatment and consent.

2 THE RANGE OF TREATMENTS

The Prison Medical Service provides prisoners with a wide variety of medical and psychiatric treatment ranging from standard primary care to sex hormone implant treatments. In particular there is substantial use of psychotropic medication (which affects mood) in the form of minor tranquillizers (which have a calming affect), major tranquillizers (anti-psychotic uses) and anti-depressants. Many of these have extremely unpleasant side effects; they can, in particular, cause dependence, and major tranquillizers can cause irreversible neurological damage simulating Parkinson's disease. The use of such psychotropic medication is sometimes necessary in the treatment of mentally disordered patients. But to ensure quality control and public confidence, outside practitioners from the NHS should be brought into the prisons to supervise and monitor these treatments.

3 TREATMENT WITHOUT CONSENT

As a matter of law there is now no doubt that a prisoner is in the same position as any member of the public in respect of his right to refuse to consent to treatment. The real questions for prisoners, however, are whether (1) they are ever in a position to give uncoerced consent and (2) whether, in practice, their decisions not to consent are respected. Both questions were answered, albeit unsatisfactorily, in *Freeman* v. *Home Office* (1984). Freeman alleged that he was given medication without his consent, and this was supported by a medical record which indicated that he 'consented reluctantly'. The Court of Appeal decided that there should be no fixed rule of law which states that a prisoner, because of general institutional pressures on him, is automatically incompetent to consent to treatment. Accordingly, prisoners are free to consent, or to refuse consent, to medical treatment. This is a desirable principle, for a prisoner should not lose his right to decide the treatment he should receive simply by reason of a sentence of imprisonment. Yet the Court appeared unwilling to consider carefully whether pressure was, in fact, put on Freeman to consent. Where a prisoner's conditions of confinement and time of release are in part dependent upon the prison authorities, and where he is subject virtually to total control, it is particularly important to ensure that his consent is uncoerced.

4 TREATMENTS WHICH ARE EXPERIMENTAL, HAZARDOUS OR NOT FULLY ESTABLISHED

Prisoners, because of their vulnerable position, are more likely to be subject to treatment which is experimental, hazardous or not fully established than virtually any other section of the population. In *Kaimowitz* v. *Michigan* (1973) a US district court held that if experimental psycho-surgery was being used, it would be impossible for a prisoner to consent to it voluntarily. The *Kaimowitz* court set up an irrebuttable presumption that no prisoner can consent to experimental treatment because of the institutional pressures on him.

In this country, sex hormone implant treatments have been administered to prisoners. Prisoners effectively have little option but to acquiesce to such treatment because they sometimes face the sole alternative of an indefinite period of confinement in prison.

5 TREATMENT FOR RESTRAINT OR DISCIPLINE

There may be times when treatment is sought to be used as a method of restraint, punishment or discipline. There are instances where sedatives are currently used to restrain prisoners. Here the prison authorities could argue that an injection is the least intrusive measure to prevent a prisoner from causing imminent harm. Alternatively, the use of tranquillizers over a long period of time may reduce aggression, and make the prisoner more cooperative and less disruptive. The medical profession, and their treatments, should never be used as a method of restraint or prevention in any of these ways. The practice of medicine and psychiatry are for the treatment of illness, and once the tools of medicine are used for punitive purposes (even where the end is arguably a just end) the legal, social and moral justifications for the practices cease to exist.

Mentally disordered offenders

It is sometimes not appreciated that judges and magistrates do not have the power to compel a hospital to admit a mentally disordered offender. Indeed, sentencers have expressed considerable frustration at the difficulties of finding a hospital bed for mentally disordered offenders. The solutions to this problem devised in the Mental Health Act 1983 – such as remands to hospital, interim hospital orders and the requirement of Regional Health Authorities to give information about the availability of beds in hospitals – are explored elsewhere (Gostin 1985a).

Figures provided by Prison Medical Officers consistently show that there are some 300 mentally disordered prisoners actually awaiting transfers to NHS hospitals, and most observers regard this as a highly conservative estimate of the numbers of mentally ill and mentally handicapped prisoners who require hospital treatment (see, for example, Gostin 1985b). The number of prisoners manifesting severe psychiatric disturbance is of the order of 5 per cent of the prison population (Guze 1976): and a recent study of prisoners remanded into custody has shown that about 9 per cent of them are psychotic, 4 per cent alcoholic and 5 per cent drug-dependent (Taylor and Gunn 1984).

Minimum standards

There is a consensus among official bodies, prison employees and prison reform organizations that prison establishments are overcrowded and fall below acceptable physical standards. If the prison system is to avoid the charge that physical and mental degradation has become a *de facto* goal of the system, and one that is routinely achieved, certain basic levels of dignity, privacy and diversity of experience must be built into that system. Prisons must be – and must be seen to be – conforming to standards of those kinds expected in any other part of society. The standards should set minimally acceptable levels of facilities, and of consistency and equity of treatment between prisoners, and between prisoners and others. They must be a benchmark against which actual conditions can be measured; and prison management must be held to account for any failure to meet them. The consequence of a lack of such standards, or a failure to implement them, is quite simply that prisoners will be subjected to the risk of physical and mental harm. It is thus our view that in order to protect prisoners from such harm it is necessary to introduce enforceable codes covering not only physical requirements for prison establishments but also the care and treatment of prisoners.

In *A* v. *UK* (1976), the European Commission of Human Rights held admissable a complaint brought by MIND that segregation of a Broadmoor patient was contrary to Article 3 of the Convention which proscribes inhuman and degrading treatment. The applicant complained in particular of the length of time he had to spend alone in a secure room (five weeks); that he was deprived of adequate furnishing and clothing; and that conditions in the room had been insanitary and it had been inadequately lit and ventilated.

As part of a friendly settlement, the Commission accepted the adoption by the respondent government of minimum guidelines concerning the use of seclusion at Broadmoor Hospital (similar guidelines were adopted at the other three special hospitals). Clearly, guidelines applicable to a secure mental hospital could not be adopted without modification to the prison context. Yet the precedent for minimum standards has now been set under Article 3 and the introduction of some of the standards enunciated in *A* v. *UK* are clearly desirable within prison settings. The mimimum standards include: the required amount of floor space; natural lighting; an individual programme of recreation, association and where necessary, nursing care and treatment; clothing; mattresses and bedding; toilet and sanitation facilities; writing and reading materials; and the reception of visitors. Let us now look in turn at the problem areas defined earlier, outlining ways in which standards might be introduced and implemented.

1 GENERAL CONDITIONS OF CONFINEMENT

The existing difficulty of directly enforcing the provisions of the Prison Rules (*Arbon* v. *Anderson* 1943; see Richardson Chapter 3) could be resolved by replacing the present Act and Rules with a new Prison Act. This would set out various physical standards of space, heating, lighting, occupation, recreation, etc. (see Casale Chapter 6). Prison authorities would have a statutory duty to comply with such minimum standards. A new Act would also establish statutory duties on the prison authorities, *inter alia*, to allow access to legal advice and medical treatment, and to provide adequate facilities for visiting and correspondence. The Act would be supplemented by codes in the form of Statutory Instruments, subject to affirmative resolutions of both Houses of Parliament, which would also set out methods for the practical implementation of the standards. For example, the Act would establish a requirement to provide adequate lighting, and the code would define this and set out the management systems for ensuring that it was complied with, e.g. regular inspection and reporting by prison staff. The advantages of this proposal over the present system are that:

(a) it would allow Members of Parliament to debate and amend the standards set out in the Act on the floor of the Houses of Commons and Lords and in committee – in contrast to their lack of power to amend the Prison Rules of 1964;
(b) it would give the courts a role to enforce the statutory duties set out in the Act using the codes as a guide. No doubt the courts would still take into account the problem of resources. However, there would no longer be doubt as to the status which Parliament intended to confer on rules governing prison conditions;
(c) it would provide a consistent standard of confinement against which independent bodies – such as the NCCL – could assess complaints.

2 SEGREGATION

Any decision to extend segregation should be on the ground that the prisoner continues to pose a danger to others, and must be for a specific and limited period of time. There should be a requirement for periodic assessment of the physical and mental well-being of the prisoner by qualified professional staff coming into the prisons from the National Health Service. Further, the justification for segregation (which must continue to be the probability of imminent harm) should periodically be re-examined by an independent authority (e.g. at weekly intervals).

3 MEDICAL TREATMENT

A major step towards the improvement of medical services for prisoners would be to transfer responsibility for their treatment from the Prison Medical Service (PMS) to the National Health Service (NHS). This would require the PMS to become part of the NHS, with District Health Authorities having the primary responsibility for providing services. This proposal is based upon the simple principle that prisoners should have the same access to the NHS and its resources as do other citizens. However, the Home Office has consistently rejected the idea of a merger of the PMS with the NHS, despite the logic behind it. As a compromise proposal it would be possible for the PMS to be designated as a special health authority under Section 11 of the National Health Act 1977. This would place a positive duty on the prison authorities to meet all reasonable requirements for medical care, where outside NHS contractors would provide much of the service. There is precedent for outside contractors to provide treatment and services for prisoners. Dental treatment is provided under the NHS scheme. Education officers employed by the local authority run courses in prisons. The expertise of an independent service with its own career, status and system of accountability can be applied to prisoners irrespective of the fact that they are confined.

This solution would still leave many problems of inequality of access to Health Service care. But it would at least ensure that the provision of medical services to prisoners was the responsibility of the Department of Health and Social Security, which is separate from the Prison Department and not concerned with matters of order, discipline and security which often conflict with the therapeutic responsibility of doctors, nurses and other professionals within the NHS.

So far as *consent* to treatment is concerned, the solution in England and Wales lies in the Mental Health Act 1983 which states that any 'patient' (i.e. any prisoner suffering or appearing to suffer from mental disorder (s.145)), even if he or she is 'not liable to be detained under this Act' (s.56(2)), cannot be given sex hormone implant treatment or psycho-surgery unless he or she consents; there must also be multi-disciplinary review of the voluntariness and effectiveness of his or her consent; and a second doctor must state that treatment is beneficial. Given the very case where treatment was unusually hazardous, experimental, or not fully established. In cases where the treatment is experimental 1983 Act applies to any prisoner to whom it is proposed to give any of these treatments. Even in those rare cases where the prison medical officers contend that the Mental Health Act does not apply, it would be expected that the courts would apply very strict standards in examining the voluntariness of consent in any broad definition of 'patient' and of 'mental disorder' (i.e. 'any other disorder or disability of mind' (s.1(2)), it is arguable that the in the sense that it is not for a therapeutic purpose, or there is a feasible alternative treatment of greater value or fewer risks, the courts could well adopt a *Kaimowitz*-type approach. (For a more detailed examination of the consent to treatment provisions of the Mental Health Act and the common law, see Gostin 1985a.)

4 MENTALLY DISORDERED PRISONERS

The treatment and care of mentally disordered prisoners is also the responsibility of the Prison Medical Service. Sometimes in the name of 'caring' for these prisoners they are placed in the most restricted forms of association (e.g. at C1 wing in Holloway Prison). In any such case guidelines accepted by the European Commission in *A* v. *UK* should apply in full. Further, to ensure that the justifications of 'therapy' and 'discipline' are not blurred, the continuous medical supervision and assessment required under the *A* v. *UK* guidelines should be undertaken by senior psychiatrists from the National Health Service and not associated with the prison. This would ensure a form of outside scrutiny, and that the standards and quality of care available to mentally disordered people outside of the prison system are maintained for prisoners.

Enforcing standards

The existing bodies with powers or duties to monitor conditions have failed to impose consistent or minimally acceptable standards. One of the reasons for this failure is the confusion between the watchdog, monitoring and adjudicatory functions of Boards of Visitors in particular. Proper enforcement of minimum standards requires one or more independent, alert bodies with clearly defined powers and duties to inquire into specific incidents as well as general conditions in prisons, and with access to appropriate research and information. One model of establishing and enforcing realistic minimum standards is set out below.

The enforcement of standards would continue to be carried out by Boards of Visitors as watchdog bodies in individual prisons, the Prison Inspectorate monitoring the consistency of standards between prisons (using the Act and codes as a yardstick) and the prisoner having an individual right of action in the courts.

With regard to the Boards of Visitors, we agree with the recommendations of the Jellicoe Committee (Martin 1975) that in order for Boards of Visitors to perform their watchdog function effectively they should be divested of their adjudicatory function (see also Morgan, Maguire, and Vagg this volume). The new boards, which we should rename *Prison Councils*, would include local councillors from the area in which the prison is based and appointed by the local authority, as well as Home Office appointees. They would continue to have powers of entry and inspection with duties to enquire into prisoners' complaints. They would have the power to convene inquiries (with teams of, say, three of their number) who could summon witnesses in the course of their investigation into a specific complaint or incident.

The Prison Inspectorate would maintain its monitoring function using minimum standards as a yardstick. Thus comparisons between conditions in different prisons could more easily be made. The thematic reviews presently carried out by the Inspectorate, for example into suicides in prisons and Rules 43, would benefit from research facilities to monitor the effect of specific regimes on prisoners.

The reports of both the Prison Councils and the Inspectorate would be published and laid before Parliament, and the setting up of a Select Committee on prisons would provide a forum for Parliamentary debate with more powers that the existing All Party Penal Affairs Group.

The prisoner would, however, still have a right of action on the basis of a breach of statutory duties. The remedy of judicial review would still apply in cases where administrative bodies have unreasonably failed to carry out their statutory duties. Moreover, a court would be better equipped to decide private law claims of, for instance, negligence if there were clear statutory duties and guidelines in the Act. This would help ensure that the standard of care of professionals was measured not solely by existing practice but by minimum guidelines set out in statute and administrative regulation.

Conclusion

It is only by setting out clear minimum standards for prisons and the care and treatment of prisoners, with effective monitoring by Boards of Visitors (renamed and divested of disciplinary powers), the Inspectorate and Parliament, that we can meet even the minimum requirement of the Council of Europe *Standard Minimum Rules for the Treatment of Prisoners*:

> 'The prison system shall not, except as incidental to justifiable segregation or the maintenance of discipline, aggravate the suffering inherent in such a situation.' (para. 57)

6
A practical design for standards

Silvia Casale

Recent developments in England and Wales

In this country no comprehensive code of standards for prisons is in operation, either as part of the legislation controlling what happens in prisons or as an authoritative and precise set of requirements for prison management. The prison system in England and Wales is the subject of diverse uncoordinated rules and regulations, which vary as to their clarity, specificity, scope, authority and status in law.

The debate in this country on standards for prison conditions recently began to take on a less abstract tone. In 1982 the government made a commitment to publish a draft code of minimum standards for the prison system. Although in late 1983 the commitment was withdrawn, with a promise to proceed by publishing building regulations for new prison establishments, by then the Chief Inspector of Prisons had called for a code of standards guaranteeing a prisoner's rights (HM Chief Inspector of Prisons 1983a) and the Society of Civil and Public Servants, Prison Governors' Branch, had presented its report on prison standards (Society of Civil and Public Servants 1983).

Against this background, the National Association for the Care and Resettlement of Offenders (NACRO) published a code of minimum standards for prison establishments (Casale 1984). Because it was intended as a first step towards a system of standards for prison conditions, the code is naturally of a rudimentary nature. It is therefore not to be regarded as the ideal for a practical design for prison standards. Nevertheless, it provides a useful starting point for discussion since it attempts to define clearly and precisely a set of criteria for practical use in measuring living conditions in prisons. Although it is by no means comprehensive, it represents the furthest move to date in this direction in this country. (The code will not be presented again in detail here. This paper addresses more general problems concerning the design and implementation of such a code.)

A practical first step

The NACRO code identifies in the first instance certain elements of prison conditions that are particulary amenable to measurement, e.g. space/occupancy, lighting, heating, ventilation, noise, cell contents, hygiene, food, exercise/recreation and safety. It will be immediately obvious that, while some aspects of these elements are quantifiable, others must be defined qualitatively. This approach necessarily suffers from certain shortcomings: important components of prison conditions may be omitted because they do not readily lend themselves to measurement.

In this country minimum standards are in their infancy and it is necessary to proceed by dealing first with variables relating primarily to physical conditions, because they offer the possibility of consensus based on technical expertise. Heating and lighting conditions, for example, exhibit these properties. It is possible to refer to medical and other authority for desirable levels of heat and light for a normal healthy environment. However, this should be regarded as only the beginning: in theory at least, *all* aspects of prison conditions might form the subject of minimum standards. The logical progression would seem to be to broaden the scope starting from this limited and more easily quantifiable base.

The fact that certain elements of prison conditions are susceptible of objective quantification does not mean that any code of minimum standards can claim total objectivity. The level at which a minimum standard is set is essentially a matter of subjective choice. There are, however, ways of making the choice more legitimate. One obvious method is to refer to other related and relevant standards already in existence. Another is to incorporate the opinions of experts.

Thus the NACRO code reflects levels agreed as basic minima in other codes of minimum prison standards (both international and in particular countries), levels recommended or required by existing rules, guidelines or statutory instruments in this country in relation to prison establishments or to other relevant areas, and levels that find approval among a wide range of concerned and experienced organizations.

The underlying notion is that the levels should reflect basic standards below which living conditions should not fall. That is ultimately a moral consideration and for that reason any code of minimum standards must be controversial.

Impractical codes

The task of establishing a viable code of minimum standards for prisons entails balancing two potentially conflicting elements: specificity and subjectivity. At times the temptation is to avoid the conflict by escape into obscurity. In order for standards to gain the official approval necessary for their translation into an authoritative instrument for change, e.g. legislation, they tend to be couched in vague language which effectively robs them of practical utility.

This is the case with the United Nations and European Standard Minimum Rules for the Treatment of Prisoners (see Fawcett Chapter 4). As expressions of general principle they serve a valid but limited purpose. The extent of their usefulness may be measured by the fact that in 1978 the UK Government was able to claim (though not without criticism) that the European Standard Minimum Rules had been fully implemented in all but two respects.

An example may serve to illustrate the problem. European Standard Minimum Rule 8 states that single cell occupancy is the preferred norm, but with the proviso 'unless circumstances dictate otherwise'. This broad qualification robs the standard of any real force.

Historically, then, at the international level the move towards codes of minimum standards for prison conditions has reached only this first stage of enunciating general propositions in language so vague and ambiguous as to detract from their practical utility.

More practical developments

At the national level the development has been more promising. Standards have been evolving which are less vague, without veering to the other extreme of reducing what is at heart a human problem to technical formulae.

In the Netherlands legislation has made single cell occupancy a practical norm. Legislation in the Federal Republic of Germany has also moved in this direction; however, there are several important exceptions to the provision for single cell occupancy, including the broad exclusion 'except . . . for only temporary periods and for compelling reasons' (Federal Republic of Germany 1976: s.18).

By far the most comprehensive and precise codes of minimum standards are to be found in the USA. The extent of the development there is due in part to a marked tendency towards codification and in part to the context in which the movement towards standards arose. The impetus came from prisoners, who on the one hand sought legal redress through class actions based on claims that certain prison conditions violated constitutional rights, and on the other hand voiced their grievances through prison riots (see Morgan and Bronstein this volume).

The response took various forms. Some courts made quite specific rulings of a practical nature: in some cases doubling-up prisoners in cells under certain size specifications was prohibited; in others the court reduced the certified capacity of a particular prison (Rutherford 1982: 169). Alternatively out-of-court settlements (consent decrees) were negotiated in some jurisdictions, such as New York City. The result was a carefully worked out schedule for practical changes to plant and regime to improve prison conditions.

As this phenomenon arose at the federal, state and local levels, systematic codes of standards began to evolve. Although the various codes apply to different kinds of correctional facilities and differ as to details, they have certain common features. They tend to be the product of a systematic and thorough approach to defining minimal levels of living conditions and they are often remarkable for their specificity.

In space/occupancy standards we find that careful attention is given in various codes (as, for example, in Standard 2.27 of the Federal Standards for Prisons and Jails (US Department of Justice

1980)) not only to minimum square footage of floor space, but also to minimum ceiling height amd minimum measurement between walls. This may sound pedantic but in practice it is of vital importance.

In our own Prison Department's Current Recommended Standards for the Design of New Prison Establishments (Home Office 1984c) the space standards for cells are limited to square footage requirements. The result is that they are open to varying interpretation. Theoretically a single cell measuring 1 metre wide and 6.3 metres long with a ceiling of 1.3 metres would conform to the published recommended standards. It is to be hoped that interpretation would not be taken to this absurd conclusion, but it is not expressly precluded.

Attention to detail bears witness to an awareness on the part of codifiers that the practical value of a minimum standard is inversely proportionate to the degree to which it is open to varying interpretation. There is something to be learnt from the specificity characterizing many of the American codes.

Comparative reference points

There are many lessons to be learnt from looking at past experience in developing standards for prisons. That experience has largely occurred outside this country and there are obvious problems in comparing phenomena in different contexts. No one would reasonably advocate a facile transference of experience in a crude, wholesale fashion without regard to context. That does not preclude the value of carefully considered comparisons.

Indeed the recent report on managing the long-term prison system (Home Office 1984b) points out that we may have something to gain from considering the new generation prison designs in the USA. In the matter of minimum standards for prisons, too, we are necessarily thrown back on comparisons with other systems, because developments in this country are behindhand. Without imitating parrot-fashion, we may extract from such comparisons useful hints on how to approach our own related problems.

Certain of the codes produced in the USA are impressive because not only do they treat elements of prison conditions with great attention to technical detail, but they also manage to avoid the pitfall of concentrating on technical detail to the exclusion of the human dimension. Any practical code of standards for prison conditions must avoid an over-simplistic approach focusing on purely physical components (plant and equipment). Conditions entail a relationship between plant and the uses to which it is put.

Thus if a code is to address standards of living in prison it cannot stop at specifying minimum provision of plant and equipment per capita; it must also address questions of access and availability. In the matter of personal hygiene it is not enough to specify minimum provision of bath/shower apparatus in relation to prison population: the standards must specify how often per week each prisoner may use these facilities.

The importance of relating physical facilities to use is nowhere more central than in space/occupancy standards. It is not enough to ensure that cells have certain minimum dimensions. It is necessary to link these measurements to the period of occupancy. If a prisoner remains in a cell for most of his or her sleeping and waking hours, the size and shape of the cell takes on a different significance than for a prisoner who spends most of the day elsewhere.

Similary lighting, ventilation, heating and contents of a cell are related to the proportion of time spent there and to whether or not the cell is crowded with other occupants. A sophisticated code of minimum standards for prison conditions would have to take the complex interrelationship between many factors into account. However, at present we are a long way from this level of refinement. The first step is the articulation of a set of basic standards relating primarily to the more tangible aspects of prison life.

Sources and references at home

Some of the material for this exercise already exists in this country, though not as a coherent and comprehensive body of legislation. Therefore the task is partly one of reiteration and compilation.

There are various rules and requirements applying specifically to prison establishments in England and Wales. The problem is that the Prison Rules are not comprehensive or specific enough to constitute an adequate set of standards, minimum or recommended. The Standing Orders and Circular Instructions are at times more specific, although by no means comprehensive (they contain, for instance, no noise standards at all); the main problem inhering in them is their status.

They are essentially directives to management. As such they sometimes set out precise and exacting requirements for the provision of certain facilities in prison establishments. Thus Prison Rule 26(1) and Standing Order 14 together provide for most of the hygiene supplies necessary for an adequate minimum standard on this point (see Casale 1984: NACRO code B1(e)).

The Standing Orders also establish obligations on the part of prison governors to ensure observance of various relevant statutory instruments, such as the Factories Act 1961, the Offices, Shops and Railway Premises Act 1963, etc. There is a great deal of material in the form of legislation in related areas on which one may draw for standards. There are rules and regulations concerning private and public places of communal working and living, such as factories, offices, hospitals and barracks.

Professional and governmental bodies publish technical guidelines on lighting, heating, ventilation, noise, nutrition and general hygiene. Many of the recommended levels are officially agreed in this country and abroad. They form a legitimate and relatively uncontroversial source to inform a practical code of minimum standards for prison establishments.

Developing a code from these materials is not solely an exercise in collating and editing. Many people see the step from these rules and recommendations to minimum standards as a quantum leap. The distinction depends upon the status of the rules and recommendations on the one hand and of a code of minimum standards on the other. The question has profound implications for the problem of implementing standards.

Prospects for implementation

One way of viewing a code of minimum standards for prison establishments might be to accord it the status of management directives and to see it as a reiteration and elaboration of existing requirements addressed to the prison service. The explicit addition would then consist in prison management being required to ensure *at least* those levels of provision. The value of such a code would lie in its incorporating clearly and systematically in one body a set of coherent minimum standards.

A code of minimum standards might, on the other hand, be enacted as law. Whether or not it expressly conferred rights on the prisoner, it would almost certainly be used as a basis for claims by prisoners that conditions not in compliance with the code violated rights implicit in the minimum standards, and the courts might hand down judgements confirming those rights.

Whether compliance is a matter of conforming to the law or to an internal administrative order, in practical terms implementation of a code does not follow automatically from its authoritative status. Legal status may promote regard for the standards and open avenues for challenge, but the prospects for implementation are more likely to be enhanced by two mundane factors: the ability to detect non-compliance and the feasibility of sanctions.

For this reason an essential component of any practical code of minimum standards is the careful provision for a system of management information operating on a routine basis. This means specifying methods for measuring and recording standard items as a regular part of administering various types of establishments.

In addition to this internal information system there is a need for external monitoring. However, there are cogent reasons for emphasizing the internal mechanism: external monitors cannot, without enormous input of resources, hope to equal the level of information achievable by an internal routine. In the end they must rely in part at least on information gathered by prison staff. They are therefore best seen as a necessary addition guaranteeing a measure of independent and impartial scrutiny.

The internal information system should not be viewed as an unnecessary imposition from without. It is potentially of considerable value to the establishment, since it is an important ingredient of proper accountability and effective management. Indeed it is difficult to see how establishments may be run efficiently and future budgets planned in the absence of this kind of information system.

The system is therefore a prerequisite both for a workable establishment and for a workable code. It forms a first step towards building the possibility of implementation into the structure of a code itself. However, one can go only so far in the direction of implementation by careful codification.

Sanctions must exist as the ultimate recourse in the event of blatant and continued non-compliance. In the USA we see that sanctions may take many forms: from the extreme of closure of parts of or entire facilities, to court orders for practical operational changes, to out-of-court settlements (consent decrees) involving compromises negotiated between prisoners' groups and prison management, to withholding or reducing central budget allocations to individual facilities (see Morgan and Bronstein, this volume).

In the end, however, implementation stands or falls on the ground floor with the staff who are faced with putting standards into practice. In the final analysis excessive codification without consultation with those persons at the centre of the work might become a useless paper exercise. What is needed is a joint effort at translating minimum standards into a detailed timetable for practical implementation at individual establishments. It would be futile to attempt this without reference to the expertise of those closest to the task. Refinement of a code of minimum standards into a working plan for change must involve a sustained dialogue within and beyond the prison system.

7

Her Majesty's Inspectorate of Prisons

Rod Morgan

Background

The first prison inspectors were appointed in 1835. They were statutory agents of central government, enforcing compliance with prison legislation by the local authorities, which at that time were responsible for all but the convict prisons. The first inspectors, however, achieved more than that: they shaped prison policy. Their published reports were voluminous, detailed and trenchant. They developed systematic ideas about the desirable shape of prison regimes and converted ministers to their cause (MacDonagh 1977; McConville 1981).

In 1878 all prisons were brought under the control of central government. The prisons inspectorate disappeared, replaced much later by an internal system of institutional inspection as part of management. Senior staff, based at headquarters, undertook inspection tasks on behalf of the Prisons Board within the Prison Department. Their reports were confidential and though their activities doubtless caused the occasional stir within the Department, they excited little interest outside. Apart from their occasional investigations into incidents (for example, the riot at Hull in 1976) the inspectorate largely disappeared from public view.

On 1 January 1981 all this changed. A new prisons inspectorate came into being, external to the Prisons Department but within the Home Office. The decision to appoint this new 'independent' body was almost universally applauded. After three years, it seems sensible to review the nature, problems and achievements of this still developing institution.

The May Committee

The proposal that there be a prisons inspectorate outside the Prison Department and answerable to the Home Secretary was first formally made in 1978 by the House of Commons Expenditure Committee. The recommendation was repeated in 1979 by the Committee of Inquiry into the UK Prison Services (the May Committee, Home Office 1979). Both committees linked their views on inspection with a concern that the prison service be more open. The Expenditure Committee Report connected inspection with a group of recommendations designed to strengthen contact between prisons and the community (House of Commons Expenditure Committee 1978: paras 162–81). The May Committee concurred that 'public sentiment requires that as many aspects of government, which includes the prison service, should be opened up to as wide an audience as possible' (Home Office 1979: para. 5.61). However, though all inspectorates are justified, *inter alia*, by appeals to public confidence, the prison service in England and Wales poses unique problems which the May Committee found their most difficult organizational issue (Home Office 1979: para. 5.50).

The problem is this: on whose behalf can a prisons inspectorate inspect? Most inspectorates act as intermediaries between central and local government, or between government and private institutions. They are concerned largely with the enforcement of statute law, some ensure efficiency and a few have additional functions (see Rhodes 1982). But in nearly all cases they act on behalf of government concerning activities for which the department exercises limited administrative responsibility. Herein lies the difficulty for prisons. Alone of all public services bar the armed forces, prisons are the sole undivided financial and administrative responsibility of a single central government department, the Home Office. In which case, can a prisons inspectorate responsible to the Home Secretary be said to be truly independent of the department being inspected?

Home Office advice to the May Committee was very clear on

this point (Home Office 1979: Evidence, Paper 15). Since prisons are the responsibility of the Home Secretary, who is answerable to Parliament for their management, there was no basis on which the inspectorate could be independent of government. Nor, in the Home Office view, would it make much sense to think of an inspectorate as independent if it were outside the Prison Department but reporting to the Home Secretary. The recipients of the reports, the Minister and his Permanent Under Secretary, would be the very persons constitutionally responsible for the service being reported on.

The Home Office distinguished between the inspection functions of efficiency and propriety (by which it meant compliance with rules, statutory and non-statutory), and argued that since both forms of inspection would, in the interests of good management, be continued within the Prison Department, the formation of an external inspectorate would unnecessarily duplicate the task. The Home Office advised retention of the existing inspection arrangements with certain modifications: institutions might be inspected more frequently and the Chief Inspector might cease to be a member of the Prisons Board so as to distance himself from operational responsibility. But the publication of reports was said to be ill-advised; such a move would simply prevent the Chief Inspector from speaking frankly.

The May Committee accepted the constitutional logic of these Home Office arguments, but their quest for greater openness led them to reject the conclusions. The Committee agreed that a Home Office inspectorate outside the Prison Department could not be fully independent of the service, but it held that it would have credibility if: the new department included personnel not recruited from prisons; its reports were published; it could make unannounced visits; and it could report on general aspects of the work of the Prison Department.

The Home Secretary announced in April 1980 that he accepted the May Committee's proposals on inspection. Later, he and his ministerial colleagues frequently pointed to the existence of the new Inspectorate as evidence of their commitment to 'opening up the prisons to public gaze'. This claim has been substantiated principally by the decision to publish in full all the Chief Inspector's reports except where matters of security have been at issue. At no stage was it envisaged that the Inspectorate, unlike, for example, Environmental Health Officers, should have enforcement powers – and they have none. The Inspectorate's role is purely advisory.

The mandate and its implementation

Brief terms of reference for the new Inspectorate were announced in April 1981. This statement was subsequently expanded to form what the Chief Inspector refers to as his 'charter' (reproduced in HM Chief Inspector of Prisons 1982a, Appendix 1). Though the Inspectorate has since been put on a statutory basis (s.57 of the Criminal Justice Act 1982 provides for the insertion of a new section, s.5A, in the Prison Act 1952), it is the charter which spells out the Chief Inspector's functions and mode of operation. The statute merely provides that: 'Her Majesty may' (not will) appoint a Chief Inspector of Prisons (s.5A(1)); refers to his duties in England and Wales only (s.5A(2)); and concentrates on his remit to 'report to the Secretary of State on the treatment of prisoners and conditions in prisons' (s.5A(3)). The charter describes other, less straightforward functions.

The Inspectorate's main task, the charter explains, is to inspect individual establishments regularly. The first Chief Inspector, William Pearce, who died in January 1982, agreed to the Home Office suggestion that 'regularly' should mean the continuation of the quinquennial inspection programme maintained by the old inspectorate. There being some one hundred and twenty institutions administered by the Prison Department, this meant twenty-four week-long inspections per year. This was the target set for 1981 and again for 1982.

Given the Chief Inspector's slender resources it was always doubtful whether this arduous target could physically, let alone adequately, be achieved. Though the Inspectorate was large enough to operate two teams, the considerable burden of twenty-four weeks in the field, preceded by briefing and followed by analysis and report writing, left little space for basic preparation or other tasks. The plan seemed unwise for four reasons.

First, the Inspectorate's terms of reference mentioned their looking at 'such other matters as the Secretary of State may direct' (*Hansard* 30 April 1980: col. 1395). The charter elaborated this as follows: 'the presumption will be that major incidents which raise questions about the management of an establishment, or of the service as a whole, will in future be investigated by the Inspectorate' (para. 7). Major incidents – riots, breaches of security, or industrial actions by staff – have been common in recent years: it seemed probable that special references to the Inspectorate would occur fairly often, with disruption of the regular inspection programme the inevitable consequence.

Second, the charter required the regular inspection programme to concentrate on 'the morale of staff and prisoners; the quality of the regime; the condition of the buildings; questions of humanity and propriety; and the extent to which the establishment is giving value for money' (para. 4). Given the poverty of information known routinely to be available on such matters as institutional costs and regime characteristics there was a premium placed on the Inspectorate devising its own criteria for the evaluation of regimes, and the efficient use of resources. Too onerous a fieldwork programme seemed likely to prejudice this spadework.

Third, the May Committee had recommended that thematic rather than routine institutional inspection should be the Inspectorate's core function (Home Office 1979: para. 5.62). The Committee argued that institutional inspections of the sort conducted by the old inspectorate should in future be undertaken by regional directors of the Prison Department. This view was acknowledged in the charter, albeit in a watered down form: 'inspections of more general aspects of the work of the prison service will normally be included in the programme of general inspections of establishments' (HM Chief Inspector of Prisons 1982a: para. 5). By design or default, serious thematic inspection seemed a likely casualty of too strenuous a routine programme of institutional inspections.

Fourth, if the objective of opening up the prison service to greater public scrutiny was to be achieved, the Inspectorate's work had to be publicized as fully and speedily as possible. Like justice, publicity delayed is publicity denied: inspection reports on institutions whose functions have changed, on incidents that have long passed, or on policies that have been amended, lose their relevance. Too heavy an inspection programme risked delays in the analysis of data and the publication of reports, calling into question the credibility of the office itself.

Despite its considerable achievements, the Inspectorate has fallen prey to all these pitfalls. The Secretary of State has twice requested that the Chief Inspector investigate incidents, both in Northern Ireland. In 1981 eight remand prisoners escaped from

Belfast Prison with the aid of firearms. The Inspectorate spent ten days in Belfast and two routine inspections were cancelled. In 1983, a prisoner breakout occurred at the Maze Prison. Thirty-five prisoners escaped and one officer was killed. For five weeks the whole Inspectorate was in Northern Ireland and four routine inspections planned for the autumn of 1983 were cancelled.

It is apparent, however, that the Inspectorate was incapable of fulfilling the quinquennial programme, even without these crisis interventions. Only eighteen routine inspections were accomplished in 1981 (four fewer than the Belfast incident explains) and an uninterrupted passage in 1982 still produced only twenty-one inspections.

Slippage also characterized the publication timetable. At the beginning of 1981 the Chief Inspector was able to sign and send routine inspection reports to the Home Secretary within four to five months. But this dispatch was short-lived. Delays of seven to eight months became the norm for the rest of 1981. By the middle of 1982, the Home Secretary could reckon on having to wait twelve months or more for reports, with publication taking longer still. At the time of writing, October 1984, nine reports on inspections conducted in 1982 have still to be published.

The explanation for these damaging delays must include processes outside the Inspectorate. Publication is a two-stage process. First, the Home Secretary receives the Chief Inspector's report. Second, the report is published, accompanied by comments indicating how the Home Secretary has acted, or intends to act, on any recommendations; publication follows deliberations within the Prison Department. At the outset in 1981 this second stage took four months or less. By the end of 1981, delays of eight months were not uncommon, matching those within the Inspectorate. Responsibility, therefore, appears to rest equally with the Prison Department and the Inspectorate. Clearly, the work of the Chief Inspector is generally accorded a low priority by the Prison Department and, by implication, the Home Secretary.

Further evidence for this conclusion emerges from scrutiny of those inspection reports where operational considerations made early publication desirable. The inspections of Birmingham Prison (November 1981) and Ashford Remand Centre (November 1982) followed scandals arising out of coroners' verdicts. In Birmingham, Barry Prosser had been 'unlawfully killed' by persons unknown, but certainly by one or more members of staff; in Ashford, James Heather-Hayes had died 'through lack of care'.

Both institutions needed a clean bill of operational health, if one could be given. The Chief Inspector's reports met that need: there were minor criticisms, but, as far as the nature of the original scandals were concerned, no suggestion of staff corruption or callousness. On the contrary the staff at Birmingham, where the unsuccessful prosecution of several officers left the deepest stain, emerged with a 'good deal of credit' (HM Chief Inspector of Prisons 1982b: para. 1.03) and the staff at Ashford demonstrated 'concern' and 'distress' in the wake of Hayes' death (1983b: para. 7.18). In both cases the reports were written, reacted to and published in less than half the time taken over other inspections during the same periods.

In 1982, following the appointment of the present Chief Inspector, Sir James Hennessy, it was decided to abandon the quinquennial programme. Henceforth there were to be only fourteen routine inspections annually, plus several thematic reviews of general policy issues across institutions. This directional shift, which accords more with the mandate recommended by the May Committee, is still taking place.

Resources

Inspection of all public services depends crucially on human skills. The question of whether the resources available to the Inspectorate are adequate comes down to two issues – personnel and information. Does the Chief Inspector have the right staff and enough of them? And do those staff have access to the data which will enable them to gauge whether what is going on in prisons is satisfactory?

The two questions seem capable of being answered separately. What fuses them is a problem not unique to the prison service: it concerns the proper and, more pragmatically, the effective balance between the independence, impartiality and expertise of the inspectors on the one hand, and their insider intelligence, credibility and experience on the other. An Inspectorate staffed by persons from outside the service, experts in management, buildings, public health or whatever, may satisfy the demand that inspection be conspicuously independent. But if the inspectors are unversed in prison culture, if they lack the confidence of prison staff, they may be blind to some of the questions which need to be asked and ineffective at penetrating the system. The dilemma confronting the Prisons Inspectorate is similar to that which preoccupies the designers of police complaints systems.

The May Committee advocated that the Inspectorate should comprise 'people with relevant prison experience as well as such others as the Home Secretary thinks appropriate' (Home Office 1979: para. 5.62). With the exception of the Chief Inspector (an ex-Chief Probation Officer), and two part-time advisers on medical and building matters, the remaining seven full-time inspectors, including the Deputy Chief Inspector, all had Prison Department career backgrounds. These personnel were divided into two teams which included a former prison governor, chief officer and prison administration officer. Some were at the end of their service careers. But this was not invariably the case; members of the Inspectorate have returned to the prison service. For example, both the first Deputy Chief Inspector and his successor have become Deputy Director General of the Prison Department.

The dilemma is obvious. Can persons recruited from the service being inspected – some of whom will return to it – so distance themselves from service colleagues, practices and attitudes, that they are able to bring a fresh, dispassionate and critical view to bear on it? It is not easy to answer the question. The inspectors maintain they are not inhibited by their past associations and, possibly, future prospects. On the contrary, they argue their experience makes them peculiarly adept at recognizing when things are awry: they imply that colleagues drawn from outside the service may find it harder to see through surface appearances. This may of course be true, though the only member of the Inspectorate to discuss the issue in public, a part-time medical inspector without previous experience of prisons, has suggested otherwise: following his resignation in 1982, he spoke of 'plea-bargaining' between the Inspectorate and local governors, of undue sensitivity to press criticism of the prison service, of deference to the views of the Prison Officers' Association, and of censorship over what the Inspectorate was prepared to discuss in published reports (Lee 1983).

These allegations are denied by former colleagues. Furthermore, at least one of the policy issues allegedly subject to censorship, namely special security units, has since been the subject of a published report (HM Chief Inspector of Prisons 1984b). But the argument about whether 'insiders' pull punches, as opposed to 'outsiders' not knowing how to throw them, may be missing a more essential point. It seems at least probable that insiders, however self-consciously critical and independent they strive to be, tend to focus on day-to-day management issues, and that they do so within the framework of 'propriety' as the Prison Department understands the term. This, after all, is what they know best. In this sense, the influence of insiders seems likely to favour the routine inspection programme which, however diminished, remains in content a management-orientated legacy of the old inspectorate.

The present Chief Inspector is well aware of these relationships. Significantly, the decision to reduce the burden of routine inspection in favour of thematic inspection, has been accompanied by efforts to increase the recruitment of outsiders. The two 'administrator' members of inspection teams are no longer former prison administrative officers. In 1983, the Inspectorate acquired the services of a research officer seconded from the Home Office Research and Planning Unit, and the Chief Inspector is currently negotiating the possibility of his recruiting more part-time inspectors. These outsiders might include commercial managers or accountants, probation officers, academics, public health or safety specialists. Their involvement should help the Inspectorate occasionally to get off the inevitably repetitive treadmill of routine institutional inspection (which will remain a core function) to make more lateral forays into broader questions of policy.

It remains to be seen whether the Home Office will allow the Inspectorate to harness these potentially challenging resources. The indications so far are not encouraging. The Inspectorate has regularly been starved of resources. In 1982, periods of eight and six months respectively lapsed before the Chief and Deputy Chief Inspectors were replaced: for a time both posts were vacant. During this and the following year there was a 50 per cent turnover of full-time inspectors, again accompanied by replacement delays. Given that it takes three months to train team members (HM Chief Inspector of Prisons 1984a: para. 1.08), this is scarcely a personnel policy reflecting Home Office concern for the Inspectorate's effective operation.

The Inspectorate appears to receive all the information it

requires. There is no suggestion of their being denied access to institutions or, during inspections, persons or documents within institutions. The Inspectorate draws up a list, well in advance, of establishments it wishes to inspect the following year. The choice is determined largely in terms of mixed rotation, but institutions are included if public concern, internal reports, or a pattern of complaints suggests that early scrutiny is desirable. The Prison Department is shown the list and occasionally adjustments are made in response to comments. The Department may, for example, request an inspection be delayed because of impending staff or functional changes. This sort of consultation seems perfectly sensible: for an inspector to be briefed adequately there could be no question of conducting full inspections without warning. Furthermore, the Inspectorate does make unannounced visits. In 1983, twenty one-day visits were made to establishments of which eleven were unannounced.

Prior to each institutional inspection the inspectors receive briefs comprising: prisoner, staff and physical capacity statistics; a statement of the prison's functions; the Board of Visitors' annual report; and reports from governors and departmental heads on their work. The Inspectorate also receives copies of all Prison Department circular instructions and standing orders, working party and research reports, and the papers and minutes of the Prisons Board. There is no evidence that the Department holds back on routine management information.

Yet the adequacy of the Inspectorate's informational base concerns more than their access to Prison Department data. It is doubtful whether the Prison Department itself possesses the information which adequate inspection demands. Consider costs data. Until recently, the Prison Department had a relatively unsophisticated accounting system; it was unable, for example, to provide the May Committee with costs for individual establishments (Home Office 1979: para. 5.35). Thus, although the Inspectorate is charged with discovering whether establishments are giving 'value for money', it has neither the information nor the expertise to make such assessments. The Chief Inspector's first annual report admitted both shortcomings. Pointing out that his staff were not accountants, he said it was 'difficult to establish whether resources are being distributed in a way that effectively achieves a desirable balance between the various activities'. His staff had to rely on 'common sense', though 'as more financial information becomes available it will be possible to adopt a more systematic approach (HM Chief Inspector of Prisons 1982a: para. 1.10). Common sense is manifestly not enough. For example, in a recently published report on Leicester Prison, the Chief Inspector drew attention to the high staffing ratio in the special security unit. This led him to question the 'appropriateness of siting such a unit in an overcrowded local prison where the conditions for the majority of the prisoners are so totally different'. However, 'lack of information about costs and other matters' meant he came to no conclusion (1984b: para. 7.05).

More financial information is now available and is supplied to the Inspectorate. But data on costs are supplied for individual establishments without comparative indices to aid interpretation. Furthermore, the Inspectorate is still without the accounting or economic skills required to process routine financial data and assess whether the sort of information now becoming available is adequate for effective Prison Department management.

Similar points can be made about information on the treatment of prisoners. From the Prison Department records, local and national, published and unpublished, it is not possible to say whether the quality of life for prisoners is improving or declining (see Morgan 1983). Published statistics on crowding and prisoner employment are indicative, but they tell only part of the story. The Prison Department does not know, generally or for particular prisons, for example, whether prisoners spend more or less time locked in their cells, whether the frequency and duration of visits has improved, or how access to basic services has changed. Except where regime features are subject to precise statutory direction, which is scarcely ever the case, the Prison Department has not stated minimum physical and regime standards (see Casale Chapter 6). The Chief Inspector has expressed regret publicly that this is so. He regularly refers to the Council of Europe's Standard Minimum Rules. But in judging the adequacy of provision his staff rely principally on their 'subjective . . . experience of life and of the Prison Service' (HM Chief Inspector of Prisons 1982a: para. 1.7). The problem with this solution is twofold. First, it remains unclear as to what criteria the Inspectorate are using. Second, for as long as the Inspectorate fail to state their criteria, and the precise degree to which the conditions they find measure up to them, the public is none the wiser as to whether conditions are equitable, or have improved or deteriorated.

Pronouncements and reactions

Neither Sir James Hennessy, his predecessor nor his staff have been prepared to make *ex cathedra* comments about their work or the prison service it is their duty to monitor. The public record of the Inspectorate comprises only the official reports, which fall into four categories: routine institutional, thematic policy, incident and annual reports.

The routine inspection reports are of interest mostly to the people associated with the institutions described. To begin with, in 1981/2, the reports frequently attracted attention from the media nationally. This is seldom now the case, unless conditions in the prison under review are criticized sharply. The local press may report the Chief Inspector's findings, the penal pressure groups sometimes take up the most recent example of a long-pursued deficiency, but for the most part institutional reports are ignored. The negligible feedback received by the Inspectorate suggests they are little read.

This is scarcely surprising. For the staff in the prisons described, routine inspection reports are history; the inspection may have taken place anything between four and thirty months previously. But whatever the delay, the governor and most of his staff will have learnt of the Inspectors' findings if not during the visit itself then shortly thereafter. The Chief Inspector has always maintained, quite properly, that staff should be advised as to the Inspectorate's tentative conclusions before they are committed to print.

The inspection team's assessment used to be written in outline form before departing the establishment. This practice was modified in 1983. On the final day of the inspectors' visit the governor is provided with an undifferentiated set of comments. The following week the team is de-briefed and their observations subdivided into those which need to be brought to the attention of the governor, regional director or Director General, whoever is operationally responsible. These observations are distinguished from formal recommendations.

In future, all observations and recommendations will be published. This will typically mean a very long list. For example, the report on Canterbury (inspected January 1984) includes three formal recommendations, one observation directed at the Director General, eleven for the regional director, and twenty for the governor (HM Chief Inspector of Prisons 1985). This is a much fuller and clearer account than has been included in reports hitherto. Discretion was exercised previously as to whether comments were reported (1982a: para. 1.14); and when they were, all were couched as recommendations no matter how serious or trivial. Despite minor changes the overall format of routine reports has remained fairly constant since 1981; thirty to forty pages long, a series of more or less standard sub-headings are used. A general assessment is followed by sections on staff, prisoners, the regime and security.

The majority of recommendations concern matters which are the responsibility of governors locally. Most involve non-compliance with statutory rules or Prison Department procedures. The most commonly cited deficiencies have been failure to: post fire regulations; hold fire-drills; provide prisoners with information; keep areas clean; record use of stripped cells, prisoner segregation or restraints; make adequate provision for prisoner exercise; and store cooked and raw food separately. In virtually all cases the Home Secretary has stated the recommendations to be accepted and implemented. Where recommendations concern Prison Department policies, involving the use of resources or the stresses on the system, the picture is different. The Home Secretary usually accepts recommendations 'in principle', but often states merely that the Department is doing its best, holding out little short-term hope of making whatever improvement to buildings, regimes or facilities are pressed.

The Chief Inspector sometimes uses uncompromisingly critical language. Overcrowding is frequently described as 'unacceptable', regimes 'barren' or lacking in 'respect for human dignity', conditions 'squalid' or 'degrading' (see, for example, HM Chief Inspector of Prisons, reports 1982a; 1982b; 1982c; 1982e; 1983c; 1983d). But when confronted with local prisons or remand centres (all of which have permanently been overcrowded for over twenty years) the problem for the Inspectorate is one of linguistic exhaustion. How often can prison overcrowding be described as unacceptable when plainly it is accepted? How frequently should the Chief Inspector spell out the solutions – reducing the population, improving facilities and refurbishing the fabric – which would make life tolerable? Most of the early reports on overcrowded prisons (Gloucester, Leeds, Stafford, Birmingham and Wormwood Scrubs) formally recommended the population be reduced. The Home Secretary's response in each case was predictable; 'the prospects for reducing the population . . . are dependent on a substantial reduction in the overall prison population' (comments published with HM Chief Inspector of Prisons 1982d). The Inspectorate seems to have decided this dialogue served little purpose. Recent reports on prisons equally overcrowded (1983b; 1983c; 1983f; 1984b) contain no population recommendations. Indeed the report on Leicester, which at the time of inspection contained twice as many prisoners as its certified normal accommodation, describes the gross overcrowding without a hint of pejorative language; the short-term solution of providing extra lavatories on landings ('the installation of integral sanitation . . . is some years away' (1984b: para. 3.05)) is recommended.

Rather than condemn conditions in successive and increasingly ignored individual reports, the Inspectorate sensibly has tended to store up its fire-power for the annual reports. Here issues can be dealt with more systematically and tellingly since the annual reports are read and reported widely.

Overcrowding is the major blight on British prisons; it is appropriate, therefore, that Chief Inspectors should have made it the focal point of their first three annual reports. No matter how often the topic is debated, the Inspectorate has rightly concluded that 'it is essential for us to continue to emphasise the price which society pays for having more people locked up than there is room for' (HM Chief Inspector of Prisons 1982a: para. 3.02). In 1982, they proceeded to do this in graphic and subsequently much-quoted terms. They pointed out what the implications of overcrowding were for: time spent in cells; prisoner employment; access to other services; and, not least, staff working conditions. They invited the reader to imagine himself obliged to stay in an hotel so overbooked that he has to share his room with two complete strangers. And in the elaboration of this imaginary exercise they shirked none of the 'degrading and brutalising' details of the existence daily faced by many prisoners (1982a: para. 3.07).

The problem with descriptive chronicles of this sort is that they may differ little from statements regularly put out by press officers within the Prison Department, usually in support of claims for more resources. However, the Chief Inspector has not allowed himself to become merely a spokeman for officially sanctioned bad news. He has followed his descriptions with brief appraisals of the degree to which current Prison Department and government programmes offer feasible solutions to overcrowding or minimize present suffering. Under both headings the Chief Inspector has been prepared to make waves.

In 1982, for example, he doubted whether the Government's prison building programme could reduce overcrowding before 1990 (HM Chief Inspector of Prisons 1982a: para. 3.12). In 1983, despite the announcement of a substantially increased building programme, he concluded that the end of the decade was 'likely to see a worsening in overcrowding' (1983a: para. 2.07). Furthermore, his judgements that any building programme should concentrate first on the local prisons (1983a: para. 2.11) and that many prisoners were almost certainly subject to greater security than they warranted (1983a: para. 2.21–2), were scarcely disguised criticisms of Government plans which gave first priority to the construction of more high-security accommodation and left local prisons till last. The Inspector's view coincided with that of several independent commentators (see Morgan 1983). Within the Home Office it became an open secret that the Home Secretary and some officials were greatly discomfited by Sir James Hennessy's report.

The annual report for 1983 is the briefest and most restrained yet. Overcrowding is mentioned but only in the form of a reminder and to point to conclusions reached the previous year (HM Chief Inspector of Prisons 1984a: paras 3.02–4). Yet the report does, by implication, discuss whether current Prison Department policy mitigates or aggravates the consequences of overcrowding. Having earlier established that the concentration of overcrowding in the local prisons is 'a result of a deliberate Prison Department policy' (1982a: para. 3.03), the Chief Inspector points out that impoverished regimes in local prisons are aggravated by staff shortages resulting from the Prison Department court escort commitment. He suggests that the principle of charging for services on an agency basis might, if applied to the escort function (a matter long debated but about which nothing has been done), 'lead to more acceptable and more economical procedures' (1984a: paras 2.05–6). Second, he doubts whether staff shift arrangements are the most efficient or flexible and he is critical of growing prison service dependence on high voluntary rates of staff overtime; he implies that the situation reflects ineffective management of staff resources which will in turn serve to undermine that effectiveness further (1984a: paras 4.05–6). Finally, following up earlier doubts about the need for so much high security, the Chief Inspector describes security classification procedures as inconsistent and haphazard, with 'security, control and allocation issues' insufficiently differentiated (1984a: paras 5.09–15).

Prison Categorisation Procedures (HM Chief Inspector of Prisons 1984e) was the subject of the Inspectorate's second thematic review. It had been preceded in June 1984 by a review of *Suicides in Prison* (1984d). Both reviews betray the Inspectorate's predominantly management orientation and limited research resources. Though both reports conclude with recommendations for change (the revision of standing orders for suicide prevention and the introduction of new definitions for security categories) the Inspectorate has so far concentrated on questions of whether Prison Department policies are internally consistent, effectively communicated or properly implemented. The results are somewhat parochial assessments of policy. For example, while the report on suicide includes statistics from other countries and a review of the research literature on prediction, there is no discussion of the possible relationship between regime characteristics and suicide. Neither is there any reference to the preventive methods employed in other institutions such as mental hospitals. Similarly, the limited bibliography and scant references to other countries in the security categorization report, are indicative of the Inspectorate's poor grasp of developments elsewhere which call into question key elements in the Prison Department's overall security strategy. Ironically, the critique of current policy offered by the Inspectorate is less incisive than that incorporated in the Prison Department's own working party report on 'Managing the Long-Term Prison System' (Home Office 1984b).

Conclusions

The new Inspectorate has lived up to the expectations of those who recommended its formation. The Chief Inspector treads a delicate path. He is not constitutionally independent of the chain of responsibility for the Prison Service. But he can and does exercise independence of judgement. His reports, particularly his annual reports, are no public relations exercise; if the measured language is decoded, the reader is drawn to the conclusion that the Prison Department does not make the best of a bad job and that conditions for prisoners are not simply the result, as successive Home Secretaries would have us believe, of too many prisoners and too few resources.

It is not possible from published reports to determine what impact the Inspectorate has had on policy. Most recommendations about matters within the managerial control of governors locally are allegedly implemented. But there is no way of knowing, for example, whether, following an inspection: fire drills are now regularly held; prisoner exercise is continued; areas are now continuously kept clean; or the use of stripped cells is recorded. However, the fact that the Inspectorate seems now less often to find fault with exercise provision or fire precautions suggests, at the very least, that governors get these areas up to scratch in anticipation of an inspection. As far as general questions of policy are concerned, the Chief Inspector's strictures do not differ greatly from those long repeated by the penal pressure groups. But the fact that the Inspectorate has added its voice to this throng has lent authority to the criticisms.

It would be self-defeating for the Inspectorate to be composed entirely of persons recruited from outside the Prison Department. They must include persons who understand how prisons work. Similarly, if the Inspectorate is to appraise policy constructively, it must maintain a close dialogue with the Prison Department; it must know how the Department sees the future as well as the present. It could be argued, as the recent reviews of security and control of long-term prisoners illustrates, that closer collaboration between the Department and the Inspectorate might on occasion make for a more effective critique of current policy.

The other side of this delicate balance is the need to draw on the expertise of persons who bring a fresh and less parochial outsider's view to prison policy. It is vital that the Chief Inspector succeed in his attempt to recruit further assistance of this sort to undertake future routine and thematic inspections.

Two aspects of the inspection process need bolstering and the results made public. First, routine inspection reports need to include more hard data about aspects of the regime, physical plant, costs, staffing ratios and the security composition of the population, etc. This information should preferably be in the form of standard appendices. If slogans of openness and public accountability are to have any meaning, the Inspectorate must enhance its role as public educator. Its routine reports must have a long-term analytical value; they must serve as points of reference. Their present value in this respect is limited.

Second, the Inspectorate must devise (or adopt) and publish the standards by which they inspect prisons. In his first annual report, the Chief Inspector regretted the absence of binding regime standards in Britain. In his second report he awaited, hopefully, the 'code of standards . . . being considered in Prison Department' which should, he suggested, 'ultimately be approved by Parliament' (HM Chief Inspector of Prisons 1983a: para. 5.11). In the event the Home Secretary decided against the publication of a set of standards for regimes or existing prisons. In his report for 1983, the Chief Inspector undertakes to review the issue in 1985 (1984a: para. 6.03): if he devises a code of standards and publishes in routine reports the gap between those standards and the conditions prevailing, it will be his most important contribution to the creation of a more accountable system.

8

Independent inspection: the role of the Boards of Visitors

Jon Vagg

Other chapters in this volume argue that prison regimes should be subjected to standards, which set out a legal and moral framework with detailed practical specifications for the treatment of prisoners. While this argument is still developing in the British case, there are several bodies which have in their own way sought to inject some principled reflection into the administration of the prisons. In particular, the role of the Prison Inspectorate has been discussed (Morgan Chapter 7).

Another watchdog body also exists, and in theory at least it should prove highly influential in penal thinking. Boards of Visitors are committees, composed of ordinary individuals, who have remarkable powers of access to institutions, records and prisoners. They are charged with a responsibility to oversee the prisons and their treatment of prisoners, and to report to the Home Secretary. These bodies, in common with many others in Britain, are both statutory (the Home Secretary is required to establish them) and voluntary (members may claim expenses and loss of earnings at a fixed rate but are not paid; neither are they elected, but join by invitation).

The work of these Boards raises a number of interesting and complex questions. Some are discussed by other contributors, and this essay confines itself to the following:

1 Who sits on the Boards; how are they appointed; and what powers do they have?

2 In their 'watchdog' capacities, what do they inspect; how; and what standards of acceptability do they apply?
3 Whom do they seek to influence; how; and with what measure of success?

and finally, since the answers to all these questions will be somewhat low-key:

4 How successful could any such body be in a watchdog capacity, and in what ways? What structural or organizational problems confront it? And, realistically, what are the prospects for addressing or resolving these problems?

The descriptive material presented here is drawn from a research project (Maguire and Vagg 1984) conducted over a period of almost three years. This chapter discusses the concerns of that report in the context of more general institutional problems.

Memberships, appointments, powers

At last count, there were 115 Boards of Visitors; one for every penal institution in the country, excepting that institutions which share sites also share Boards. They have between them about 1,500 members, the typical Board containing twelve to sixteen visitors. Members are appointed by the Home Secretary, usually from lists of nominations produced by the Boards themselves who thus have some influence on recruitment. The membership as a whole would not be untypical of many other voluntary bodies. Our 'census' of the 1981 membership, carried out from Home Office files, showed that 83 per cent were involved in at least one other voluntary body; slightly more than half were over 50 years old; slightly less than two-thirds were men; and less than one in ten were manual workers. The major distinguishing characteristic of the membership was that 43 per cent were also magistrates. It was only in 1971 that the all-magistrate Visiting Committees of local prisons were brought into line with the Boards of Visitors already existing in the other establishments, and in changing their name (the functions were identical) admitted non-magistrates to their ranks. There is still a statutory requirement for each Board to contain at least two Justices of the Peace.

The latest Home Office figures show that this composition has begun to change. For example, the proportion of ethnic minority members, of whom there were only a handful in the early 1970s, rose to 2.3 per cent in 1981, and at the end of 1983 stood at 5.2 per cent.

The duties and powers of Boards are laid down in the Prison Rules. Principally, the duties are to 'satisfy themselves as to the state of the prison premises, the administration of the prison and the treatment of the prisoners'; to hear any complaint which a prisoner wishes to make; and to conduct certain disciplinary hearings. Others include the authorization of segregation under Rule 43, the making of annual reports to the Home Secretary, the appointment of some of their number to parole Local Review Committees, and the tasting of food. They thus have minimal executive powers (so far as their watchdog role is concerned) but have access to their establishment at any time, access in private to any prisoner, and access to records. Their observations and comments are made principally to governors or to the Prison Department, and it is the Department which in practice deals with the annual reports mentioned above. But Boards have a right of direct access to the Home Secretary, and we discovered several cases in which this right was exercised either by letter, telephone or personal contact.

Criticisms

Some commentators have suggested that Boards are not adequately fulfilling their watchdog role, through either sheer ineptitude or through constraints created formally or informally by prison administrators. In 1975, the Jellicoe Committee concluded that inspections were 'superficial' and quoted one governor's evidence that a Board member conducting an inspection was 'nothing more or less than a casual visitor to the prison' (Martin 1975). Thomas and Pooley (1980) considered that any members who question prison administration seriously might find themselves edged out of the Board by 'judiciously placed frustrations'; the implication being that the majority of members support or at least accept a status quo in which they perform no more than a symbolic role. Home Office reports on disturbances at Hull and Wormwood Scrubs have also levelled criticism at those Boards for complacency prior to, and inaction during and after, riots in 1976 and 1979 (Home Office 1977; 1982). Finally, some Board members have 'come out'; most notably the Strangeways Board, which published a newspaper article detailing their frustrations.

This chapter is not intended specifically to substantiate or rebut these allegations, though it will be argued that serious deficiencies do exist. The immediate purpose is to identify the causes of these deficiencies, and the considerable practical and organizational difficulties entailed in rectifying them.

Doing inspecting

Within British prisons, formal standards of establishment performance exist only for management purposes. They are laid down in the Prison Rules, Standing Orders, Circular Instructions and other internal documents, and are intended to be management tools rather than publicly accepted minima or routine criteria for the acceptability of regimes or treatment. Boards, however, are free to adopt and apply any standards they wish; Prison Rule 94 expressly enjoins them to do so in stating that Boards shall 'satisfy themselves' as to the state of the prison premises, administration and the treatment of prisoners. But to our knowledge, no Board has laid down any explicit criteria for what will satisfy them. This lack appears to have several consequences for the ways in which Boards perform their task. It means that Boards have no coordinated sense of what they should be looking for. This in turn creates a situation in which the practice of inspection, ossifying into a tradition which is passed on to new members, formulates the objectives of inspecting rather than vice versa. Great reliance is placed by default on the management-created standards for institutional performance, while the issues considered by Boards are likely to arise from information given to Boards by management, members' own observations on visits, or complaints from prisoners. And these points in turn suggest that Boards are essentially reactive rather than proactive, discussing issues which arrive on the Boardroom table rather than seeking to check aspects of regimes which they themselves might consider important. The various parts of this cameo are laid out below.

Boards obtain information from a number of sources. One of these, though arguably not the most important, is for members to devise a rota and visit the prison on a regular but unpredictable basis. All Boards are required under Prison Rule 96(1) to arrange such visits at least monthly, and most in fact do so at least fortnightly. While the visit is intended to be unannounced, and at least one Board followed this as a matter of principle, most give the prison about half an hour's warning of their arrival so as to be sure that an officer will be available to escort them round the establishment. While this may seem strange to outsiders, it was intended to ensure that members did not have to wait in the gatehouse for long periods while staff were found to escort them. In practice, however, the call was often only acted upon when the member appeared – thus leading to such a delay. Again, it might be argued that while this might have enabled staff to tidy away anything or anyone that would give a bad impression, our research, both in visiting with members and without them (to interview staff and prisoners) indicated that Boards were simply not regarded as important enough for this to occur. This in turn may be because the visits themselves are often less than searching – or, to put it another way, the major problems such as overcrowding cannot be hidden, while many petty things that members may wish to criticize, such as delays in obtaining library books, simply would not be observable on a visit.

Visits varied in scope and duration; yet three general points may be made about them. First, despite the intrinsic value of seeing the physical plant, the visitor will only be able to obtain limited types of information. Typically, he or she will be able to notice things which are noticeable – dirt, broken guttering and the like. But many aspects of regimes which may give cause for concern are related to performance rather than plant; for example, the routine administrative decisions to which prisoners are subject. Visits are less than likely to capture these unless visitors are told about individual cases – and check to see whether a number of prisoners are similarly affected. Second, this implies that visitors should create situations in which prisoners may talk to them. One problem in this context is the discipline offence of 'making a false and malicious allegation' (Rule 47(12).[1] However, Board members can and do make themselves available to prisoners by visiting at times when prisoners congregate, in workshops or on exercise. Visits are most often made during the day, when these activities occur; and visitors usually direct themselves to the communal areas. Less attention is paid therefore to cells, dormitories and areas above ground level. Consequently prisoners on the upper landings, for example, locked up through lack of work, might only see a Board member by making a specific request to see one. Third, and perhaps most crucially, the lack of explicit standards places importance on what individual members regard as worthy of their attention. In our interviews with members, those who felt they could articulate what they were looking for described their concerns as 'cleanliness and tidiness', 'being accessible to prisoners', 'sensing the atmosphere' and the like. They described their planning for visits as simply deciding where to go within the institution, with the thought that 'something will come up', or simply that they might 'learn more about the establishment'. It would not be extreme to characterize many visits as predominantly learning exercises; the methods of visiting appear to have defined its aims.

This last point also characterized the conduct of the monthly Board meetings. Members' reports of visits, routine statistical information collected within the prison, and a briefing by the governor are all part of the agenda. But it is the governor who is able to interpret for the Board the significance of their observations, often by adducing a context within which the points raised may be seen as unimportant, or by informing the Board that he has noted the matter himself and is already taking action. While neither of these governorial responses can be seen as attempts to dupe Boards into thinking something is being done where it is not, they do raise two points. First, they imply that situations and attempts to resolve them must be monitored over a period of time. It often becomes difficult for Boards to determine the point at which they should decide that the institution's management efforts have failed or floundered. If a problem is recognized by the governor and is constantly subject to his attempts to improve it, Boards may wait for many months before concluding that their initial decision to 'wait and see' was, under the circumstances, perhaps not for the best. Second, reliance on the governor to interpret information to and for the Board entails by default a reliance on managerial judgements of the acceptability of situations. Boards are often in the position of having to create standards of acceptability *post hoc*, in the light of Standing Orders and Circular Instructions which management is seeking to implement. Boards are, then, handicapped by their lack of explicit and prescriptive standards based on their own judgement rather than that of management.

If such standards were forthcoming, would they improve the situation? The answer must be a qualified yes. Boards would be able to direct their attention systematically to regime performance. The continuing availability of library books, periods of association, and so on could be monitored on a routine basis. Boards might also be able to develop their own information bases, arranging for the collation and presentation of data which are useful to them, rather than relying exclusively on figures produced and designed for management purposes and goals (Maguire and Vagg 1983b). For example, one Board in our study began to require information on the number of Rule 43 men in the establishment together with the first date on which they went into Rule 43 segregation. They were alarmed to find that a proportion of the men had been segregated, albeit on their own request, for over a year. To take a hypothetical example, figures for workshops produced to Boards show, usually, the number of hours per week that each shop is open. Such information may be better presented as the proportion of men available for work who have worked in any given week, together with an indication of the number of hours worked – what proportion worked less than one full day, two full days, and so on. This might prove a more reliable indicator of the extent of purposeful activity (of one kind) provided for inmates.

At the same time, standards are only as useful as their interpretation in, and applicability to, concrete situations. Any form of words relies on the discretion of the evaluator as to what 'hygienic', 'adequate', 'freely available' and so on, mean in particular contexts. To take one illustration: in a prison we studied, a problem arose over cleaning. A group of prisoners had been issued with scrubbing brushes, rather than the more usual long-handled mops, for cleaning their cells. The brushes were no doubt adequate for the job, were freely available to inmates, and allowed a high standard of hygiene to be maintained. In every respect, relevant managerial standards were being met. But the prisoners complained that their human dignity was being abused, both because other prisoners had 'better' materials, and because of the association of 'hands and knees cleaning' with the treatment of young boys in Detention Centres – or, for that matter, boarding schools. In such cases, standards are only of value if they can be used to interpret the moral symbolism of the issue.

The major conclusion to be drawn from this discussion is that members appear to have subordinated rational inspection goals to actual practice. However, while the adoption of standards may lead to improvement in practice it can only augment, and not replace, fine judgement and a sense of purpose.

Influencing people

If Boards have difficulties in obtaining and evaluating information, how do they fare in fulfilling their second, 'whistleblowing' role? Their executive powers are minimal. They may authorize the use of Rule 43, though if they refuse to do so it may be authorized over their heads by the Home Secretary. Their powers of access to information, records and prisoners are facilitating rather than executive, and limited in one important respect by Rule 47(12).

Their powers and responsibilities, in any meaningful sense, are thus concerned with influence rather than action. Whom do they seek to influence, how and over what issues? And what would 'successful influence' mean in this context?

First, members we interviewed were quick to point out that they had no managerial brief and would not 'interfere' in day-to-day management. Their comments and arguments were reserved primarily for the governor; a situation implied in Prison Rule 94(5), which demands that they consult the governor before taking action in any sphere concerning discipline, which effectively means in any sphere of prison life. Moreover, members generally felt that this was a proper constraint on them, and indeed took care not to express their opinions on the running of the prison to prison officers. This frequently led to a situation in which uniformed staff were left in ignorance of the views expressed in the Boardroom. As one commented: 'What do they talk about up there for four hours? It's all a closed book to us, like a secret society.' Their response appeared to be twofold. Staff either viewed Boards as secretive (and criticized them for this), or they considered that since information on the Board's activities was so scanty, they must be ineffectual.

What results from these *in camera* discussions with the governor? We have already noted that governors interpret or contextualize information to and for Boards. It is hardly surprising that this kind of influence on their thinking leads to a situation in which governors themselves are rarely directly criticized, although the simple fact of asking questions might on occasion exert some leverage on the prison administration. The meetings we were able to observe produced issues as disparate as cleanliness and discipline, and on most of these the governor could announce measures already being taken. Alternatively, where, for example, the standard of catering had fallen due to the retirement and non-replacement of a catering officer, or where hot water for washing had to be rationed, or indeed where a particular prisoner was creating constant discipline problems, then a solution was often thought to lie with regional or national management rather than the governor. A staff appointment, or a building programme, or strategic rather than local management of an inmate's 'penal career' appeared to be necessary.

In many ways it would be true to say that this situation reflects the high level of institutional management and managers. More cynically, it may reflect the abilities of governors to manage their Boards and use them as a lever to obtain resources from regional management. Many mundane problems (for management) and indignities (for prisoners) do have their roots in matters of resources or policy over which governors have little control; and, as one governor put it: 'They can help you get things done. A letter from the Board is a useful weapon.'

One would expect, therefore, that Boards put a good deal of effort into directing their comments to regional or national headquarters. Such comments, at least in the form of letters, were rare. The Boards we studied sent such letters about twice a year, and did so in full knowledge that the reply would be along the lines of 'this problem will be resolved if or when more resources become available'. At the same time, a number of issues where reasonable prospects of improvement were thought to exist, such as the speedy filling of a staff vacancy, were the subject of informal discussions between Board chairmen and senior managers at conferences. One Regional Director we spoke to said that he would expect to 'have his ear bent' over two or three issues at every Board conference he attended.

Finally, to what extent do Boards question 'policy'? Our interviews with members revealed that the majority thought it outside their area of responsibility; their role was to see that whatever it was, it was implemented fairly. Moreover, the term appeared to cover many issues which we ourselves regarded as no more than institutional habits. However, some Boards have had a degree of success in forcing reviews of policy. One queried the limits on the amount of cosmetics women prisoners could buy each week, and ultimately the limits were raised. Another demanded to know why Rastafarians were having their dreadlocks cut on reception as a matter of routine, whereupon, as one member put it, 'a new ruling came on the heels of our enquiry'. But in such cases it is difficult to know the extent to which the Boards' queries and arguments directly effected the changes in policy. For the most part, it appears that 'policy' is a term, like 'security', which can cover virtually any aspect of prison life; that Boards have little inclination to question it; and that many policy issues – for example, the location of mentally disturbed offenders in prison – are simply not under the exclusive control of the Prison Department and therefore not amenable to speedy change.

An effective watchdog?

The points above give rise to a single, central question. Can Boards, or any analagous body, be effective watchdogs? We suggest a three-part answer. First, Boards face some structural organizational problems which limit their potential. They cannot be 'solved'; only 'lived with'. Second, analagous problems would face any similar inspection body. Third, Boards could do much to help themselves live with their problems.

The organizational problems which have been implicitly identified in the discussion are listed below.

1 *The relationship with the Home Secretary*. Boards are appointed by and responsible to the Home Secretary; their sphere of interest lies only within the establishments for which the Home Secretary is also responsible; and their liaison in practice is with the Prison Department rather than its political master. At the same time, many of the issues which concern Boards cannot be solved within the institutions or indeed the Department. Their role is thus to feed information and comment to the Department; policy formulation or interdepartmental action is con-

ducted wholly within the executive. To this extent, the influence of Boards is dispersed. The Boards are fragmented, each one making its own comments in relative ignorance of others, information from each being collated within the Department. And there is a qualitative difference between the Home Secretary reporting at an annual conference that a particular problem has been mentioned in the annual reports of a majority of Boards, and the Boards announcing to the Home Secretary that the majority of prisons face operational difficulties as a result of a particular policy decision (or lack of one). The latter case puts Boards in a much stronger position to make waves by presenting a fully-formed and systematically argued case to the Department.

2 There is an important sense in which the *flow of information to Boards bears on their credibility which in turn bears on the flow of information*; the same might also be said of their influence. These interlocking circles can be broken, but little thought appears to have been given to them. For example, prisoner's complaints form one source of information. But complainants may be inhibited as long as it appears that nothing is done when the complaint is made, while the apparent inaction will affect a Board's credibility adversely, leading to fewer complaints. At a more public level, the provisions of the Official Secrets Act preclude Board members from making open statements about, for example, security problems or the treatment of individual prisoners. Yet at the very times a Board's credibility is questioned – for example, during or after a disturbance – it is precisely these sorts of questions which will be the subject of public debate. To what extent are the Home Secretary's watchdogs, by implication or by necessity, also public watchdogs whose actions and views should be known by, among others, prisoners and the press? In order to acquire information and, hopefully, influence, Boards will have to give information and opinions – and then act in accordance with them. In order to improve the efficiency of the Boards, the Home Secretary will have to accept that he should not possess a private watchdog which reports to him alone. Lastly, the willingness for this move towards greater openness has also to be found among the members themselves.

3 *A lack of explicitly agreed and adopted standards*, together with the realization that local problems have national causes mentioned

above, appear to have led to a reliance on the prison governors, on management information, and a feeling of being 'part of a team' within the institution and against the higher reaches of the Department. Despite the difficulties associated with the adoption of standards, such a move may lead to sharper local inspections, incisive views on the causes of problems, and the formulation of criticisms of policy. However, the extent to which these improvements in Board practice could effect changes in the prisons would depend crucially on their willingness to rethink their 'hands-off' approach to policy-making.

These three problems have served to limit the value of a body which in principle could be extremely influential. But precisely because they are structural problems of inspection it is unlikely that any other body would avoid them, or that they can be 'solved' by the introduction of a new inspection and complaints mechanism. Morgan (p. 107) has argued that the Prison Inspectorate face an analagous difficulty in their line accountability to the Home Secretary and has outlined the practical difficulties in moving from institutional to thematic inspections. A prisons ombudsman (Birkinshaw Chapter 11) offers the possibility of systematic and standardized evaluation of complaints and the identification of systemic problems through them, but would be unable to monitor routine regime performance in the way that Boards do. In short, the conclusion must be that if Boards did not exist, they would have to be created.

Proposals for change

If, as we have argued, Boards fill an important gap in the structure of inspection and complaint, and yet face structual problems as a result of that very position, how could these be dealt with? The key points of the discussion above can be restated as proposals. They are:

1 *Boards should obtain more control over the way in which information from them flows to the Department.* For example, we found a great deal of dissatisfaction among members with the current arrangements for the Boards of Visitors' annual conference. It was not uncommon for members to describe it as 'stage-managed' by the Prison Department, and lacking in opportun-

ities for them to question senior staff or ministers thoroughly about major problems. But this kind of questioning requires a permanent organization through which Boards can speak with a collective voice. This could be facilitated if a standing committee of members were to be formed, with its own permanent office managed by the Boards themselves. The committee's staff might be the same civil servants who currently liaise between Boards and the Department, but would be accountable to the Boards rather than the Department, while having ready access to a career structure in the Department. In many respects they would have the same problems that face Prison Inspectorate staff (Morgan p. 113) but this is only to beg the question of why the liaison staff do not already have them.

2 *Boards themselves should argue that it is in the Home Secretary's best interest that Boards 'go public'*, especially with regard to their concerns and views. The Home Secretary could make their task easier by explicitly allowing Boards to breach the convention of not discussing individual cases where a prior interest exists, such as the reassurance of the public over the treatment of individual prisoners after, for example, a riot. If this measure led to an increase in the Boards' credibility among public and prisoners, then it can only be to the good – and it may ease the task of collecting information if it makes prisoners more willing to supply information to the Boards. By the same token, Rule 47(12), which makes it a disciplinary offence to lay a false and malicious allegation, should be withdrawn.

3 *Boards themselves should discuss, codify and adopt sets of standards for regime performance* which, in the terms of the prison rules, will 'satisfy them'. The value of this may be limited to policy questions rather than individual complaints, but this in itself would be an advance if it leads to discerning judgements as to whether a governor or a policy is at fault, and then to appropriate action.

Conclusions

Much of the criticism levelled at Boards of Visitors in the past has rested on assertions and assumptions about the conservatism and inaction of individuals who happen to constitute the membership of the Boards. Their ineffectiveness, too, has been formulated in terms of their inability to change prisons rather than influence prisons policy, perhaps because change is easier to measure than influence. The purpose of this article has been to argue that while many of the problems identified by the critics are correct, they are aimed to some extent at the wrong target; the problems are systemic and likely to affect any inspectorial group which occupies the ground and assumes the functions given to Boards. Neither are there any easy ways of solving these problems, though undoubtedly some accommodation to them and the redirection of individual and group efforts may ease their effects. But if Boards of Visitors are to change, and to become more influential, the systemic issues raised here must be addressed in practice. And it is the members who must find the willingness to do this. Influence cannot simply be granted by the Home Secretary; it must be created by the Boards themselves.

Note

1 Rule 47(12) makes it a disciplinary offence for a prisoner to lay a false and malicious allegation and inhibits complaints about the actions of staff. Essentially, any allegation may be investigated only if it is written, and any written allegation will be investigated by the governor. If it is found to be false and may also be malicious, it can then result in a disciplinary charge. And as one prisoner said to the researchers, 'any complaint is at some level a complaint against staff'. The practical difficulties that flow from this are examined in Maguire (p. 146).

The above paper is based on research funded by the Home Office. The author gratefully acknowledges the source of the funding.

PART 3

AIRING GRIEVANCES

9

Prisoners' grievances: the role of the Boards of Visitors

Mike Maguire

Ostensibly at least, prisoners in the UK have a wide range of opportunities for the expression of complaints about their treatment. The right to make a formal complaint through *internal* channels – in a 'governor's application' or a petition to the Home Office (see Ditchfield and Austin Chapter 10) – has been routinely established in all prisons for well over a century. Newer *external* avenues, such as actions in the divisional courts, complaints to Members of Parliament or the Parliamentary Commissioner, and applications to the European Commission of Human Rights, while appropriate in relatively few cases and suffering from several defects, have become easier to use as barriers to access and communication have been removed (see Richardson, Birkinshaw, Fawcett, respectively, this volume). In addition, there is a very long tradition of the *independent hearing of grievances at a local level*: as early as 1681, for example, the City of London provided for the annual election to Newgate prison of 'two curates and two commoners, to inspect the prison in order to hear prisoners' complaints' (Bassett 1943), and from even earlier times the official duties of Visiting Justices in many county gaols included the investigation of grievances. While the executive powers of the Justices were substantially reduced after the nationalization of the prison system in 1877, sufficient importance was accorded to the principle of an independent local channel for complaints, for the duty of hearing them to be retained by a lay board or a committee of visiting magistrates attached to every establishment.[1]

The present-day inheritors of this tradition are Boards of Visitors. Such Boards have a number of separate tasks and responsibilities: their 'inspectorial' role is discussed in Chapter 8 by Vagg, while Fitzgerald outlines recent court developments concerning their role as adjudicators upon disciplinary charges. In this chapter, however, we are concerned primarily with their handling of grievances, which they receive from prisoners in the form of 'applications' put to individual members, to panels or 'clinics', or to the full board. It will be asked to what extent Boards of Visitors enjoy the confidence of prisoners, in how much depth complaints are investigated and with what results, and, ultimately, whether the system can be said to form an effective remedy for grievances. Readers may also be interested to compare the British system with that existing in the Netherlands – with which it has some parallels – as outlined later by Nijboer and Ploeg (Chapter 16).

Strengths and weaknesses

The three features of Boards of Visitors which make them potentially one of the most important elements of the complaints system as a whole are:

1 that they consist of unpaid and, to an arguable extent, independent outsiders;
2 that they have the freedom to speak to any prisoner, inspect any record and comment in any way they like, including questioning established rules and standards; and
3 that they can handle large numbers of grievances quickly at a local level.

While Boards have virtually no executive powers to overturn decisions or order redress,[2] they have sufficient weight to create discomfort for staff at any level if they make strong enough representations to the Secretary of State. In the final analysis, they could exploit the powerful threat of embarrassing Ministers by making their dissatisfaction known publicly, or even resigning *en bloc*. Boards of Visitors appear, then, to form a central pivot of the complaints system, offering prisoners a unique opportunity to put their case even on relatively minor matters to an outside body, while at the same time avoiding the protracted procedures involved in litigation or other external avenues of complaint.

Unfortunately, virtually all the evidence available about the work of Boards of Visitors suggests that they have consistently failed to fulfil their potential. They have been shown to enjoy little confidence among prisoners and to be regarded by staff as uninformed and superficial in their approach (English 1973; Martin 1975; Maguire and Vagg 1984; Austin and Ditchfield 1985). JUSTICE (1983: 27) goes as far as to say that 'they are not a sufficiently independent body for the handling of complaints'.

Explanations for this apparent failure have been put forward primarily on two levels. The first is that the 'wrong kinds of people' have been appointed and that many members, through lack of time, lack of will, lack of understanding of prisoners and prison life, or lack of critical awareness, have failed to carry out their duties in a resolute and independent spirit. The second involves the deeper argument that, however conscientious individual members or Boards may be, there are serious problems inherent in their statutory role, their 'amateur' status, and their relationship to the prison authorities, which make it difficult (if not impossible) for them to act either independently or effectively. There is also a third, although generally neglected, set of contributory factors, which to some extent straddle the other two. These have been discussed most fully in Maguire and Vagg (1984), where it is argued that, while changes in role and personnel are necessary if more effective Boards are to be created, attention should also be paid to weaknesses in the routine ways in which Boards conduct their business and communicate with prisoners: at present, a great deal of well-intentioned work put in by individual members tends to be negated and wasted through simple organizational deficiencies.

The social composition of Boards of Visitors has been discussed in some depth in Maguire and Vagg (1983a) and is summarized by Vagg (Chapter 8). Here, it will simply be reiterated that, in common with many other voluntary bodies, Boards suffer from a serious imbalance in terms of the social class and age of their membership and to a lesser extent in terms of gender and ethnic background: where grievances are concerned, the social distance between most members and most prisoners can be a handicap both to mutual understanding and to the confidence of prisoners in the Board's impartiality.

This chapter will concentrate instead upon the other problematic areas outlined above. The following will be considered in turn:

1 'constitutional' and other fundamental problems involved in the achievement and demonstration of genuine independence;
2 limitations upon the depth of investigation of complaints and capacity for bringing about redress;
3 organizational deficiencies in the way that applications are handled.

1 INDEPENDENCE

The achievement of independence in practice depends not only upon the existence of formal relationships or a statutory framework which allow freedom of action and comment, but also to a large extent upon 'attitudes of mind'. In the case of Boards of Visitors, it will be argued that three aspects of the relationship between them and the prison authorities, while not ruling out a genuinely independent approach towards grievances, certainly hinder its achievement by making it difficult to avoid the assimilation of management values and attitudes.

The first concerns ambiguities in the formal definition of their role. Boards are officially appointed and trained by, and are responsible to and report to, the Home Secretary, who is himself the head of the organization it is their task to monitor. They are further obliged to report directly to the governor 'any matter which calls for his attention' and to pass on promptly to him any request made by a prisoner (Rules 94(3) and (8)). Their statutory position is therefore such that Prison Department literature is able to describe them as 'the eyes and ears of the Secretary of State', and further that many members come to regard themselves almost as the eyes and ears of the governor. Perceived in this way as a local watchdog on behalf of the higher prison authorities, a Board's duties in handling complaints may be said to cease at the point of satisfying itself that local staff have acted in accordance with the regulations (Rules, Standing Orders and Circular Instructions) laid down by the Home Secretary and/or Prison Department. Yet at the same time, Rule 94(1) states that it is the task of Boards to 'satisfy *themselves* as to . . . the treatment of prisoners' [my emphasis], which may be interpreted to mean that, as representatives of the local community, they should also act, quite independently of the Home Office, as watchdogs on behalf of the *public*, judging complaints by *external* standards – a role with very different implications (see also Vagg Chapter 8). For example, if a prisoner complains about not being allowed association or about a refusal to issue certain items from his property, neither of which break a specific regulation but which could be seen as unreasonable treatment in a more general sense, the Board may, rather than simply accept the right of staff to use their discretion freely within the regulations, decide to challenge such decisions on wider moral grounds. Moreover, this wider interpretation of their role would allow Boards to challenge not simply discretion within the regulations, but *the regulations themselves*. There are certainly some precedents here: Vagg quotes examples of complaints (e.g. about the forcible cutting of Rastafarian prisoners' hair) which, supported by Board members in a letter to the Prison Department, have led to changes in Standing Orders.

However, Boards in our experience very rarely took complaints any further than satisfying themselves that no regulations had been breached. Although lip-service was quite often paid to their representation of the independent outsider's viewpoint, the direct relationship and responsibility of Boards to the Home Office and to local governors clearly led many members to feel that they were in some senses 'part of the team', with a stake in the system, working within it and accepting its rules and values. Thus a common attitude to applications was that, however much one might sympathize with the complainant, it would be wrong to 'interfere in management' by seriously questioning discretionary actions, while the majority felt that questioning the rules was not part of the Board's functions. Generally speaking, complaints were viewed as no more than an opportunity for prisoners to 'let off steam', and it was felt that there was little that could or should be done about the vast majority: as one member put it, shrugging, 'we all have to live by the rules'.

A second major contributory factor to the tendency of Boards to adopt an 'insider's', managerial viewpoint when dealing with complaints has been their dual role as 'watchdogs' and as adjudicators upon disciplinary offences. The Jellicoe Committee report (Martin 1975) argues unequivocally that these functions are incompatible, a conclusion echoed by, among others, Zellick (1978), JUSTICE (1983), and Douglas (1984). In dispensing punishment, a major objective of which is the maintenance of order and security, Boards are stepping into an administrative role and are acting to some extent as an arm of the very authorities they are appointed to keep an independent eye upon. Not only is this likely to increase individual members' orientation to institutional goals at the expense of a wider viewpoint, but the two roles can become dangerously intertwined when Boards hear complaints arising out of incidents which have led to charges against prisoners, or, again, when an unsubstantiated complaint to a member results in a charge of making 'false and malicious allegations' (Rule 47(12)) which is then heard by members of the same Board. This last rule has been criticized in many quarters, and there have been numerous calls for its abolition (see, for example, Zellick 1982a; Marin 1983). There are few, if any, equivalents in prisons in other Western democracies, and it seems both unnecessary and highly damaging to the general principle of accountability in prisons.[3]

A third obstacle to the development of genuine independence is the difficulty which virtually every Board faces, whatever theoretical view it may take of its role, in maintaining sufficient social distance from the senior staff of the prison, particularly the governor, to remain capable of making firm critical comments when these are needed. The fact that governors or their representatives are present at and play a full part in Board meetings, and sit in on the hearing of most applications made to the full Board, almost inevitably results in close relationships being formed. The natural accumulation of personal warmth and respect (and not infrequently friendship) had clearly led some members we interviewed into an attitude of mind whereby serious questioning of staff actions would be regarded almost as 'disloyalty'. This pattern is exacerbated by the reliance upon the governor which many Boards develop for the acquisition of information. As discussed at length in Maguire and Vagg (1984), the infrequency of visits by individual members and their general lack of investigative expertise gives them little alternative to accepting the versions of events provided by the governor at monthly meetings. While we found no evidence of governors deliberately misleading Boards, they naturally place their own interpretation upon the facts, seeing them primarily from the point of view of a manager's concerns. The governor will know more than members about the background of almost any given complaint, and the practised professional ease with which he describes it tends to lull all but the most critically-minded into the belief that if he says that all is well, there is little to worry about. While this may be true in the vast majority of cases, a dangerous complacency can easily creep in, with the governor's account being regarded almost as infallible. The events at Hull prison in 1976 (see, for example, Home Office 1977; Thomas and Pooley 1980) and at Wormwood Scrubs in 1979 (Home Office 1982), when Boards failed to pursue justified complaints after serious incidents when reassured by governors that they were unfounded, provide good examples of such complacency.

2 ACTIONS IN RESPONSE TO COMPLAINTS

Board members are not trained investigators and they cannot be expected to know enough about the intricacies of prison life to be able to investigate complaints in depth, even if they wished to do so. Moreover, close inspections of records and formal interviewing of witnesses are not traditional Board practices and, although they have a right to engage in such actions, neither they nor the prison authorities perceive them as a realistic option. Serious allegations by prisoners against officers are dealt with through professional inquiries, and if a complaint of this nature is made, members normally warn the complainant of the 'false and malicious' rule and advise him, if he wishes to pursue it, to see the governor and make a formal written allegation. The Board then takes no further part in the matter, except perhaps to be kept informed.

Where less serious grievances are concerned, Boards have a duty to bring them to the governor's attention and can comment in any way they like. If not satisfied with the governor's response, they can ask him to reconsider and, if necessary, can make their dissatisfaction known to the Secretary of State. However, in practice, both these courses of action are rare and the vast majority of complaints are taken no further than being recorded for the governor's attention. Prisoners are generally well aware of the low chances of a complaint resulting in any change or redress, and few have faith in the independence of Boards or their willingness to support their case against the governor. Typical comments from those we interviewed were:

> 'It's common knowledge that if you apply to the Board, all they do is take it up with the Governor, who's already said no. They're next to bloody useless.'

> 'They fall over backwards to tell you you're wrong and the prison's right.'

> 'I can't see the Board supporting a prisoner in any serious case, and in serious cases all other channels close up.'

Our research confirmed the rarity of occasions on which complaints led to concrete results. Only a handful of the hundreds of applications we monitored resulted in the granting of a prisoner's request or in a change in practice, and among the 208 prisoners we interviewed, only 11 could recall what they considered a 'successful' application to a Board. We uncovered a number of reasons for this. Undoubtedly, one is the close identification of many members with administrative goals and values and a general lack of willingness to criticize staff or to 'interfere' in management. We witnessed several applications where the Board thought that the prisoner had a very good case, but did not press the governor to change his mind. This might be simply because what seemed to be a bad decision made by landing staff – for example an unsuitable work allocation – had already been upheld in complaints at wing PO (Principal Officer) or governor level and members felt that it would 'undermine discipline' if a complaint to them were seen to change it; or because if the complaint were upheld, it would cause administrative inconvenience. For example, a complaint that remand prisoners were not being given proper access to the library was answered by the governor explaining that their sudden departures for court resulted in books being lost or left around the prison, an argument surprisingly meeting no disagreement from the Board. Again, when acceding to a reasonable demand from an individual prisoner might cause problems elsewhere, Boards tended to take a managerial viewpoint. Thus when one man complained that he had been kept in 'stripes' for too long (i.e. wearing the uniform of a potential escaper, with a consequent loss of privileges), the governor agreed that he no longer posed a risk, but felt that it would be problematic to remove the restrictions while not doing the same for the man's close associate, who *did* pose a risk. The Board accepted the governor's argument that wider disciplinary considerations should take priority over the individual's legitimate grievance, and took the matter no further.

However, even where members were prepared to adopt a more independent and challenging approach, several other factors prevented them from making a determined effort to change an unsatisfactory situation. First of all, a large proportion of complaints concern matters on which Boards have normally considered that there is little effective action they can take. In particular, complaints against verdicts or awards at governors' adjudications, which made up about 10 per cent of applications to Boards in our sample of prisons, are dealt with in a standard way, by advising the prisoner to petition the Home Office. Complaints about delays in transfers or about allocation decisions, which accounted for about 14 per cent of applications at a local prison, are largely seen as the unfortunate result of the chronic overcrowding situation, and apart from requests to Regional offices to consider deserving cases sympathetically, Boards again feel there is little they can do.

Boards are reluctant, for different reasons, to take any action in a third substantial area of complaint, accounting for 17 per cent of all applications sampled: that of complaints about medical treatment or decisions by prison doctors. The main reason here is obviously the general social taboo against questioning a doctor's professional judgement. And finally, complaints by 'Rule 43' prisoners that they are being held in segregation against their will (particularly on the grounds of 'good order and discipline') tend to be almost routinely disregarded. Members have to sign forms authorizing such segregation, and there is only one known case of a refusal to do so (in the event, another member signed the form), the general view being that the governor is the best judge of whether prisoners pose a risk or are at risk from others.

While the above categories of complaint clearly pose difficulties for Boards, it is submitted that they could in fact take a more active approach in all these areas, if only by asking more questions. Certainly, one Board made a point of considering complaints against governors' adjudications *as if* they had the power to overturn them, and were not slow to let the governor know if they had any reservations about his decision or about his general disciplinary policy. Transfers for long-termers, likewise, could be speeded up if a Board strongly supported an individual's case. One Board we studied did not shrink from questioning the prison doctor closely, particularly in cases where prisoners claimed that they had been denied treatment they had been receiving outside. (In fact, this prison doctor was perfectly willing to respond to their enquiries, unlike two others who refused to accept that the Board had any right to query their decisions.) And finally, while the 'Rule 43' issue is clearly one of the most difficult (and might be better dealt with through some system of review using professionals – see Gostin and Staunton Chapter 5), Boards could at least press governors harder for a full explanation of the circumstances behind each case.

Apart from the above, the most common categories of complaint were found to concern other kinds of discretionary decision by staff, and food or living conditions. Between them, these subjects accounted for about 40 per cent of all applications. These are all areas which Boards perceive as very much within their responsibility to oversee, although as mentioned earlier they took positive action in few cases.

Two of the main reasons for Boards' reluctance to challenge discretionary decisions have been discussed above (wariness of interfering in management and identification with institutional goals rather than individual prisoners' rights). A third, reliance upon governors for the definitive version of events, has been mentioned in the previous section, but deserves some illustration here. Not unexpectedly, prisoners often give only part of the 'story' behind their complaint, and quite often the governor will add some information which substantially changes the picture. In some cases, this will consist simply of a statement or inference about the character of the complainant ('A troublemaker'; 'We have heard a lot from Mr Bloggs lately') or the imputation of hidden motives behind the application ('He keeps these battles going so he's got something to look forward to. He'd have a heart attack if we actually granted his request'; 'He's trying to get back at Mr Smith'). In others, for example where access has been denied to a particular facility, it will consist of a specific reason why it would be unwise to change the decision. Thus a prisoner who complained that he had been barred from the gymnasium 'for no reason' was said to be likely to provoke others to attack him. It is difficult for Board members, who have no easy way of checking such assertions, to do anything other than accept the professional judgement of the staff.

Where complaints about food are concerned, governors tend

to argue either that the complainant represents a minority opinion, or that unusual problems arose in the kitchen on the day in question. Again, unless members have been examining the food regularly themselves, they have little alternative but to accept the explanation given.

Overall, then, it is only very rarely that a complaint emerges in which members feel they are standing on sufficiently firm ground to argue strongly that some remedial action should be taken. While there were a fair number of cases in which an application to the Board was the first official approach by a prisoner on a particular issue, and was thus treated and satisfactorily resolved as if it had been an ordinary wing or governor's application, we found only a handful of cases in which representations from a Board actually led to a change in a decision already made.

If, as seems clear from the foregoing, Boards of Visitors are not an effective channel for complaints in terms of 'getting results', it can still be argued that they are important at least as a 'safety net' for ensuring that prisoners wishing to make a complaint are not prevented from airing it officially, and as a 'safety valve' for the need to 'let off steam' even when no practical results can realistically be expected. The very fact that prisoners continue to make applications in considerable numbers (our survey of Board chairmen indicates that nearly half the Boards of adult prisons recorded over 100 applications in 1982 and it is clear that many more were not recorded; altogether, we calculate that Boards deal with over 6,000 applications annually, about half the total number of petitions made to the Home Secretary) suggests that the facility is important to them. This being the case, it is important for Boards to take grievances seriously and pay them proper attention, and to demonstrate to prisoners that they do so.

3 ORGANIZATIONAL DEFICIENCIES

Maguire and Vagg (1984) identified four common weaknesses in the practicalities of the applications procedures used by Boards of Visitors, which contributed to the lack of confidence most prisoners felt in them, and improvements in which would almost certainly make Boards a more effective channel for complaints (see also Maguire 1985).

The first was a lack of attention to the accessibility of members to inmates. About 30 per cent of Boards took the view that prisoners should put in to staff a formal request either to address the Board at its next meeting or to see the next member to visit the prison, some Boards refusing to consider applications unless they were received through such formal channels. As Board meetings take place monthly, and 46 per cent of Boards arranged only monthly or fortnightly rota visits by members, this could mean substantial delays before the complaint was heard. Moreover, many prisoners were either unfamiliar with the procedure or reluctant to face the formal occasion of a Board meeting. A much more satisfactory arrangement was a regular weekly 'clinic', manned by members on a rota basis. In training prisons, with their more settled populations, it was fairly simple to ensure that inmates became familiar with this kind of system, although less so in local prisons with their large turnover. However, only 21 per cent of all Boards had instituted clinics, and many of these were held only fortnightly or monthly. And, even then, the problem still remained that some prisoners felt intimidated by staff asking them the nature of their complaint before registering their request to see the panel.

While applauding the establishment of clinics, Maguire and Vagg concluded that these should be regarded as a useful addition to, and not a substitute for, more informal ways of receiving applications. To their credit, most female and local prisons had traditions of openness towards 'casual' approaches made by prisoners to members carrying out their rota visits of inspection. Although there was resistance to the practice from staff in some of these establishments, the argument being that prisoners were 'cutting across' the normal internal channels and wasting time with trivial complaints which staff should have been given a chance to deal with first,[4] we would argue that inconvenience is much less important than maintenance of the principle that inmates should have immediate unfettered access to the Board. It should also be added that many members tended to forget the existence of prisoners locked up during their visits (particularly non-working remand prisoners in local prisons), and access could be improved if cells were opened on a regular basis to ask if such inmates had any grievances.

A second common practice which should in our opinion be avoided is that of hearing applications in the presence of staff – either the escorting officer during rota visits or the governor in applications to the full Board. Over 60 per cent of Board chairmen stated that the governor was 'always' or 'usually' present at the latter and only 6 per cent that he was 'never' present. Escorts also frequently 'listened in' to applications during visits, a situation which several prisoners mentioned as a deterrent to approaches to members:

> 'They're difficult to talk to. I've seen some go round with the PO who won't go away. He's there to weed out timewasters.'
>
> (Local prison)

> 'One lady asked if there's anything we want to say, but we're scared of the officers – they listen.'
>
> (Junior detention centre)

Some members argued that a staff presence could be helpful for resolving simple problems on the spot, but it seems equally simple, and important to the demonstration of independence, for members to hear the application in private and to bring in staff at a later stage if necessary.

The third deficiency concerns the criticism of Boards voiced most frequently by inmates. This was that they had not received replies to applications. Typical comments were:

> 'I'll look into it – that's the kiss of death for your application. You won't hear any more.'

> 'I've never heard. I was told they'd look into it. They ask the PO, who says we're playing up. They don't bother.'

Such criticisms appear to be fully justified. Chairmen in over one-third of all establishments stated that their Board relied upon staff to convey answers to all or some applications. Prison officers rightly pointed out that this should not be their task, and it was clear that they did not do so on many occasions. The Parliamentary All-Party Penal Affairs Group (PAPPAG 1982) has recommended that Boards should be responsible for giving replies and that these should be made in writing. In 1982, only 5 of 106 chairmen surveyed stated that their Board employed the latter practice: its wider adoption seems an important step towards overcoming a major source of discontent among prisoners. It would also ensure that members actually considered all applications put to them. In many cases, they were simply recorded in an 'applications book', in which a member of staff (usually a busy assistant governor) later scribbled a brief reply, and were then completely forgotten.

The fourth and final deficiency noted is related to this last point. Many prisoners were convinced that Board members did not investigate grievances at all, simply taking the governor's word that there was nothing amiss. Even when members had questioned staff quite closely about a particular grievance before agreeing that nothing should be done, the prisoner had no indication that this had occurred. The problem could be solved quite simply by not only giving a reply, but stating clear reasons why the request had been denied.

Two other practices adopted by individual Boards deserve brief mention as possible improvements which could be copied by others. The first is that of giving each member responsibility for oversight of a particular wing of the prison, where he or she can get to know staff and inmates better, 'dropping in' informally on a more regular basis. This provides a useful opportunity for receiving applications. Second, one Board had a system of 'starring' or 'double-starring' applications recorded in the book, indicating the level of priority the member attached to them. Double-starred applications required an answer in person by the governor at the next Board meeting.

Concluding remarks

It should be clear from the foregoing that Boards of Visitors believe there is little they can or should do about the great majority of prisoners' grievances, that they rarely investigate them in depth (if at all), and that prisoners have little faith in their independence or efficiency. Even so, the very existence of this particular channel, however ineffective in practice, is of some importance in prisons, both as a reminder to staff that their actions are subject to scrutiny by outsiders, and as at least a minimum form of reassurance to prisoners that they can articulate grievances. While it is difficult to deny that Boards of Visitors, as presently constituted, are a far from satisfactory safeguard against improper treatment, either on a small or a serious scale, and that developments in other directions (e.g. the creation of a prisons' ombudsman, changes in the 'hands off' philosophy of the courts, and the abolition of Rule 47(12)) are far more important in principle and also more likely in the long run to produce major and long-lasting changes in conditions or treatment, it would almost certainly be a mistake to conclude that Boards should be disbanded. Despite all the obstacles, efforts should be made to reform them and to make them more effective.

Notes

1 Committees of Visiting Magistrates continued to oversee local prisons until 1971, while other types of establishment were served by Boards of Visitors. In that year, local prisons were brought into line with the rest, non-magistrate members joining the new Boards of Visitors instituted in each. However, the involvement of magistrates continues on all Boards: there is a statutory requirement for at least two Justices of the Peace to sit on each Board in the country, and in 1981 43 per cent of all members were magistrates.

2 Boards have executive powers to:

(a) permit an unconvicted prisoner to have in his cell (at his own expense) furniture, bedding or utensils different from those normally provided (Rule 25(a));

(b) relieve an unconvicted prisoner of the duty of cleaning his cell (Rule 25(b));

(c) allow a prisoner an additional letter or visit in special circumstances and direct that a visit may extend beyond the normal duration (Rule 34(6));

(d) authorize or refuse to authorize the use of Rule 43 (concerning removal from association);

(e) authorize or refuse to authorize the use of Rule 46 (concerning physical or mechanical restraints).

In practice, the first three powers above are very rarely used (and indeed many members we interviewed did not know they possessed them), while authorization of Rule 43 has become virtually automatic on the governor's advice.

3 As Marin (1983: 319) has pointed out, the 'dual role' problem can apply to governors as well as to Boards of Visitors. If a complaint involves the manner in which the governor heard an earlier charge, it is likely that the same governor will also rule, or at least comment, upon the complaint.

Two well-known cases illustrate other unsatisfactory aspects of the rule. *Kiss* v. *UK* (1976), which was decided by the European Commission of Human Rights, involved an allegation in a petition to the Home Secretary that a prisoner had been struck in the back by a prison officer. Kiss was charged and found guilty under Rule 47(12) even before the Home Secretary replied to the petition. While the Commission did not challenge Rule 47(12) itself, it said that the applicant had a right to sue for the injury sustained in the incident. This case highlighted at least the contradictions in allowing such charges to be heard by a body connected with the prison system, and raised the interesting point that Kiss might have won his case when sueing for injury, yet would still have had no redress against a then manifestly unjust award for making a false and malicious allegation.

The second case involved a prisoner who lost six months' remission for alleging that there had been an improper relationship between a prison officer and Myra Hindley in Holloway prison. The officer was later tried in a criminal court.

However, perhaps the strongest argument against the existence of the rule is well put by Marin (1983: 320), who contrasts the British system unfavourably with the American acceptance of the principle that there should be no retaliation by the authorities against complainants, primarily because of the powerless situation of those held in custody:

> 'The conditions of captivity breed complaint. As a child may tattle to attract attention, the prisoner, reduced to childlike subservience, may complain for the same purpose. Of course, no one likes to be falsely accused of anything, particularly when his employment may be put in jeopardy. Prison officers may thus be justifiably sensitive to complaints by persons whom they do not regard as being very truthful. However, to suppress complaint is like compressing a volatile chemical. It is not good to be around when the explosion occurs.'

4 Two of the ten prison governors we interviewed had strong views against permitting 'casual' applications to members. One argued that he should always have 'first bite at the cherry' and the other that members were encouraging too many trivial requests: 'the currency of applications has become devalued'.

The above paper is based on research funded by the Home Office. The author gratefully acknowledges the source of this funding.

10

Internal ventilation of grievances: applications and petitions

Claire Austin and John Ditchfield

Introduction

As has been stressed many times in this volume, prison inmates are extremely dependent upon other people for the fulfilment of their needs and the resolution of their problems. The series of formal procedures they are obliged to go through to bring their requests and grievances to the attention of prison staff and prison authorities are therefore an important part of prison life, and the satisfactory operation of these procedures plays a crucial role in the management and control of prisons. A successful system means that prisoners feel their requests and complaints are being dealt with quickly and fairly, whether or not the outcome is satisfactory to them.

In 1983, the Home Office Research and Planning Unit undertook a study of grievance procedures in six closed prisons for men – two local prisons, two training prisons and two dispersal prisons. The following chapter will draw on the findings of this study. It will describe the principal stages in the procedures and will assess, briefly, both the extent to which they were found to enjoy the confidence of staff and inmates and any changes to policy and practice which seem desirable and necessary.

Grievance procedures at wing and Governor levels

In the first instance, inmates' complaints and grievances are registered in the same way as routine and administrative requests – by making an 'application'. Typically, an inmate will queue up to see his wing senior officer or principal officer to make his application. If it is a minor problem (for example, checking his eligibility for extra visits or letters, replacing inadequate or worn kit, etc.) then the officer may well deal with it himself. The problem might be more substantial – for example, a request for a change in work allocation or to check the condition of a hospitalized relative – but because the two share a good relationship the officer might still agree to investigate the matter himself. Usually, however, the more substantial problems are referred upwards to the next tier of the hierarchy, the 'duty governor', that is the member of the governor grades with the responsibility for taking applications on any particular day. This may be the Governor himself (the 'No. 1' Governor as he is often referred to by staff and inmates), the deputy governor or one of the assistant governors.

Certain subject matters *must* be referred to the duty governor, for example applications for home leave, permission to send out photographs, permission to make a telephone call; in these cases the wing officer does not have the authority to make the decision and when the inmate makes his application at wing level it is in the nature of an administrative formality whereby he simply asks to be 'put down to see the governor'. Sometimes, however, the referral of the complaint to the duty governor is a means of appeal against a wing decision; for example, an inmate might ask the principal officer for permission to have a china cup allowed out from his stored property for personal use, and the officer might refuse on the grounds that it could 'be used as an offensive weapon'. The inmate would then have the choice of either accepting this ruling or taking the matter to the duty governor in the hope of obtaining a different decision.

Thus applications are more varied and unpredictable at duty governor level than at wing level. They represent substantial matters that are best dealt with by the governor, matters that must be referred because of their subject matter, and matters that are in the nature of appeals against decisions made at wing level. But applications might also be referred up for other reasons: 'personal' – because the inmate does not wish to disclose a particular problem to a particular officer or assistant governor; 'litigious' – because the inmate wants to pursue the problem or complaint through all channels available; 'psychological' – because the inmate has a desire not to 'get lost in the crowd' and to get the governor to remember his face; 'a need for reassurance' – because the inmate wants someone to listen to his problem and express interest or sympathy, and so on. Because of these and similar reasons, many of the applications referred to duty governor level concern matters that can be satisfactorily resolved at wing level (indeed many of them are eventually referred back), but staff are usually prepared to accept this as a necessary consequence of being accessible.

Inmate confidence in grievance procedures at staff levels was lowest at the two local prisons. The characteristic problems of locals – rapid turnover of population, commitment to court duties, and long lock-up periods – meant that staff were unable to devote as much time and resources as in other prisons to dealing with inmates' requests and complaints in any depth and inevitably these limitations were reflected in inmates' responses. Only a small proportion of the inmates interviewed felt that their requests and grievances had been dealt with at all positively or sympathetically by wing staff or governor grades. Mostly they felt that their application had been dealt with matter-of-factly or off-handedly and that staff were uninterested and sometimes hostile. Some of the comments received were: 'he was nasty to me and told me to get lost – he thought I was being funny asking to see the Governor'; 'I made a mess of it (petition) and wanted to re-write – he was angry about finding a new sheet'; and 'he was no help whatsoever'. At the same time the prospect of imminent allocation (or of serving only a short sentence) tended to reduce their urgency; as one inmate said 'it's a local prison and people are coming and going – they will be here only a few weeks so they feel it's not worth complaining'.

Provisions for dealing with complaints and grievances were more developed at the two training and two dispersal prisons. Access to wing staff was on a more informal 'open-door' basis, whereby inmates could see the wing senior officer (and/or the wing principal officer) at more or less any time they were available, although there was still a clustering of applications at morning 'unlock' and before evening association.

The greater informality of these regimes and their more developed state of staff/inmate relations also meant that a larger proportion of applications might be dealt with informally, i.e.

not be made the subject of a formal record. For example, at one training prison an inmate came into the wing office and asked the senior officer for advice about a complex situation involving the police and judiciary; the inmate's problems were discussed at length and advice was given (and taken) but no note or record was made of this 'application'.

These differences in practices seemed to be reflected in inmates' opinions. Their confidence in grievance procedures, while varying somewhat from prison to prison, was much higher at the training and dispersal prisons than at the two local prisons, both in respect of the help they received with their individual problems and the way staff dealt with complaints generally: 'any genuine complaint is dealt with reasonably' and 'in this prison I'd give it (grievance procedures) a 95 per cent rating' were reasonably typical of inmates' comments about how their complaints were dealt with at these prisons.

As previously noted, the governor responsible for taking applications is very often not the Governor of the prison, but his deputy or one of the assistant governors. Where this happens there is an understanding that if an inmate insists on seeing the Governor then he will be given access. However, few inmates are sufficiently assertive or confident enough to insist on such a right, and in the three prisons studied where this duty was normally delegated inmates were very critical of the practice: 'getting to see the No. 1 in this prison is like going to the other side of the moon', 'wing staff won't let you see him, you have to beg to see the assistant governor, let alone the No. 1', were some of the comments made. At the same time inmates were well aware that such access was unlikely to make any difference to the outcome of their applications; rather they wanted to assure themselves that they had discussed their problem with the highest authority in the prison and could therefore regard the decision as final and definitive – 'he's the ultimate boss' as one of the inmates put it.

Finally, it should be mentioned that if an inmate is dissatisfied with the way his problem or complaint has been dealt with at governor level, he might consider taking his case to the Board of Visitors. The various procedures by which inmates can make applications to the Board of Visitors, together with an evaluation of the effectiveness of Boards, are described by Maguire (Chapter 9), and will not be discussed in detail here. However, it is interesting to note that both Maguire and Vagg (1984) and the present study have identified similar shortcomings in their practices and procedures. Both studies reached the general conclusion that Board members need to be more critical and interventionist in their attitude to prison authority, and to 'distance' themselves more conspicuously from the Governor and some staff, an argument which meets little resistance from serving governors. As one Governor in the present study said: 'I constantly urge them not to worry about me and be more critical.'

Petitions to the Home Office

Inmates also have the option of submitting written petitions to the Home Secretary. These are processed by staff of the Prison Department within the Home Office and carry the authority of the Home Secretary. Inmates can petition about any subject but, in practice, a large number of petitions are referred to the Home Office, either because it alone is empowered to deal with the matter (for example, problems about parole, queries about conviction or sentence, and representations against decisions to deport), or simply because it is a long established Home Office custom to deal with that particular subject (for example, permission to have photographs taken, compensation for lost or damaged property, permission to attend court hearings, certain forms of temporary release, etc.). The former can be thought of as petitions requiring compulsory referral and the latter as those which are subject to customary referral. In both instances the petition acts more or less as a formal request mechanism and the role of prison staff is mostly to provide the necessary information and advice on which the Home Office can reach a decision. In most other instances the petition acts as an appeal mechanism whereby the inmate tries to persuade the Home Office to countermand or set aside a local decision. Problems concerning inmates' allocation and requests for transfer occupy a somewhat ambiguous position in this respect. The number of establishments to which the allocation unit of a local prison can send its inmates (i.e. taking into account their security category and length of sentence) is usually very limited. Consequently, decisions about allocations are not local decisions in the same way that decisions about privileges and local conditions are, and appeals against such decisions cannot really be classified as appeals against local decisions either.

The researchers analysed the petitions forwarded to the Home Office from the twenty inmates interviewed at each of the six prisons. Of the 120 petitions forwarded, 30 per cent required compulsory referral, 18 per cent were of the customary referral type and only 12 per cent were appeals against local decisions. The largest category – slightly less than 40 per cent – concerned problems of allocation and transfer, a large proportion but reflecting the fact that two of the prisons were local prisons.

Only 6 of the 120 petitions were granted by the Home Office. The first was a straightforward request to attend a magistrates' court hearing for guardianship proceedings; another was a request for an early parole review on the grounds that the inmate's co-defendant (who had received an identical sentence) had been granted parole. The third inmate requested a transfer to a prison nearer his home on the grounds that it would facilitate visits from his family. The fourth petitioner requested a transfer for accumulated visits and to have photographs of himself sent out to relations who could not visit him since they lived in Australia and Scotland. The fifth case was more routine: it concerned an application for back pay whilst on remand at Brixton. The final case was a request for compensation for a radio which had been damaged during a cell search.

All inmates' petitions are accompanied by a report, prepared by a governor or principal officer, which indicates whether or not the petition is supported. In all but one of the six cases listed above, the petition had been accompanied by a supportive report. The actual replies to the inmates' petitions were available for analysis in 90 of the remaining 114 'unsuccessful' cases. The most common form of reply (accounting for just over one half of the sample) was an 'expanded' reply, i.e. a reply which noted the subject matter of the petition and which contained some form of 'personalization', however brief. A typical expanded reply was:

> 'Your papers have been re-examined in the light of your third and fourth petition. The review of your case for parole was correctly carried out and I can assure you that it was not prejudiced in the way that you suggest. A decision was reached after only a very full and equitable assessment had been made of all the aspects of your case. The Secretary of State regrets that he is unable to justify the direction of an early review.'

Approximately one half of the expanded replies were in response to petitions about parole.

The next most commonly used form of reply (used in about one third of the cases) was the 'stock' or standardized reply. An example of this was the 'nil request' reply which gave the subject matter of the petition, but otherwise limited itself to a simple comment that the case had been 'fully considered':

> 'The Secretary of State has fully considered your petition but is not prepared to grant your request for a transfer.'

Most 'nil request' replies were in response to petitions requesting transfers.

The 'no action' stock replies were even briefer, being mostly in the format:

> 'The Secretary of State has fully considered your petition but can find no grounds for taking any action in regard to it.'

Interestingly, dissatisfaction with the amount of detail in Home Office replies was expressed by the majority of both inmates and staff. This was surprising since the analysis of replies to petitions showed that most were in a more expanded form than this criticism would suggest. So, there would seem to be an important distinction between replies which are expanded or explanatory and those which give the reason for the decision reached and/or which specifically counter the inmate's submission by showing that the points raised in the petition have been taken into consideration. In the words of one inmate: 'the Home Office are defensive to hide behind a photocopied answer. No doubt they have reasons on file. Even the Appeal Court gives reasons for refusals.'

Contrary to expectations, dissatisfaction with the time taken by the Home Office to reply to petitions was not widespread. Moreover, what dissatisfaction there was amongst inmates was as much associated with rapid replies as with slow replies: this was because inmates felt that a rapid reply might mean that the petition had not been properly considered and even that it might not have left the prison. For example, an inmate who had requested a review of his security categorization and who had received a reply within days complained, 'it only took ten days and I did not think it had left the jail; others can take months'.

The small proportion of petitions granted by the Home Office reflects the fact if a prison is both willing and able to grant an inmate's request, then it will generally do so. Thus, most of the petitions forwarded to the Home Office consist of requests and complaints that are not supported by prison staff or over which they have little influence – e.g. problems concerning parole or conviction; these are also matters in which the authorities are unlikely to interfere with the decisions made except for the most compelling reasons.

These considerations gain support from the analysis of the reasons why the 82 inmates in the sample who had withdrawn their petitions had done so. The most frequent reason given was that they had been satisfied with some form of action or intervention by prison staff. In practice, therefore, the petition system would seem to be more effective as a procedure for obtaining action at a local level than as a means of obtaining central redress of grievances.

11
An ombudsman for prisoners

Patrick Birkinshaw

If the title to this chapter were descriptive, it would be misleading, as there is in the UK no special ombudsman for prisoners. The Parliamentary Commissioner for Administration has responsibility for the investigation of complaints against Government departments and certain governmental agencies, and the Home Office and its Prison Department fall within his jurisdiction, but as will be shown, prisoners' complaints form a very small part of his workload. I hope, however, that the chapter title will be seen as prescriptive and add its voice to the burgeoning demand for a special prison ombudsman.

Ombudsmen: powers and limitations

In many countries, there is a tendency to see ombudsmen as panaceas for abuse of public power and high-handed or inefficient bureaucratic decision making in an ever increasing range of public and even private institutional frameworks. Their growth over the last decade, not least in the form of specialist correctional investigators for prisoners, has been little short of staggering (Anderson 1982). Notable examples of special ombudsmen for prisoners are afforded by various states in the USA and a federal ombudsman for Canadian prisons (see Anderson (1981a) and Canadian Correctional Investigator (1974) for details of the latter's powers and establishment).

Outside the UK, even ombudsmen who are not specialists on prison matters have shown considerable success in taking up prisoners' grievances and achieving wide-ranging reviews of penal policy and administration (Anderson 1978, 1981a, 1981b; Wener 1983). Invariably, the scope of investigation of these ombudsmen is wider than that of the British Parliamentary Commissioner for Administration (PCA), as they are more often fully independent and their powers of investigation are not restricted basically to matters of procedure, as is the case with the PCA. In the UK, the PCA was established in 1967 in order to assist Members of Parliament in their constitutionally allotted task as trouble-shooters for constituents. As the PCA was originally introduced as a supplement to Members of Parliament (MPs), it was insisted that he could be contacted only *via* an MP, whom a citizen must ask in writing to pass his complaint to the PCA. This restriction on direct access has remained almost unique among ombudsmen. However, since 1978, citizens have been able to write to the PCA, who, if he believes the matter to fall within his jurisdiction, may send the complaint to the citizen's local MP asking him or her to re-submit it officially.

The second significant restriction on investigations by the British Ombudsman relates to the fact that he can investigate only 'maladministration', which includes delay, incompetence, oversight, rudeness, arbitrariness and the like – that is, essentially procedural matters. He is *expressly prohibited* from questioning the merits or policy elements of a decision. Nor is he meant to question the exercise of discretion if there is no maladministration. His ability to question rules, such as the Standing Orders of the Prison Department, is also strictly circumscribed: he is meant to criticize an individual decision and not a rule. It is true that a circuitous procedure has sometimes been adopted whereby the PCA can ask a department to review a rule causing 'hardship' (see *Knechtl*, below), but his ability to criticize 'bad rules' *per se* remains extremely limited. Finally, the PCA has no power to enforce his decisions against departments, which 'negotiate' a settlement around his recommendations, possibly making an *ex gratia* payment or offering apologies to a victim of maladministration. This is not a question of legal right, but governmental 'grace and favour'.

On the positive side, it should be said that the PCA does have wide powers to call for departmental papers and evidence and to examine witnesses, and that government departments cannot rely upon any immunities to demands for information from the PCA which they could rely upon if they were a party to legal proceedings. Any interference with his investigations which, if the investigation were a judicial proceeding, would amount to a contempt of court, can be transferred to the High Court for that court to punish as a contempt. Moreover, his pronouncements are at least made public. Reports of his investigations are sent to the MP, the principal officer of the department concerned and to any other person 'who is alleged in the relevant complaint to have taken or authorised the action complained of'. Quarterly selections of his investigation reports are published and he makes an Annual Report to Parliament.

Despite these qualifications, the extent to which the British PCA's remit and powers are limited is confirmed by glancing at those of ombudsmen elsewhere. For example, the Canadian Correctional Investigator can make unannounced visits to all Canadian penitentiaries and can arrange private interviews with inmates who wish to meet him (Canadian Correctional Investigator 1974). Ontario has its own provincial ombudsman with power to investigate 'decisions, recommendations, acts or omissions' which appear contrary to law, or are 'unreasonable, unjust, oppressive, or improperly discriminatory'. The American prison ombudsmen, though with variations between jurisdictions, also tend to possess considerably greater powers (Anderson 1981a).

Volume of cases

The British PCA received only 133 complaints on prison matters from 1967 until June 1980, of which 107 were investigated. In 1981, he made twelve investigations, in 1982 five, and in 1983 just one, while JUSTICE (1983) was informed that between 1976 and 1980 the PCA had found no cases of maladministration in prisoners' complaints. In a prison population which stood at over 40,000 for much of this period, these seem staggeringly low figures. The number of complaints to the PCA from *all* quarters between 1967 and 1980 varied between 1,259 in 1978 and 548 in 1971, much lower figures *per capita* than those for comparable institutions overseas. In 1977, JUSTICE pointed out that the PCA had investigated a total of 252 cases in 1974 from a population of

55 million, while in New Zealand the ombudsman had investigated 414 complaints from a population of 3 million; for the same year the Public Protector in Quebec investigated 2,369 cases from a population of about 6 million. With regard to special prisoners' ombudsmen, the Canadian Federal Correctional Investigator received from prisoners 782, 988 and 1,057 complaints respectively in the first three years of operation (JUSTICE 1983).

It is interesting to compare the number of complaints to the PCA with the number of petitions to the Home Secretary from prisoners. Many agree that this latter procedure is excessively prolix, is seldom successful and, for prisoners, extremely frustrating (Ditchfield and Austin Chapter 10). Petitions rarely lead to an inquiry by the Home Office, which limits itself usually to a perusal of the information appended to the petition by the Governor (JUSTICE 1983). However, despite prisoners' lack of faith in the system, in 1976 something approaching 9,000 petitions were made (Prescott 1976), while by 1983, the figure had risen to about 12,000 per annum (JUSTICE 1983). In the context of figures of this magnitude, the contribution of the PCA seems minimal indeed. He has asked to be judged by the quality of his investigations,[1] and their painstaking and time-consuming nature has been seen as one of the reasons why he can deal with so few (Harlow 1978). However, no matter how important an impact he may have in one or two specific areas of prison administration, it is clear that there are numerous other areas which he has left untouched.

Achievements to date

It would be difficult to claim that the PCA has made a significant impact upon the administrative practices of the Prison Department. The overall conclusion of JUSTICE (1977) was that: 'An important area in which the PCA has failed to live up to his expectations is that of prison administration' – a point made with special reference to 'oppressive or brutal treatment by prison officers' and to a lesser extent to denial of privileges and transfers. Nothing has occurred since 1977 to allow this view to be seriously disputed.

There are several illustrations of the limitations and indeed timidity of the PCA relative to other avenues of complaint open to prisoners in the UK, in particular cases, where a subsequent decision has gone much further towards providing a remedy. Over a decade ago, in the *Knechtl* case, the PCA found no case of maladministration against the Home Office when the latter had insisted that prisoners alleging injury resulting from medical treatment received in prison would have to make out a *prima facie* case of negligence before being allowed to contact lawyers (for a fuller discussion of this case, see Wener 1983). The PCA merely suggested that the Home Office should review their rule, which it did and duly reported that it was satisfied with its content. It was left to the House of Commons Select Committee on the PCA to urge upon the Home Office further review, which eventually led to easier access to lawyers on this specific issue 'unless there are overriding considerations of security'.[2] It remained for the European Commission and Court of Human Rights, and indeed the English High Court, to achieve more fundamental change on access to lawyers (Fawcett; Richardson this volume). Similarly, the PCA criticized, but then approved, amendments to Standing Orders concerning censorship of prisoners' correspondence, which were subsequently ruled in breach of our international legal obligations under the European Convention of Human Rights (*Silver and others* v. *UK* 1983). The same decision condemned a breach by the UK of Article 13 of the Convention, inasmuch as the PCA had not constituted an 'effective remedy' for breaches of the Convention because he could not enforce his decision against a Government Department.

Perhaps the main achievement of the PCA has been to draw attention to some of the serious shortcomings in the internal methods of investigating complaints within prisons. Censure from the PCA on this matter is not uncommon and on occasion it has been quite severe.[3] His investigations have covered delays in responding to petitions to the Home Secretary; inadequate educational facilities and medical treatment, including failure to keep records of medical treatment dispensed in one prison;[4] refusal to allow prisoners to institute legal proceedings; calculations of parole eligibility dates; and refusal of compensation for lost items of property.[5] In several of these cases, the PCA has acknowledged the difficulties facing prisoners in having to prove their case against the authorities,[6] while in Inv. C258/80,[7] he wrote:

> 'I have criticised the Home Office for the disparity between the system of making Governors' applications in operation at the

> prison, and that prescribed by the Home Office and set out in the cell information cards. . . . I am also concerned about the occasions when the Home Office gave wrong or misleading information to the complainant's MP.'

It could be said that the fact that officials know that the 'long-stop' of the PCA exists, and that they might have to face searching questions and have any errors made public knowledge by the Parliamentary Select Committee on the PCA, contributes over the long term to more attention being given to the fairness of their procedures. It is also true that he has criticized 'extreme' conditions in local prisons[8] and has revealed some of the more petifogging rules on privileges.[9]

However, such achievements are only minor in comparison with the vast range of important issues in which he could become involved, and are anyway offset by the outright refusal of the PCA to challenge rules made by the Prison Department (for example, on making contact with a marriage bureau[10]), to question seriously why the Home Office will not give reasons for refusing petitions but resorts to 'stock replies',[11] or to censure the inconsistent application of censorship criteria on prisoners' letters.[12]

What reforms are necessary?

The most immediate issue for reform is to make the Ombudsman more accessible to prisoners than he is at present. In his 1979 Report,[13] the PCA noted that Home Office instructions to prisoners informed them that they could not write directly to him. In August of that year, the PCA observed that the Home Office had reworded the instructions to make it clear that they could write to him on the same basis as MPs (see above). Since then the House of Lords and the High Court have liberalized prisoners' access to outside legal advisers to such an extent that a prisoner does not even have to raise a complaint with the authorities before seeking legal advice with a view to possible litigation, let alone *exhaust* internal grievance procedures before being allowed access to lawyers outside prison. However, as regards access to the PCA and MPs, the position is still covered by the Standing Orders which stipulate that a prisoner must notify the authorities of a complaint before contacting either, although since 1981 a prisoner does not have to exhaust internal procedures. It is submitted that prisoners must be allowed the same access to the Ombudsman and to MPs as they possess to lawyers. A liberal reading of s.9 of the Parliamentary Commissioner Act 1967 could possibly allow this, but the situation should be clarified beyond a peradventure. It is particularly important in the case of prisoners to remove the unnecessary MP 'filter', for it adds yet another barrier to the already difficult matter of contacting outside agencies.

This should be only the beginning of a much-needed package of reforms. To begin with, there is a desperate need for an effective, impartial complaints mechanism operating *within* prisons. At best, some form of local complaints panel might be established on which membership of a prisoner, elected in secret ballot by inmates, as well as, possibly, a senior officer, would be a positive step forward. Other members would be totally independent of the Prison Department and prison disciplinary bodies. Models in the USA and Saskatchewan show what can be achieved (Keating 1975; McGillis, Mullen, and Studen 1976; Birkinshaw 1981). The internal procedure would operate to deal in a swift, responsive and accessible manner for the majority (possibly a substantial majority) of cases, which could be resolved at a relatively early stage.

For more resistant complaints which the grievance procedure has not resolved, there is a pressing need for a special ombudsman operating for prisoners, and not simply an extension of the powers of the present PCA to take more account of prisons.[14] Such an office should not be grafted on to that of the PCA because – and here I borrow from models operating outside the UK – a prison ombudsman should have full powers to question the merits of Departmental policies, rules and standing orders and to criticize them openly when they are simply bad. Moreover, there should be no necessity for a prisoner to go through an MP, but access should be direct once the complaint had been raised with the authorities. This would allow the governor to attempt a resolution but it would not hinder access to the ombudsman in any manner. Abolition of Rule 47(12), which allows punishment for 'false and malicious' allegations by prisoners would be a further beneficial development (see also Maguire Chapter 9, p. 146). Correspondence between prisoners and the ombudsman should be uncensored. The ombudsman should have power to visit prisons, unannounced if he so desires; to interview prisoners; to conduct investigations on his own initiative; and to have access to all necessary papers and individuals.

With nearly 120 institutions within his jurisdiction, the prison ombudsman might well be assisted by a duty solicitor, such as exists in HM Prison Strangeways, who could liaise with the prison complaints panel and maintain regular contact with the ombudsman (Hall-Williams 1984), suggesting, when appropriate, the need for his attendance. The duty solicitor scheme in question is still in its infancy, but the arrangement outlined for contact between the solicitor and the ombudsman could be provided for in the statute establishing the ombudsman, leaving to the parties themselves the initiative for developing their respective relationships. He would publish reports of his investigations, annual reports, and special reports if necessary; all of these would be presented to Parliament, whose officer he would be.

The suggestion of JUSTICE (1983) that he should be backed by a Parliamentary Select Committee – a Penal Affairs Committee – also has merit. The ombudsman should have power to seek judicial enforcement through the courts of his decisions in the event of these proving unacceptable to the authorities. This would place him in a peculiar position in relation to present British ombudsmen, although the Northern Ireland Commissioner for Complaints has power to seek judicial enforcement of his decisions against recalcitrant public bodies. (This might prove to be the most unacceptable of these recommendations to the Home Office.) Jurisdiction of the PCA over complaints by prisoners would cease on the establishment of a special prison ombudsman, after the necessary transitional arrangements had been settled.

Finally, there is the question of complaints which raise issues impinging upon collective or systemic features of prison life. At present, the Chief Inspector of Prisons is charged with the duty, *inter alia*, of conducting special inquiries (e.g. on prison suicides), making visits, and examining the pattern of complaints, to see if there is any revelation of a defect in administration (Morgan Chapter 7). He does not investigate individual complaints. If an aspect of policy is raised by a complaint while the ombudsman is investigating, then it should be perfectly in order for him to make appropriate criticism if he believes this to be necessary. If, however, independently of investigation into a complaint, the ombudsman wishes to criticize policy, then he should be empowered to hand his findings and views to the Chief Inspector. If the latter chose to do nothing, which is unlikely, then his findings and comments might form an appropriate subject of a special report to be presented before the Select Committee.

One should not expect wonders overnight from these reforms. It is better to regard them as basic components in a broader package of changes which are necessary in prison administration. Chief among these must be the incorporation of the European Convention on Human Rights into British Law.[15] This Convention, and decisions of the European Court and Commission of Human Rights, have increasingly made their presence felt in British public administration and judicial decisions, not least in relation to prisoners (Fawcett Chapter 4). Incorporation would provide a broader basis upon which legal protection could be afforded to 'civil rights', and not merely to 'civil liberties'.

In New Zealand (Anderson 1981b), Canada (JUSTICE 1983), Scandinavia (Gellhorn 1966) and the USA (Anderson 1981a), ombudsmen have helped, with varying levels of success, to achieve wide-ranging reforms in prison administration, or have been established with more complete powers than in our own model. The efforts of the PCA have clearly been timid, if not timorous, by comparison. At present, he operates within a constitutional and cultural framework which Whitehall created for him when very few MPs understood the manner in which his prototypes operated in Scandinavia and New Zealand, or what their powers were and what they did. It is time for a new culture, a new framework, and a new ombudsman.

Notes

1 HC 312 (1977–78); HC 246 (1977–78) p. 48.
2 2nd Report, Select Committee on PCA, 1970–71, p. XII and Cmnd 4846.
3 Inv. C 258/80: HC 470 (1980–81); Inv. C 837/80: HC 8 (1982–83) and C 187/81: HC 484 (1981–82).
4 Inv. C55/81: HC 327 (1981–82).
5 And see the trenchant criticism in Inv. C 133/79: HC 526 (1979–80).

6 Inv. 2/388 77: HC 524 (1977–78); and the PCA's sardonic comments in Inv. 2/476/77: HC 111 1978–79. Complaints about Rule 43 confinement (removal from association) feature prominently and do little to dispel the presumption that the rule is used as a punishment without the minimum protection of a disciplinary adjudication: Inv. C 242/T: HC 281 (1973–74); C 483/T: HC 49 (1974–75); 2/392 77: HC 524 (1977–78); 2/499/78: HC 211 (1979–80).
7 Inv. 258/80: HC 470 (1980–81).
8 Inv. C 249/77: HC 126 (1977–78).
9 Inv. C 249/77: HC 126 (1977–78); Inv. C 193/J: HC 405 (1974–75); HC 402 (1979–80).
10 Inv. C 455/68: HC 129 (1968–69).
11 Inv. C 242/T: HC 281 (1973–74).
12 Inv. C 622/V: HC 46 (1976–77); and see Inv. 660/V HC 46 (1976–77).
13 Parliamentary Commission for Administration (1980) Annual Report for 1979. HC 402. London: HMSO.
14 The May Committee's *Inquiry into the United Kingdom Prison Services* (Home Office 1979) was lukewarm about extending the powers of the PCA in relation to prisons. Why, the Report felt, should he have greater powers in relation to one department than others, as this would create constitutional problems? If the special ombudsman for prisons had the same powers as the PCA, then why not stick with the PCA? (paras 5.56 to 5.57).
15 At present, the Home Office has been toying with the idea of drafting a Code of Standards for treatment of prisoners (see Casale Chapter 6). Such a code, if it incorporated the substance of our international obligations, might constitute a useful bench-mark for standards of administration for the ombudsman.

Note: Notes 1–2 refer to Parliamentary Commissioner for Administration (PCA) documents, London: HMSO. (HC stands for House of Commons.)

PART 4

MANAGEMENT AND DISCIPLINE

12

*Management accountability in the prison service**

Christopher Train

Following the report of the May Committee a variety of initiatives was undertaken to strengthen the management of the prison service both at headquarters and in the field. Attention has recently focused upon drawing the threads of these together to produce a coherent structure of management accountability throughout the service. This is a developing area of work, which makes it difficult to produce a definitive statement of the contemporary position. However, shortly before this book went to press, the Director General of the Prison Service set out the current intentions of the Prisons Board in an address to the 1984 Governors' Conference. The relevant sections of that address are set out below.

The Prisons Board has been working hard to get into position the sort of planning and management machinery which should enable the Service at all levels to keep on course. What follows describes a central element of that machinery, and in doing so, picks up and carries on from my opening address to last year's Conference.

I described then how I saw the Prisons Board performing the traditional strategic management role. I said:

*With appendices 'Prison Board Statement of the Task of the Prison Service' and 'Prison Board Statement of the Functions of Prison Establishments'.

'What still remains to be done is to link the management of establishments with the priorities and the strategy which the Board is developing. Governors will always, in one sense, have to operate from day to day, seeking to catch the breezes as they blow. But in the conditions of today, it will only be possible to do that sensibly by reference to a well considered set of objectives for each establishment as a whole.

I concluded by saying:

'I attach central importance to finding ways of securing that the objectives of individual establishments are linked to the view which the Prisons Board takes of the strategic needs and obligations of the Service. I confess that is a tall order. But I judge we have already made considerable progress towards it through the way Board business is now organised and through the efforts that have been put into the various management initiatives such as operational assessments. I look forward to further progress with these managerial tasks in future.'

This year I propose to set out the progress that has been made. But before I do so I want to make some general introductory points. I am concerned to give the Service a sense of unity, a common purpose. And that is in direct response, as I said last year, to the message which I had got then, and continue to get, from the Service at all levels – 'the Service wants leadership: it wants to know where it is going and how it is proposed that it should get there'. Second, and to counter the obvious objection to that notion, I should emphasize that the institutions I shall be describing are neither static nor centralist in their purpose.

All organizations should be dynamic. If they are not they are dead. Nor do I believe it possible, or desirable, to produce a blueprint for action, precise and inflexible in every detail. The Service is too heterogeneous and too complex for that. I would also acknowledge and emphasize that in any organization there are inevitably tensions between the theory and the practice, between the ideal and the actual, and particularly so in one in which the most junior officer may take action for which a Minister may have to answer to Parliament, and where on occasion instant decisions have to be made on the ground without reference to anyone else.

A final preambular point. I take as given and as understood the statutory and procedural framework within which and according to which the Prison Service works; as also the relationships, both hierarchical and advisory, that exist between Ministers and the Service. For the present purpose I shall refer to the instructions, rules, norms and so on which have been and are generated thereby as 'the Department's policies'. So I am concerned with how the Department's policies in that sense are delivered in each establishment and how their delivery is monitored, audited and accounted for. In terms of management theory, therefore, I am concerned with management accountability and audit.

The key manager in the Prison Service is the governing Governor. The Department's policies are delivered by him and his staff in the establishment for which he is responsible. In the final analysis, that is what matters. Now how is this to be done?

There are two principal ingredients to the mixture: on the one hand a general framework in which the operations of individual establishments can be set and on the other a piece of machinery which enables the Governor to be accountable for the operations of his own establishment.

The general framework for the future management of the Service is to be provided by a statement of the task of the Service and, depending upon and from that, a statement in broad terms of the functions of Prison Service establishments. I shall return to both of these later, but they set the context for the infusion of the second ingredient in the mixture. For taken together they will provide the framework in which individual establishments' functions may be defined, performance monitored and account rendered. And – this is the central point – it is that framework which produces a unity of purpose, a sense of direction, for the Service as a whole. But within that framework room is given for individual establishments to deploy their own resources in the way that most suits their individual characteristics.

For the future then (and this is already beginning to happen), the formulation of individual establishments' tasks will be undertaken between the Governor and his Regional Director. Once arrived at bilaterally in this way, that formulation – the establishment's terms of reference – will form a sort of 'contract' between them. It will not automatically be nullified by change of Governor or Regional Director, nor may any third party, from Headquarters or elsewhere, intervene to modify it without consultation with both of the others. So, it will be the basis upon which the Governor, through his Annual Report, will answer to the Regional Director and through him to the Deputy Director General and Director General for the discharge of his functions. It will provide the bench mark against which he will monitor his establishment's performance and which Region will use for setting objectives and evaluating performance, through operational assessments.

In arriving at the terms of reference, the Regional Director and Governor concerned will, of course, take account not only of the need to fulfil the establishment's general functions and to deliver the Department's policies but also of the resources available in the establishment. These are resources not just of staff and of money, but also of inmates and plant. So the constraints deriving from these factors are likely to, indeed will, produce a different balance of regime as between individual establishments. That may require decisions about the disposition nationally of resources, in particular, of staff and regime services. Where local decisions have to be taken which are likely to affect national policy, the relevant headquarters' Directorate may need to be involved. In particular, where regime services are at issue, the point of contact in the first instance will be the Directorate of Regimes and Services Management Unit (DRSMU).

For the future, that Unit will be the arm through which the Director of Regimes and Services discharges his responsibility for ensuring that the regime resources in his Directorate are used to the maximum advantage across the whole system. While it will remain possible, indeed desirable and essential, for Prison Service Industries and Farms (PSIF), for example, to develop a particular industry in a particular prison either on its own initiative or on the Governor's, it will not be open to PSIF or to the Governor to do that without reference to the way in which that will affect locally, regionally or nationally, the balance of regime resources or the agreed means of delivery of the Department's policies in that establishment. Region and the DRSMU, as appropriate, will have a part to play in striking the most effective and efficient regime balance.

Similarly, those responsible at headquarters for the maintenance of the specialist professional standards to be attained by those who provide regime services, education or physical education for example, may, and indeed should, visit individual establishments to satisfy themselves of the quality of performance of that service. But, in accordance with the process that I have described, they may not unilaterally, or bilaterally with the Governor, make adjustments to the agreed quantity of that service in that establishment.

Once the terms of reference for his establishment have been set in this way the Governor will be able to use the resources at his disposal, of course within the general rules of financial propriety and regularity, to discharge his functions and to meet his objectives, reporting annually in this frame of reference as I have said.

To sum up so far, we have here a management system which will work broadly on the following lines. Each Governor will run his establishment on the basis of explicit terms of reference. These will set out how the Department's policies in relation to an establishment of that type are to be applied in that particular establishment, having regard to all the circumstances there. The terms of reference will be formulated (and reviewed periodically) in discussion between the Governor and his immediate line manager, the Regional Director, taking account of the responsibilities of and consulting as necessary on issues of national policy with Headquarters Directorates. Once the terms of reference are set the chain of accountability will be up the line through the Regional Director to the Deputy Director General and Director General; it will not be to the Headquarters Directorates. The Regional Director will use operational assessments to audit the Governor's performance and the latter will account formally for it in his annual report.

I would like to make two further comments. First, the formal establishment of this system, almost as a side effect, fits into a co-ordinated pattern a number of major management initiatives started after the May Report (Home Office 1979) – accountable regimes, the costing system, some aspects of the Management Structure Review, operational assessments are the main examples. This provides the opportunity to draw some threads together and, in some cases, to tie them off.

Second, these arrangements are entirely in line with the principles and practice of management accountability set out in the Government's Financial Management Initiative. Each establishment will have a clearly defined set of functions to perform that are specific to it but flow from the Service's functions: security; court commitment; the feeding, exercise, and education (both academic and physical) of inmates, and so on. Over time it should be possible to devise a recording and reporting system which, on the one hand, displays each establishment's annual discharge of these functions by appropriate measures – numbers of escapes or absconds, numbers of inmates to court, inmate physical education hours, numbers of inmates through education classes or vocational training courses, and so on (much, if not all, of this information is already routinely collected) – and on the other, using the costing system, attaches costs to these discrete activities.

I return now to the statements of task and functions of the Prison Service and Prison Department establishments (which are annexed). I would like to make some general and some particular points.

The statement of the task of the Prison Service is already established in place and being used by the Prisons Board as a means of keeping under review at the strategic level on a regular basis the Service's discharge of its functions. On it depends the statement of the functions of establishments. These two statements are logically linked. As I said last year on introducing the statement of the task of the Service, the approach is essentially pragmatic. It does not include 'aspirational' language. That is not because the Prison Service should not have a clear vision of and be motivated by the need to care for, to help, and if possible to influence for the better the prisoners who are sent to it. But those intentions have to be translated into language that is precise enough for the purposes that I have described in the first part of my address – that is to determine whether functions are being fulfilled and objectives met annually or by target date. These documents are management tools, at national, regional, and local level.

The statement of the functions of prison department establishments is an attempt to fill what I believe is at least a partial vacuum so far as Headquarters' guidance is concerned. Regions and establishments have, I know, been attempting to fill that vacuum in their own way but on a somewhat piecemeal basis. So the statement is intended first to be definitive, second, to apply uniformly throughout the system, third, to be authoritative and lastly, to be congruent with the Board's more general statement of the task of the Prison Service. It has been drawn up by a working group comprised of Regional and Headquarters' representatives and has been endorsed by the Board. It provides the national framework within which Regional Directors and Governors can formulate the statements which relate to individual establishments, and within that discuss and set objectives and targets for the period ahead in the way I described earlier.

Its formulation is not, in fact, especially innovative. As I have said, there have been various attempts in the past, with which people will be familiar, for example one formulated by Mr Bainton[1] a dozen or so years ago. And a number of establishments have had such statements drafted for them specifically in the context of inspections. But the Bainton statement does not seem to have become firmly established for operational purposes, and the inspection statements were made piecemeal. As I say, we aimed for something definitive and authoritative for the whole system.

Second, the statement, like the statement of the task of the Service, does not try to make a declaration about the purposes of imprisonment or to take a position on the continuing debate about the treatment and justice models. Additionally, 'aspirational' language of the kind used in some of the existing documents, including some of the rules, has not been used. I have indicated the reasons for that. The functions are formulated in a way which will make it possible to assess performance by some objective measure.

Third, the statement does not refer to the management of the prison estate or to the management, training or care of staff. These matters are not functions of the establishment; they are not what the establishment is for. They will, of course, be matters to which the Governor and his senior management team will have to give very great attention, but they will do that as a means of fulfilling the establishment's functions and not as an end in itself.

Fourth, and on a somewhat similar point, the statement makes no reference, as the statement of the task of the Service does, to the efficient use of resources. The function of an establishment is not to use its resources efficiently. Efficient resource use is a condition of adequate performance of function. The statements for individual establishments will, as I have indicated earlier, take account of the resources (staff, inmates, money, and plant) that are available to that establishment and it will, clearly, be for the Governor to use his resources as efficiently as he can to discharge his establishment's functions. The Regional Director will decide the level of performance of functions that can and should be achieved with the resources available, and the Governor will be accountable for that. Let me emphasize: the statement of functions does not generate demand for resources.

Finally, it is to be noted that there is one composite statement of function which can be applied by selection of the elements to any individual establishment. The Working Group had originally contemplated providing statements of function for different types of establishment, but concluded that there was so much in common between so many establishments that it was easier and more economical to go for the single statement.

What I have tried to do in this talk is to take us forward a further step together. Last year I spoke of the development of the Board's role in managing the Service. This year I have made the link between that and the role of the key manager in the Service, the Governor of the establishment. I have thought it right to use the occasion of your conference to explain this to you personally. This explanation symbolizes my own concern and that of the Prisons Board that the Service should be a unity, should have a common sense of purpose, and should have a vision of a future which it can and will attain.

Note

1 A. Bainton was Controller (Operations) on the Prisons Board until December 1972.

Prisons board statement of the task of the prison service

The task of the Prison Service is to use with maximum efficiency the resources of staff, money, building and plant made available to it by Parliament in order to fulfil in accordance with the relevant provisions of the law, the following functions:

1 to keep in custody untried or unsentenced prisoners, and to present them to court for trial or sentence;
2 to keep in custody, with such degree of security as is appropriate, having regard to the nature of the individual prisoner and his offence,

sentenced prisoners for the duration of their sentence or for such shorter time as the Secretary of State may determine in cases where he has discretion;

3 to provide for prisoners as full a life as is consistent with the facts of custody, in particular making available the physical necessities of life; care for physical and mental health; advice and help with personal problems; work, education, training, physical exercise and recreation; and opportunity to practise their religion; and

4 to enable prisoners to retain links with the community and where possible assist them to prepare for their return to it.

Prisons board statement of the functions of prison department establishments

CUSTODY OF UNSENTENCED PRISONERS

1 To receive and keep in custody prisoners awaiting trial or sentence, civil prisoners and any other persons lawfully committed to their custody.

2 To release such prisoners from custody on the directions of the court or other lawful authority or when the conditions of bail have been met.

THE COURT COMMITMENT

3 To ensure that prisoners are produced at court as required.

4 To provide the requisite reports and documentation.

5 To provide staff required at the Crown Court and Court of Appeal (Criminal Division) and keep prisoners there in custody.

CUSTODY OF SENTENCED PRISONERS

6 To receive sentenced prisoners and keep them in custody.

7 To calculate and implement release dates.

8 To assess prisoners for the purpose of determining or recommending (a) an appropriate level of security and (b) an appropriate allocation.

9 To keep each prisoner's security category and allocation under regular review. In the case of life sentence prisoners, to maintain regular formal Review Board procedures.

10 To give effect to the provisions relating to parole and release on life licence.

SECURITY, SAFETY, AND CONTROL

11 To maintain a level of security appropriate to the prisoners who are or may be held at the establishment.

12 To maintain good order in the interests of the operation of the prison, and take such steps as are necessary for the safety of its staff and inmates.

SERVICES AND FACILITIES FOR PRISONERS

13 To provide in accordance with the statutory provisions and Departmental instructions: (a) accommodation, (b) meals, (c) facilities for personal hygiene and sanitation, (d) clothing, (e) opportunities for exercise, and (f) access to privileges.

14 To provide a service for the diagnosis, treatment and prevention of physical and mental disorders and the promotion of health.

15 To provide help and advice with personal problems.

16 To enable prisoners to practise their religion.

17 To provide, with a view to occupying prisoners as fully as possible throughout the whole week, a balanced and integrated regime, which may include work, education, physical education, access to libraries and individual and collective leisure activities.

18 To enable prisoners to spend the maximum possible time out of their cells.

COMMUNITY LINKS AND PREPARATION FOR RELEASE

19 To enable prisoners to maintain contact with the outside world and in particular to communicate with their families, friends and legal representatives.

20 To operate the home leave scheme.

21 To assist prisoners to prepare for release, which may include (a) providing such opportunities as are practicable for them to go out into the community on temporary release, (b) providing pre-release courses, and (c) putting prisoners in touch with the probation service and other external agencies.

22 To make arrangements as required for prisoners' after-care.

13
Control in prisons

Roy D. King

It is best to acknowledge at the outset that there is no solution to the control problem in prisons, nor can there be. The control problem – of how to maintain 'good order and discipline' – is inherent and endemic. For as long as we have prisons – and an institution that has become so entrenched in our thinking shows no sign whatever of becoming disestablished – then we will continue to hold prisoners against their will. At bottom that is what it is about.

One does not have to share Foucault's (1977) visionary analysis of the prison at the centre of the 'carceral city', a web of interlocking mechanisms designed to fabricate the disciplinary individual, to see it as a vector of power in society. Even at the most mundane level how could it be viewed otherwise? At some times it is more evident than at others – during 1984, for example, when I was researching aspects of maximum security confinement in the USA, prisoners were occasionally 'delivered' to me for interviews with hands cuffed behind their backs, and accompanied by two or three officers – but it is never absent. Indeed Foucault's concern with the prison arose because the worldwide prison riots of the late 1960s and early 1970s were not merely against 'cold, suffocation and overcrowding, against decrepit walls, hunger, physical maltreatment', but also against 'model prisons, tranquillizers, isolation, the medical and educational services'; 'against the warders but also against the psychiatrists'

(Foucault 1977: 30). As Kassebaum, Ward, and Wilner (1971: 324) wryly concluded in one of the books that signalled the beginning of the end of the twentieth-century flirtation with treatment and rehabilitation as a serious goal of imprisonment: 'It seems likely that both the flexibility and the benign visage of treatment will continue to be of value to social control agencies.'

The plain fact is that most prisoners do not much care for being incarcerated. They do not like the loss of freedom, they get frustrated by the lack of heterosexual contact, they contrast the drab restrictions of the custodial life with the excitement of the real world outside. The response that they should have thought about that before they committed their crimes is not so much wrong as beside the point. In fact many prisoners did think about the consequences, and either discounted them or accepted them as part of the price to be paid – the occupational hazard. But this in no way alters the daily fact of imprisonment and its inherent propensity to problems of control. It is not an issue of desert: rather it is a question of what are the appropriate conditions of confinement once it is decided that imprisonment is the appropriate sentence. One thing is certain about imprisonment: all prisoners have to find some way of coming to terms with it. Perhaps the most astonishing thing about it is that so many of them, for so much of the time, show a daily acceptance of the most bizarre of living conditions, often achieving an impressive kind of dignity in the process.

Nevertheless, to mis-coin a phrase, one cannot control all the prisoners all the time and probably all prisons conduct their business against the perceived constant threat to good order and discipline which from time to time erupts into what is still quaintly described in this country as mutiny. Indeed, for many staff, maintaining good order and discipline is rightly perceived as their only business. At the heart of maintaining good order and discipline in prisons is the disciplinary system itself – the discovery of alleged offences and their processing through investigation, charge, hearing, adjudication, punishment and appeal. These matters are discussed by others elsewhere in this volume. In this chapter, I propose to discuss Prison Department policy in relation to control in prisons which falls short of actual disciplinary proceedings. My concern is with administrative procedures which bear on 'good order', or what the Prison Officers' Association, in a remarkable *volte face,* has recently disparaged as the 'underground' or 'alternative' disciplinary system (Prison Officers' Association 1984).

Probably the most widely held view, both inside and outside the Prison Department, is that the worst control problems have been generated by comparatively few peculiarly difficult, recalcitrant and dangerous prisoners, some of whom may be psychologically disturbed. These prisoners are typically thought of as including terrorists, strong-arm men and leaders of criminal gangs, serving very long sentences of imprisonment: men who are as dangerous inside prison as they are outside. The unpublished report of the working party set up by Robert Carr following the Albany riot of 1972 distinguished between prisoners who were merely 'troublesome' and those who were 'troublemakers', a hard core of prisoners 'who set out to subvert the regime, or actively to disrupt it, who organize or coerce their fellows to acts of indiscipline and drag in those who would otherwise serve their sentence in comparative quiet' (Cox Report 1973). It would be irresponsible and naive to deny that such men exist. Of course they do. But I do wish to argue that conceptualizing the control problem as the product of 'difficult' or 'disturbed' individuals, and developing a reactive policy towards them, has been both partial and self-defeating. Partial in that it ignores all the structural, environmental and interactive circumstances that generate trouble, reducing it to some inherent notion of individual wilfulness or malfunction. Self-defeating in that the policy itself becomes part of those very circumstances that generate the trouble: it is likely that among those who get defined as troublemakers there are some who are made into troublemakers as a result of the way they are dealt with in prison, just as there are some who come to prison as troublemakers.

A wider analysis of issues that have a bearing on the dynamics of control is given, for example, in Cohen and Taylor (1972), King and Elliott (1978), Irwin (1980), and Johnson and Toch (1982), though space precludes review here. In any case it is unlikely that there is a finite number of troublemakers. The probability is that when some are 'dealt with' others take their place. A more rational approach would seek also to obtain a closer knowledge of the circumstances which generate disorder, and to develop a proactive stance towards prison conditions generally that would make it less likely that *any* prisoner should shift from being merely troublesome to becoming a troublemaker.

Fortunately there are signs, in the recent Report of the Control Review Committee (Home Office 1984b), of a more radical re-thinking of the control issue within the Prison Department. However, in a climate of law and order, and on such a sensitive issue as administrative measures of control, one can hardly fail to be aware of the need for caution, and for concern about accountability. There is a very long way to go.

Problems of control in prisons cannot be separated from wider issues of criminal justice policy. Before looking in detail at policy and procedures designed specifically to deal with the control problem it is worth addressing issues about sentencing and parole which set the context for this discussion.

Sentencing, parole, and the problem of control

First, I take it to be self-evident that if control problems are endemic to prisons, and one wishes to minimize them, then one must minimize the use of imprisonment: other things being equal prisons should contain the fewest prisoners for the shortest terms (King and Morgan 1979, 1980). The most recent advocacy of a reductionist strategy in this country has come from Rutherford (1984a, b) even though it is running against the current political tide. Dignan (1984) has traced the subtle changes which have taken place in offical thinking about prison avoidance in recent years, making it plain that the Thatcher Government does not see the reduction of the prison population as a desideratum. In fact, in spite of all the efforts to reduce it, Ashworth (1983) has reported a slight, steady rise in the proportionate use of immediate imprisonment since 1974.

If and when efforts to reduce the prison population are resumed, it is vital that they should involve *both* the diversion from custody of lesser offenders *and* the reduction in sentence lengths across the board and not just at the lower end of the sentencing range. If this does not happen, the process of 'bifurcation' in penal policy discussed by Bottoms (1977) between the 'mad' and 'bad' on the one hand and more 'run of the mill' offenders on the other will continue – with possibly disastrous consequences for the prison system. The effect of a sentencing policy in which 'leniency' with one group is matched by a corresponding, if more occasional, 'toughness' with others is to 'stack up' long-termers in the prisons. In the decade since 1971, receptions under sentences of three months or less have more than doubled, while long fixed sentences of four years or more have increased much more modestly by a little over 10 per cent, although life sentences have gone up by about half. But comparing the prison population of adult males under sentence on 30 June 1981 with that on 30 June 1971, the short-term population has hardly changed as a proportion of the total, whereas there has been a proportionate decline in medium-term prisoners and a proportionate increase in long-termers: prisoners serving 18 months and under increased from 45.5 per cent to 46.7 per cent; those serving 18 months to 4 years fell from 38.1 per cent to 32.5 per cent; while those serving over 4 years increased from 16.4 per cent to 20.8 per cent. Long-termers now comprise more than a fifth of the adult male prison population.

The significance of these changes is that they are *seen* as making the control problem worse. This happens, I suspect, regardless of whether long-term prisoners are more dangerous and more troublesome than they used to be. We are dealing with perceptions of changes, rather than, or as well as, the changes themselves, and the perceptions become the mainspring for action in Prison Department policy. Without the most stringent controls on sentence length it is likely that if Rutherford's (1984b) scenario of a prison system with a capacity of 22,000 and a population of 21,000 were to come about by the end of the century, it would be seen as containing the most violent and wholly intractable offenders.

Second, I take it to be no less self-evident that the most important motivator of behaviour in prison is the prospect of getting out – the light at the end of the tunnel. The perception that long-term prisoners are the least tractable is based, however, not merely on the correct observation that they have a longer tunnel through which to pass, but also on the largely erroneous assumption that they have the least to lose. In fact, until the Home Secretary's announcement of parole changes in 1983, the reverse was true. Shorter sentence prisoners have always had the least to lose from misbehaviour – for apart from getting an additional sentence, the worst that could happen would be loss of remission in the final third of their nominal sentence. Since remission was proportional to length of sentence, the longer the sentence the more remission there was to lose. That, of course, still obtains.

The introduction of parole in 1967 extended the same principle to supervised release during the middle third of the sentence. For all its many defects, the beauty of the parole system lies in its proportionality – the system allows for a reduction in custody, while maintaining both fairness as between prisoners and the relativities of the tariff imposed by the Courts. True, especially in its early days, the Parole Board was reluctant to use its full powers for long-sentence prisoners but as the scheme became established, so more and more prisoners came to look on the prospect of parole as a real possibility – remote perhaps, but certainly not to be discounted.

In October 1983, at a stroke, the Home Secretary undermined this by announcing changes to parole (see Maguire, Pinter, and Collis 1984), the legality of which has only recently been upheld by the Law Lords (November 1984). Nevertheless, it is hard to imagine a package of measures more calculated to produce trouble inside prisons. For the first time, they give the longest serving prisoners the least to lose. True, it can be argued that the Home Secretary's measures are somewhat less draconian than appears at first sight. It is quite possible that the 20-year minimum terms for certain categories of life-sentence prisoners does no more than confirm as a matter of policy what was in any case happening as a result of Court judgements and Parole Board decisions, however regrettable that might be. The sentencing cut-off point of 'over 5 years' for violent offenders at which they can expect little or no benefit from parole produces a somewhat smaller net than had it been 4 years and over, which remains the normal definition of long-term prisoners. And, of course, these severe measures were 'balanced' by the halving of the minimum qualifying period for parole for non-violent offenders. But what all these measures do is dramatically increase the process of bifurcation in penal policy by polarizing the prison population between lesser and greater offenders. The real danger, of course, is that through the grievances and tensions that will be created it will become self-validating. At present there is no wholly convincing published evidence that long-term prisoners as such are more troublesome than anyone else. These measures may make them so and , if and when that happens, will then be seen to have been 'justified'. New measures will then be required which will almost certainly make matters worse. It is quite regrettable that the Parole Board accepted, however reluctantly, such changes. In the interests of all concerned it is to be hoped that they will be reversed at the earliest possible opportunity.

It was against this depressing background that the Control Review Committee was established in 1983 to 'review the maintenance of control in the prison system; including the implications for physical security, with particular reference to the dispersal system, and to make recommendations'. The Committee immediately acknowledged the effect of the Home Secretary's measures to be one of 'redistributing the load between the long-term prisons and the rest of the system' and they noted that the measures would at one and the same time 'increase the number of long-term prisoners' and 'reduce the range of incentives that bear on their behaviour' (Home Office 1984b: para. 2).

The evolution of a control policy

It is ironic, but beyond dispute, that the worst control problems in the UK prison system are perceived to be in the maximum security dispersal prisons. Annex D of the Control Review Committee Report (Home Office 1984b) gives brief details of ten major incidents between 1969 and 1983. Two were in Parkhurst in October 1969 and March 1979; two in Albany in August 1972 and May 1983; two in Gartree in November 1972 and October 1978; two in Hull in August/September 1976 and April 1979; and two in Wormwood Scrubs in August 1979 and June 1983. Of the dispersal prisons, only Long Lartin and Wakefield have functioned over a period of time without serious outbreaks of disorder. Frankland, at the time of writing, has functioned as a dispersal prison – the first to be purpose-built – for only eighteen months and so far without apparent incident.

I shall leave on one side, for the moment, whether this constitutes an accurate portrayal of the control problem in prisons – it is clearly the most dramatic and publicly acknowledged part of the problem. The question is, how are such incidents perceived to arise? Are they inevitable or policy related?

As recently as the early 1960s, when the prison system passed from the Prison Commission to the Home Office, there was no perceived problem of security in the system, nor one of control. With the escapes of the train robbers and of George Blake in the mid–60s, the hurried establishment of the 'special security wings', and the appointment of the Mountbatten Inquiry, the problem identified was rightly one of security. Mountbatten's solution was parsimonious: categorize the prison population by security risk and send them to prisons of appropriate security status (Home Office 1966: para. 212). What this meant, in 1966, was the building of one new high security prison. Control was not addressed, because it was not a problem, and there was no special policy towards it. Fears about control becoming an issue in Mountbatten's never-built fortress, where it was assumed that the regime would be necessarily harsh and spartan, led the Government to follow the advice of the Radzinowicz Report (Advisory Council on the Penal System 1968). This sought to solve security and potential control problems in a single compromise policy, by dispersing high security risk prisoners among the general population of several maximum security prisons. The dispersal prisons would offer a relaxed regime within a secure perimeter (1968: para. 48). The control problem, as seen by the Radzinowicz subcommittee, was essentially a by-product of the method of dealing with high security-risk prisoners. Such prisoners, convicted of major crimes and serving very long sentences, were seen as notorious. If placed together, in an escape-proof fortress, they would develop an 'end-of-the-line' mentality and be uncontrollable. Their notoriety was not to be pandered to, lest it feed their sense of power. Instead, they were to be treated as 'normal' – as far as possible like the other lower security-risk prisoners amongst whom they would be dispersed. By breaking up the high security-risk prisoners, and spreading them among several prisons, the control problem was thought to be 'diluted'. It is clear that in this analysis control-risk prisoners were regarded as essentially the same persons as high security-risk prisoners. The secure perimeter would keep them in: if they abused the relaxed regime then Radzinowicz recommended the provision of physically separate segregation units to deal with them (Advisory Council on the Penal System 1968: para. 164).

From the very beginning the dispersal prisons experienced control problems. I have critically reviewed the dispersal policy frequently and in some detail (King and Elliott 1978; King 1979; King and Morgan 1980) and it would be tedious to rehearse all the arguments again. But it is necessary, briefly, to review the way in which control strategies have developed in the context of dispersal policy, from the first reactive stance of the Cox Report in 1973 to the proactive approach of the Control Review Committee in 1984.

The first review of dispersal policy came in the immediate aftermath of the Albany riot of 1972. It was undertaken by a working party chaired by W.R. Cox, then Director General of the Prison Service. As we have seen, the Cox Report, which was never published, distinguished between the 'troublesome' and the 'troublemakers'. It set about identifying the latter by asking dispersal prison Governors to nominate their most difficult prisoners, and by asking the Department's psychologists to carry out research. It soon became apparent that security risk and control risk were not coterminous categories as had initially been assumed: 72 'hard core' subversives were identified, of whom half were from Category A and half from Category B. The Cox Report recognized that the identification process was hazardous, and but one facet of the larger whole. In particular it noted the greater opportunities for creating trouble in the dispersal regime, even while it acknowledged that 'whatever the Radzinowicz Report says, the emphasis in dispersal prisons is on control' (Home Office 1973: para. 41).

Nevertheless, Cox concluded 'that there is nothing fundamentally unsound' about the dispersal system from either the point of view of security or control (Home Office 1973: para. 138). True, not all staff were reconciled to dispersal policy. They had to be shown that 'it will work and that it is going to be made to work' (1973: para. 38). There could be no return to the fortress concept for security risks, as Mountbatten wanted, and certainly not for control risks, as the Prison Officers' Association wanted (1973: para. 122). The main problem was that the policy was not fully operational: not all the dispersal prisons were yet established and the failure to provide completely separate control units, as Radzinowicz envisaged, meant that the administrative use of segregation under Rule 43(2) could actually provoke as much trouble as it solved. With repeated use of segregation being ineffective, transfers between prisons, or 'ghosting', as a control measure had become commonplace: 94 transfers, involving 63 subversive Category A prisoners, had occurred since the system started, and a handful had 'done the rounds of the dispersal system' (1973: para. 93).

Two additional facilities were recommended to deal with the

residual control problem. The first was the creation of two special control units – one at Wakefield, the other intended initially for Parkhurst and later for Wormwood Scrubs – with a purposely spare regime, to which hard-core subversives could be transferred and where they would have to display sustained good behaviour in order to get out. The second was the provision of special cells in selected local prisons to serve as a temporary relief for the dispersal prisons, and to which prisoners could be transferred for a cooling-off period under what became known as Circular 10/74. The Cox Report also acknowledged the part played by Grendon and by Parkhurst C Wing in dealing with mentally disturbed offenders, who while not perceived necessarily as troublemakers could none the less become involved in serious control incidents.

Control in dispersal prisons was next considered in the Chief Inspector's enquiry (the Fowler Report) into the Hull riot of 1976 (Home Office 1977). By this time the control units proposed by Cox had been tried and abandoned after public outcry; and a challenge to their legality was mounted in the case of *Williams* v. *Home Office*. The Wakefield unit, opened in August 1974, received only six prisoners: the opening of the unit at Wormwood Scrubs was postponed indefinitely. The Fowler Report said little about hard-core subversives as a cause of the riot – perhaps because 60 per cent of the Hull population was involved. Instead attention was focused on the inherently problematic mix of the dispersal population, and the process whereby staff withdrew from involvement in the prison community to supervise from a distance (Home Office 1977: paras 250, 256). Nevertheless, Fowler concluded that: 'We may not have the dispersal system right – but we have not got it all wrong'; and he argued for more dispersal prisons, more direct supervision from Headquarters, and special training for staff (1977: paras 361, 364). That special training related to riot control and led to the creation of Minimum Use of Force – Tactical Intervention, or MUFTI, squads whose use in Wormwood Scrubs in 1979 resulted in injuries to more than fifty prisoners.

The May Committee of Inquiry could hardly fail to address the control problem in the dispersal system: it was set up shortly after the second Gartree riot, and before it reported there were major incidents at Parkhurst, Hull and Wormwood Scrubs. In any case the issues were placed on the agenda by my own evidence (King 1979) as well as by the Treasury and the Committee accordingly commissioned a paper from the Prison Department on the subject (Home Office 1979). By this time the Dispersal Prisons Steering Group had been established within the Department as well as a permanent Working Group on Control in Dispersal Prisons. Once again the Department confirmed its commitment to dispersal – but now more because it was there than as a matter of principle. It argued against concentration of security risks, apparently because it could not dissociate this idea from Mountbatten's discredited design for a fortress. But so many questions were raised about the wastefulness of dispersal as a policy for security problems and its ineffectiveness as a policy for control problems that the May Committee concluded: 'we are not satisfied that the Home Office has struck the right security balance' (Home Office 1979: para. 6.70). While the Committee did not recommend 'either a partial or total reversal of dispersal policy', its tying of this statement to the proviso 'in present operational conditions' left the door ajar for possible future change (1979: para. 6.72).

Five years later, the Control Review Committee (CRC) opened that door. When it was appointed the Home Secretary was about to announce his parole changes and there had been further incidents at Albany and Wormwood Scrubs. In a climate of law and order, and with the continuing failure of dispersal to cope with the control problem, strong pressure was expected for the reintroduction of control units. In these unlikely circumstances the Committee nevertheless managed to produce recommendations which, if implemented in their entirety, could at last provide a framework for dealing with both security and control in a coherent, parsimonious and defensible manner. While the Committee did indeed commit itself to the creation of a series of special 'long-term prisoner units', intended to provide a varied and flexible facility to deal with a range of different control problems (Home Office 1984b: paras 51, 56), it was careful to distance itself from the earlier control units, not merely in terms of the technical breach of the Prison Rules exposed by the Williams case (*Williams* v. *Home Office* (No. 2) 1981), but from their whole philosophy (para. 52). And the proposal for the new special units was in the context of a much more proactive stance towards the issue of control generally.

The extraordinary achievement of the Control Review Committee was that it managed to accept the present existence of dispersal without regarding it as inevitable, and to map out an alternative future without attacking the reasoning that sustained it in the past. The key that enabled the Committee to open this hitherto locked box was an architectural one. In visits to the USA members of the Committee became aware of 'new generation' prisons which build into their design features intended to minimize the problems of control, but without the usual oppressive hardware of maximum security facilities. The new prisons do away with the long corridors and galleries, or the staircases and nests of cells, and so avoid the territoriality in which staff and prisoners develop their own spheres of influence. Without constant resort to physical barriers and televisual surveillance, staff and groups of about fifty prisoners share easily supervisable central areas of living units which have the cells dispersed around the edges. In principle there seems no limit to the numbers of units that could be linked together to form an institutional complex: the possibility of separating and combining groups of prisoners in a variety of ways without involving regime deprivations offers great flexibility.

In the high security context these new designs offer a humane alternative to Mountbatten's fortress, and ingeniously the Committee argued that this changes the debate over dispersal and concentration. So long as the old architectural constraints applied it was right to favour dispersal, but now the Committee went as far as it possibly could in changing direction:

> 'We do not flatly recommend the replacement of the dispersal system by a small number of new generation prisons since that concept of prison design still has to be evaluated in the U.K. Nevertheless we do not conceal our hope that this is the way in which the matter will develop. . . . What we can say is that the dispersal system seems a precariously balanced structure to carry our hopes into the next century, and that a small maximum security system must surely be cheaper than a large one' (Home Office 1984b: para. 127).

As an immediate step the Committee recommended the removal of two prisons, including the hopelessly inappropriate Wormwood Scrubs, from the dispersal system.

Taken as a package, and to its logical conclusion – admittedly some way down the road – what the Control Review Committee (CRC) recommendations could amount to is a move towards greater concentration for high security-risk prisoners in prisons designed to minimize control problems: and a move towards the provision of a range of complementary units, with more or less systematically varied and constructive programmes, from a revived Parkhurst C Wing at one extreme to the inevitably close confinement of those who have killed in prison at the other, allowing a flexible response for the authorities when things go wrong but without entailing undue regime disadvantages for prisoners. Moreover, this is set within a wider context of more rational planning for long-term prisoners (Home Office 1984b: paras 31, 32); a more consistent system of security categorization (1984b: paras 82–5); and an attempt to relate the parts to the whole of a system that would send the right signals to prisoners and reduce the opportunities for manipulation (1984b: paras 89–108).

It would be foolish to exaggerate either the originality of the CRC's achievements, or to expect too much too soon. The decision that Frankland and Full Sutton would be replacement dispersal prisons rather than additional ones had already been taken. The Department had long been embarrassed by Wormwood Scrubs, and a question mark had been over Hull, for example, since the Fowler Report. And there is much in the CRC Report that has been refurbished from the Cox Report. But the CRC has put these matters together in a new and coherent way, and shifted policy from a *post hoc* reactive stance to a proactive approach that tackles both security and control head on. The question is how far, and how fast, can the CRC Report be implemented?

Clearly much depends on the Department's ability and willingness to establish new generation prisons in the high security context. It is important to remember, though, that architecture alone is no panacea. Who can forget the grandiose claims for the Panopticon: 'the Gordian knot of the Poor Laws not cut but untied – all by a simple Idea in Architecture' (Bentham 1791: 1)? The success of new generation prisons in the USA, for example the maximum security facility at Oak Park Heights in Minnesota where I spent much of last year doing research, is as much due to the backdrop of ACA standards, a very carefully drafted set of operational policies and procedures, and their professional implementation by a well-trained, well-motivated staff, as it is to the design. Nevertheless, the establishment of such a prison is vital and could provide the occasion to move forward on all these fronts. The worst possible scenario now would be a botched compromise of implementation: no new generation prisons (too expensive or simply no scope in the already committed building programme); no reversal of dispersal (too risky); no relating the parts to the whole (too complex); instead just a proliferation of special units that degenerate into control units under another name. That must not be allowed to happen, and it need not: at its best, and taken to its logical conclusion, the CRC has provided a blue-print that offers the most reasonable solution to the security and the control problems that we are likely to get.

Control and accountability

The recommendations of the Control Review Committee provide a framework within which control problems are less likely to arise. But it will not eliminate the need for control measures, and the question of accountability will always be there. In the interim, while we continue to live with a creaking dispersal system, and in a context of a rising long-term prison population facing bleak parole prospects, great vigilance will be required about the way control measures are used. This section will raise more questions than it answers – but at the heart of accountability are considerations of publicity, standards and external review.

Perhaps the first point to make is that the Report of the Control Review Committee, unlike the Cox Report, has been published. Details of control units and MUFTI squads only emerged after the event. It must be hoped that we can yet move in the direction of making all operational policies freely available, except where they bear strictly on security, as for example are virtually all Program Statements in the US Federal Bureau of Prisons. Given the traditional secrecy of the Home Office, the CRC has made welcome moves to open the system up to outside researchers and advisers. But this cannot be a substitute for fuller public information. In a defensible system there should be nothing to hide, and there is no surer way of getting a defensible system than exposing it to public view.

As things stand at present it is hard to know even the extent of our control problems, though I am grateful to the Home Office for supplying some of the statistics quoted below. Major disturbances certainly occurred in our dispersal prisons, but none was on a scale comparable to Attica or Santa Fe. In any case these constitute the tip of an iceberg: beneath the surface, throughout the system, is a broader base of routine daily threats to good order and discipline. Most will be dealt with through the disciplinary process but many are dealt with administratively – and clearly there is a trade-off between the two approaches. The number of administrative options is wide, ranging from judicious allocation to, and transfer between, prisons and cell and work locations within prisons; through the confiscation of property (Rule 41) and the use of force (Rule 44), restraints (Rule 46) and temporary confinement (Rule 45); to administrative segregation (Rule 43) and the transfer from dispersal prisons to special cells in local prisons under Circular 10/74. But in respect of what kinds of activities are these measures used? In spite of a chapter entitled 'The Problem' the CRC gave little indication of the nature and extent of the control problem apart from the major dispersal disturbances. One searches the literature in vain for detailed analysis of the nature of everyday incidents, the circumstances in which they arise, or any assessment of their danger to good order and discipline. One instinctively supposes the problems to be less severe here than, say, in many US State systems – but one does not actually know. More research is needed if we are to get control problems into proper perspective.

It is, meanwhile, impossible to determine the extent of the problem in any sense which is independent of the attempts to control it – and even then the information is either not available or else is presented in unhelpful ways. Presumably this is because, unlike disciplinary offences and punishments, for many administrative control measures there is no statutory obligation to present statistics. One area where more detailed reporting would be valuable concerns the use of hypnotic and psychotropic drugs, especially where they are administered forcibly. While drugs are not formally part of the apparatus of control, the boundary between medical problems and disciplinary problems in the prison setting is inevitably difficult: and the published data often conceal as much as they reveal (Owen and Sim 1984). On other matters the Home Office cannot always account to itself just what is happening, and sometimes the gap between an identified problem and the measures to control it is intriguing. Thus the Cox Report initially identified 72 hard-core subversives: in a more systematic search 371 were subsequently reported to the Adult Offender Psychology Unit. After one year, a third had been transferred, apparently as a control measure, a fifth had been re-classified or released, and about 45 per cent remained in the parent prison – but it is not clear whether they were subject to control measures. On the other hand, if one looks at the 122 prisoners who, in 1980, had received the most severe control measures – multiple transfers, or some combination of segregation, prison transfers, or circular 10/74 cooling off periods – then only 43 had been entered in the original Governor's list of disruptive prisoners.

Possibly the most severe administrative sanctions now in use are the administrative segregation for good order and discipline (GOAD) and the transfer of prisoners around the system, known as 'ghosting'. Both seem to be on the increase. In 1983, there were 1,454 incidents of segregation for GOAD – a rise of 26 per cent over 1982 which could not be accounted for by the rise in prison population alone. Such incidents involved 1,119 prisoners of whom 40 per cent were long-termers. While Category A, and the dispersal population, were both over-represented they nevertheless accounted for less than a tenth, and less than a fifth, respectively, of the total incidents. The use of segregation apparently varied considerably by region, and by prison, both inside and outside the dispersal system, independently of population characteristics – which suggests that local policies and traditions play an important role. About three-quarters of all segregations were for less than a month, but there were 92 lasting more than three months, of which 5 were for more than a year. Some 101 prisoners were segregated twice in the year, and 53 were segregated on three or more occasions. Over the period 1980–82, some 21 long-term prisoners, one short-term prisoner and one remand prisoner had been segregated on five or more occasions – though by no means all of these were within the dispersal system. Almost half of prisoners placed in administrative segregation in 1983 were transferred to another institution on removal, though it is hard to get any broader picture of the use of transfers for control purposes because of the way the statistics are reported. It is, however, commonly said that some dispersal prison governors now regard three months as the maximum period they are prepared to take some disruptive prisoners before sending them on the rounds. There were some 45 recorded transfers under the Circular 10/74 procedure in 1983, almost certainly an under-reporting.

Clearly the use of administrative procedures for control purposes is inevitable in any prison system. In some sense and to some degree, virtually every decision has some implication for control. Their use becomes problematic when they entail serious deprivations from the normal regime – though even here neither the *Williams* case, nor that of *McAvoy* (1984), who was transferred without warning, suggest that the Courts are likely to intervene. In any case, in circumstances where regimes may legitimately vary from prison to prison – though most are more or less impoverished – and where there are no standards laid down either as to normal regimes or segregation, then it may be hard to determine what constitutes deprivation outside the context of the European Court. But in circumstances where 'ghosting' approaches what the Americans call 'jails on wheels' and where the threat of 'smelling diesel' becomes an automatic resort, rather than a last resort, then it is hard to see how that could be construed as a normal regime. Nevertheless, it is clear from the CRC Report that the Department wants to move away from the repeated use of transfers and segregation if it can; and after the experience of the 1974 Control Units it is sensitive to criticism and anxious not to repeat mistakes.

There are, of course, some safeguards built into the use of some of these measures – Boards of Visitors are involved, for example, in authorizing and monitoring the use of segregation under Rule 43 (Morgan 1982), as well as various forms of restraint. While there is clearly room for reform, and more stringent review of decisions once made (Gruner 1982), it is worth noting that not all systems have this degree of external involvement. It is hard to disagree with the Prison Officers' Association's recent advocacy of more due process, by the integration of the disciplinary system with the criminal justice system, and the reduction of use of administrative measures. But that would be even more convincing if the POA were to cooperate, for example, with the requirements to report the circumstances where the staff are obliged to use force. On a day to day basis, if not in any ultimate sense, the greatest safeguards lie in the professional integrity of staff.

14

Prison management and prison discipline: a case study of change

Peter M. Quinn

Control and the struggle to stay the same

However prison managers conceptualize their objectives, be they punitive, reformative or warehousing, such objectives are often subsumed by the overall goal of 'running a quiet nick'. In sociological terms, the prison fulfils the criteria of the mechanistic organization (Burns and Stalker 1966). Control is hierarchical with responsibility vested at the top. Communication tends to be vertical and, traditionally, loyalty to superiors is stressed. The mechanistic organization is best suited to stable conditions. Change, particularly rapid change, is threatening. When this is seen as advantaging prisoners at the expense of staff, management may come to believe that their long-established systems of discipline and control are in danger. Whilst it was possible to encapsulate people in customary roles – governor, staff, prisoner – each with their own 'script', management was simple. When role relationships are disturbed, most recently through successful prisoner challenge in the courts, stability is threatened. Mechanistic responses may not suffice in restoring the balance and may, indeed, exacerbate the instability.

The culture which, classically, formed the basis for the perceived stability was that of the quasi-military. This implied a degree of aloofness between the Prison Commission and the governors, on the one hand, and staff on the other. Strains were evident from time to time, seldom more so than when staff stepped out of role during the gestation of trade unionism (Thomas 1972). But if one cliché could sum up something of the relationship between the different groups, it was that everybody knew where they stood. The same could be said of prisoners. They were not universally compliant; there were riots at Lewes and Wandsworth and the mutiny at Dartmoor in the first third of the century. But these incidents were relatively isolated. The potent force of Du Cane's separate and silent system affected prisoner/prisoner and prisoner/staff relationships long after it had fallen into disuse.

It may be thought from some of his public statements that Du Cane was content to see the rule of law extended to prisons. For example, he told the International Penitentiary Conference in 1872 that:

> 'It is above all things necessary that the prisoners should feel that the rules are carried out justly and fairly – that the officers are simply administering the law, and that in the case of any abuse of power on the part of an officer, he will be held answerable for it.'

Yet when Du Cane was asked to account for alleged irregularities at a prison, his terse response indicated that, wherever he believed accountability might lie, it did not lie outside the prison:

> 'It seems to me to throw a certain amount of discredit on the administration of the prisons and the care of the officers to imagine that they require the interference of persons outside to secure attendance to their complaints.'
>
> (Du Cane, quoted in Rose 1961)

He, and his contemporaries, could not countenance an environment where the officer 'would be at the mercy of people of lost character' (Du Cane 1865). On the very rare occasions that prisoners did manage to gain access to a court it became clear that the judges were anxious for the managers of prisons to retain control. The development of the 'hands off' doctrine assured that, apart from gross infractions of the law by the authorities, the courts were reluctant to intervene. As recently as 1972, in *Becker* v. *Home Office*, Lord Denning MR was to state that: 'If the courts were to entertain actions by disgruntled prisoners, the governor's life would be made intolerable.'

But now, as in Du Cane's day, the principal responsibility of management is to hold inmates under the authority of the warrant addressed to the governor. Prison Rule 1[1] and all that stems from it is grafted on to this responsibility. The corollary of holding inmates according to the law is that governors must respect their rights. We know, from the judgement in *Raymond* v. *Honey* (1982), that a prisoner retains all those rights that are not taken away either expressly or by necessary implication. In the latter instance, management has scope for manoeuvre. If a prison community is to be run upon orderly lines it must be under staff direction. If management is to be effective in regulating life in a captive community, then encroachment upon untested 'rights' becomes a reality. Thus correspondence becomes subject to controls, there are restrictions on visits, property in possession is regulated, and so on. In one sense, the prisoner becomes less important than the regime. He becomes subject to the plethora of handbooks, manuals, circular instructions, notices and local rules which, while not forming part of the law, may be regarded as having equal effect. In total, a ponderous control structure has been established, the implications of which are far reaching. So, for very many years, staff regarded the Secretary of State as having a wide discretion as to whether or not prisoners might communicate their grievances to those outside, including their lawyers and the courts. Prison Rules provided for this. Control, of a significant degree, was maintained. Even after the *Golder* judgement (1975) which would have appeared to remove encumbrances, devices like prior and simultaneous ventilation of complaints meant that the full force of the decision was avoided.

Now, following the decisions in *Raymond* v. *Honey* (1982) and *Anderson* (1984), the prisoner is in substantially the same position as any other citizen who wishes to take legal advice. Staff are not yet used to the new climate. The General Secretary of the Prison Officers' Association (POA), speaking to the 1983 annual conference of the Scottish POA, believed that the Home Office had not 'fought its corner in Europe'. One commentator (Logan 1982) suggested that management itself had been taken by surprise:

> 'Until that time [the Hull riot of 1976] the concept of prisoners' rights was alien both to the Prison Service and the Home Office. The view of both could be encapsulated in the view expressed by a senior prison governor that the only right a prisoner had was to be released at the end of his sentence.'

The question of retaining control in the face of change has caused concern to some. Thus, a governor (Wood 1983) has written:

> 'There seems to be a strange inconsistency between calls by the House of Commons majority for longer sentences for prisoners and current moves to ensure that they have legal representation when facing adjudications. On the one hand, prison staff are expected to contain prisoners; on the other, prison staff are expected to maintain control in a situation in which the prisoners' position is increasingly improved in relation to that of the officers.'

The point thus raised, that of assistance for the prisoner at adjudication, presents an interesting case study of change, of management reaction to change and of staff reaction to that.

Assistance at adjudication: a long and winding road

Offences against prison discipline are listed in the Prison Rules. Rudimentary procedure is outlined and this is supplemented for the information of adjudicators, staff and prisoners in a variety of publications. Stated succinctly, if an alleged offence is classified under the Rules as 'grave' or 'especially grave', it will generally be referred to the Boards of Visitors; otherwise, under Rule 51(2) serious or repeated offences may be so referred. Boards of Visitors are independent bodies appointed by the Secretary of State and their powers of punishment or 'award' are greater than those of the Governor. There are about 70,000 reported offences against internal discipline annually, about 4.5 per cent of which are dealt with by Boards of Visitors.

Prison Rule 49(2) states that: 'At any inquiry into a charge against a prisoner he shall be given a full opportunity of hearing what is alleged against him and of presenting his own case.' The last phrase of the Rule had, traditionally, been taken to imply that assistance or representation for the accused was excluded. This could lead to hard cases and the arguments countering the traditional stance are many. Hobhouse and Fenner Brockway (1922) drew attention to possible inequities:

> 'One of our witnesses, who is a chairman of quarter sessions as well as an experienced magistrate, gives it as his strong conviction that it is the exception for the prisoner to get a really

> fair trial [*sic*]. Several magistrates have also pointed out to us that the accused prisoner is in an unfair position compared with the warder, or warders, on whose report he is usually charged. Thus one magistrate writes: "There is difficulty in that the prisoner's offence is often supported by several warders, whilst he is alone in his defence." '

The *Howard Journals* of the 1930s carry several pleas 'for a "Prisoner's Friend" to speak for prisoners charged with serious offences against discipline' (Liverman 1938). The proposal found an early parliamentary protagonist in Rhys Davies MP who recommended it at the second reading of the Consolidated Fund (Appropriation) Bill of 1938. Further parliamentary debate took place prior to the enactment of the Criminal Justice Act 1948. In November of that year, the Secretary of State appointed a committee under the chairmanship of H.W.F. Franklin to review, among other things, existing punishments and procedures in prisons. Using a logic to which the passage of time has lent a quaint touch, the committee rejected arguments for representation:

> 'The character of some recidivist prisoners is such that they would be prepared to risk a flogging by striking an officer in order to have the opportunity afforded by legal representation of maligning the character of individual officers or of discrediting the prison authorities.'
>
> (Franklin Report, Home Office 1951: Part I, para. 127)

In 1964, during parliamentary debate on the proposed new Prison Rules, the Secretary of State, Henry Brooke, disposed of arguments for assistance at adjudications by stating that: 'A man who has got himself into prison cannot hope to have all the advantages that a free man would have outside.' In 1970, a similar proposal was found not to be 'necessary or practicable' by the Home Secretary (English 1973).

More recently, argument in favour of assistance or representation for the prisoner at adjudication re-emerged. It formed one of the principal demands of PROP (Preservation of the Rights of Prisoners – a prisoners' pressure group) on its inauguration in 1972, and the following year, *The Guardian* newspaper carried pieces both by its columnist Malcolm Dean and by a group of prison staff who favoured the idea.

In 1975, the matter came before the courts. In *Fraser* v. *Mudge* the Court of Appeal declined to make a Declaration that a prisoner was entitled, as of right, to such assistance and refused to issue an Injunction to prevent a Board of Visitors adjudicating. But also in 1975, a Home Office working party under the chairmanship of T.G. Weiler was meeting, having been required to report upon adjudication procedures. As regards representation and assistance, Weiler suggested that there should be no departure from standard practice in the main. The committee recommended, however, that an experiment should be mounted in a number of prisons where a prisoner would be given assistance in preparing, though not presenting his case (Home Office 1975: paras 61–6). The results of the experiment have been published (Smith, Austin, and Ditchfield 1981) and a noteworthy feature from a point of view of institutional response was that participants in three of the four selected prisons withdrew their cooperation.

But influential opinion was shifting. The *St Germain* case (1979) established that Boards of Visitors' adjudications are subject to judicial review by way of *certiorari*. The Royal Commission on Legal Services (1979) recommended that a prisoner should have the opportunity of being legally represented were he to be at risk of forfeiting seven or more days remission. In *Mealy* (1981) Hodgson J was openly critical of a procedure under which

> 'the prisoner was at a substantial disadvantage when compared with someone facing an ordinary criminal charge. The prisoner need not be allowed legal, or other, assistance and in this case, the applicant had not had any assistance at all. . . . The prisoner could not be expected to have the flexibility of a trained legal mind.'

There was an abortive attempt to secure, for prisoners, the right to advice and representation at disciplinary hearings with the introduction, to the Commons, of a private Member's bill in 1981 (Dubs 1982). Further, Ministers came to realize that there might be inequity in denying assistance where a prisoner was not proficient in English. On 7 June 1982 Lord Elton, Minister of State at the Home Office, informed Parliament that 'where a prisoner has difficulty in understanding English he is given assistance, whether by members of the adjudicating panel, prison staff, other inmates or an interpreter to enable him to participate in the proceedings'.

As these developments were taking place there were growing challenges, at law, to institutional decision making. The courts, since the late 1970s, have shown themselves prepared to scrutinize internal practices more rigorously than in the past. The dicta in *Raymond* v. *Honey*, referred to above, have informed a number of subsequent judgements. The detail of these is to be found elsewhere in this volume (Fitzgerald). In brief, however, it was held in *Tarrant* (1984) that, whereas a prisoner had no right to assistance or representation at adjudication, the Board of Visitors had a discretion to allow them. In *Campbell and Fell* v. *UK* (1984), before the European Court of Human Rights, it was held, *inter alia*, that Article Six of the European Convention on Human Rights accorded a *right* to assistance and representation in certain circumstances. Current domestic litigation may well be a precursor of prisoners at governors' adjudications being offered some form of assistance (*King* 1984).

Doubtless, this question will be addressed by the Departmental Committee under the chairmanship of Mr Peter Prior, the establishment of which was announced by the Secretary of State in October 1983 (see Morgan, Maguire, and Vagg, this volume). The Committee is charged *inter alia* with making recommendations about the adjudication system, used both by governors and by Boards of Visitors.

Sixes and sevens

The kind of change brought about by *Tarrant* and by *Campbell and Fell* had been foreseeable for a number of years. Yet for those working within the prison system, it would have been reasonable to conclude that change had come upon us suddenly. The mechanistic organization does not respond readily to rapid change and the planning to accommodate it was not effectively communicated to the field. This led the POA to conclude:

> 'We believe the present disciplinary system is in a state of irremediable crisis and that if this crisis has been precipitated by the legal decisions . . . it has been aggravated by the failure of the Prison Department to anticipate them.'
>
> (Prison Officers' Association 1984)

At many levels there was faith in the survival of 'hands off'. To this was added the fruitless hope that prisoners' rights issues would, somehow, go away. In 1979, one prison governor told the writer that to contemplate assistance for the prisoner at adjudication would be to regard 'legal niceties as more important than seeing justice done'. Again, in 1982, a senior governor wrote to me that 'a more detailed and intimate knowledge of arguments pertaining to rights and (inmate) litigation . . . could not be seen as essential to the work of the Department and would be of limited direct benefit'. Attitudes such as these were to lead the POA to write of apparent 'official complacency' (Prison Officers' Association 1984).

But there had been contingency plans to deal with post-*Tarrant* practice. After the judgement was handed down, hasty communications did take place between the Home Office, chairmen of boards and governors, with an invitation to share advice with staff. Amended procedure was recommended. Unfortunately, however, speed led to certain misinterpretations of the judgement and some incorrect advice was passed down. This has since been rectified.

But hasty and inaccurate as some of the advice was, it was more than the POA received when they, quite properly, sought the acquisition of professional skills in a new and vital area. HM Chief Inspector of Prisons (1983a) commented that such training, as with police officers, is a requirement of a good disciplinary system. But when the General Secretary of the Association wrote to the Prison Department in January 1984 to ask about plans for training staff in the particulars of evidence in the new circumstances, the reply, though lengthy, was dismissive. Policy has now altered and a comprehensive training package has been distributed to institutions (Prison Service College 1984). This will be supplemented as necessary. But my own discussions with members of the POA National Executive Committee reveal that staff felt thoroughly bruised by the first response. At least three institutions, thereafter, decided to mount their own training programmes, the result being an undesirable variation in tuition and resulting practice.

And on the threes and fours?

It is necessary not to allow the extent of change to be overemphasized. One of the POA's early concerns, expressed in their *Magazine* in April 1984, was that legal representation would be granted to every inmate who asked for it. This has not happened;

the number of cases where a solicitor is present is in the order of about one in twenty Boards of Visitors adjudications. However, there is no place for further complacency. Whatever the courts decide and however the Prison Department devises policy, it is how this is experienced in the prisons that is of the essence for staff and for inmates. If the Governor is to be able to continue to run his 'quiet nick' it is important that all within the prison have confidence in the systems that are operating. Foremost among these is the need for the internal disciplinary system to be seen as speedy and fair. Not only is this important to those in the prison, but it has also been seen as axiomatic by the courts. Since the *Tarrant* judgement, which has the potential to enhance the status of internal proceedings at law, a number of issues militating against this have become manifest. Paradoxically they tend to be in the areas of speed and fairness.

The POA has suggested that the 'corrosive anxieties' created by the recent judicial decisions may lead, or may have led, to the use of alternatives. Underground systems may bypass the formal disciplinary procedure completely. Thus a troublesome prisoner may find himself affected either by overt alternatives ('ghosting' or temporary transfer, segregation under Rule 43 for the sake of good order and discipline, etc.) or by covert alternatives which cannot be challenged (adverse reports to the Local Review Committee of the Parole Board, etc.) (Prison Officers' Association 1984). But, even where the formal procedure is employed, there may be diversion from a Board of Visitors. Rutherford (1983) wrote of the possibility that a staff, lacking confidence in a Board, might divert charges to the lower level of governor. This might be achieved, for example, by reducing the nature of the charge, say from assault to attempted assault. In such circumstances the effect could be that a guilty prisoner might be punished more severely than by a 'lenient' Board. Other effects would be that the decision would not, at present, be subject to judicial review by way of *certiorari* and the prisoner would be denied legal or other assistance. But diversion need not be to achieve a sinister purpose. The mechanistic organization aspires to certainty and to that which it knows best. A member of senior management in a local prison described it to me thus:

> 'Following the *Tarrant* case, headquarters issued urgent guidance to boards of visitors on the criteria for allowing inmates to be legally represented at the adjudication and suggested an

appropriate procedure to be adopted. This imposed a need for boards rapidly to familiarize themselves with the criteria and revised procedures under the spotlight of intense legal and media interest. Their professionalism would also be scrutinized by the prison community. The boards were not obliged to follow the Department's guidelines and often modified them significantly. Board procedures could not be changed without making different demands upon prison regimes. This required discussion with management and, at times, referral by management to headquarters. Change of this nature is inevitably time consuming. An adjudication conducted under procedures not yet finalized would produce difficulties. It is not, therefore, surprising that during this transitional period, cases which could legitimately be conducted by the governor tended not to be referred to the board.'

But, whereas prisons are now becoming more familiar with the new requirements, in the cases where assistance or representation is granted the question of delay is posing a serious problem. The reasons are many. Prisons are not always conveniently placed in terms of being able to provide adequate facilities. In one case, a Board is faced with recommending to a prisoner who requests legal assistance that he should seek a transfer back to the nearest local prison if he is to make effective use of that opportunity. Some of our prisons are isolated and thus, by definition, remote from solicitors' practices. Solicitors themselves must master not only a novel procedure but also an environment for practice previously kept hidden. Becoming aware of the nuances of prison jargon can, itself, be frustratingly time consuming. A management perspective on the results of such difficulties, in practice, can be gleaned from the following statements, both from senior members of their respective management teams:

'A local solicitor was appointed as governor's representative. He came to the prison, consulted with various members of staff, saw witnesses' statements and discussed procedure. He withdrew from the case on the grounds that he lacked sufficient experience and another local solicitor was appointed. . . . At that point, fifty days had elapsed since the incident occurred.'

And again:

'In the end, the prisoner had been a year in chokey.[2] Staff didn't give a sod what the award was as long as he was found guilty.'

Boards, too, share similar concern. Conveniently placing the blame on the lawyers, the chairman of one Board of Visitors was reported in *The Guardian* on 2 October 1984 to say:

> 'There is an average of eleven weeks delay before the hearing when prisoners are represented and this is a serious retrograde step. Lawyers must put their houses in order and find ways of preparing cases more quickly because these delays are just not acceptable in the prison context.'

Yet it is precisely that prison context that can help to bring about delay. One case of which I am aware, both from the governor and the prisoner's legal representative, remain part heard some nine months after the prisoner instructed his solicitor. The alleged offence took place in a Midlands prison. The solicitor was in practice south of London. This created problems of communication. Procedural difficulties regarding access to written records led to adjournment. Delay was compounded by non-availability of Board members. The prisoner was transferred, though he had to return to face the renewed hearing. Other cases have involved a number of co-accused prisoners, or various witnesses who might have been either segregated pending adjudication, or transferred or even released. In one instance several prisoners were charged with involvement in an incident. Individually, their legal representatives wished to call different witnesses, some of whom were charged with complicity, some of whom were not. Delay built up as new panels of Board members were convened so that each could come to the adjudication with a fresh mind. One governor told me: 'The trouble with those multiple charge prisoners was that we used up all our experienced Board members. At the end, Board members were very inexperienced.' The nature of this inexperience can lead to a wariness of the whole process. One senior manager told me: 'If legal representation is granted, we have difficulty finding Board members who are available.'

Some of the delay, therefore, has been brought about by the understandable need, on the part of Boards, to become adept in the new procedure of which they are the masters. Boards, and staff, have, on occasion, had to wrestle with difficult problems of evidence. As an internal quasi-judicial tribunal a Board is largely freed of the rules of evidence that apply in a court. The principles of natural justice apply, but within those parameters, a Board has considerable freedom. So it is, for example, that hearsay evidence is given and accepted relatively frequently. Other facets of the evidence question are producing contention and thus delay.

Since Boards cannot subpoena witnesses, their attendance cannot be guaranteed. A prison officer could be placed on a disciplinary charge for refusing to attend or to give evidence, or indeed, as in *Fox-Taylor* (1982), an adjudication might be overturned if he conceals evidence. But no sanction can be brought against a prisoner or a member of the public who refuses to give evidence. Specialists employed by the Prison Department are in an anomalous position. As part of their duties they must attend if required, but the degree of disclosure of information to which they are subject is not as rigorous as in court proceedings. A Board member has access to the records of the prison under Rule 96(3). But whether he or she can order their production at an adjudication remains a moot point.

Staff do not yet feel confident with post-*Tarrant* practice. Most have not experienced it at first hand. One group of assistant governors had it: 'There is a genuine fear of questioning by legal representatives within internal hearings' (Milligan *et al.* 1984). Fear has no place in the adjudication room. The mechanistic organization can adapt, but it needs time and it needs certainty. The latter depends upon the former. Prisons find the change to more scrutiny by the courts and more accountability quite threatening. But, already, there are hopeful signs that change is being welcomed. An assistant governor at the first prison to experience a legally represented prisoner at adjudication wrote to me: 'The rough and ready methods which have traditionally served the prison service so well have long outlived their usefulness.' Prison staff now look to the recommendations of the Prior Committee to reinforce their professional competence and confidence.

I would like to thank George Owen, Tutor at the Prison Service College, Wakefield, for his expert help and advice during the preparation of this chapter. I would also like to thank the many prison governors and officers who patiently responded to my enquiries.

The views expressed are those of the author. They do not necessarily represent those of the Home Office or of the Prison Department.

Notes

1 Prison Rules 1964 (SI 1964 No. 388) as amended. Prison Rule 1 states: 'The purpose of the training and treatment of convicted prisoners shall be to encourage and assist them to lead a good and useful life.'

2 'Chokey' is one of several pieces of prison jargon used in place of 'segregation'. Prisoners are often segregated before an adjudication to prevent the possibility of collusion or intimidation.

15

Overhauling the prison disciplinary system: notes for readers of the Prior Committee's Report

Rod Morgan, Mike Maguire, and Jon Vagg

At the time of writing, the Prior Committee is still considering what changes should be made to the prison disciplinary system in England and Wales. The Committee is expected to report in the autumn of 1985. Now is not the time to discuss the paucity of information about existing arrangements available to the Committee (the result of resistance within the Home Office to independent research on adjudications in the past and pressure on the Committee to report quickly now) nor is there much to be gained from speculation about what detailed recommendations the Prior Committee may make or the Government accept. However, it may be useful to consider what factors do and should govern prison disciplinary systems and review some of the written evidence submitted to the Committee which may shape their general proposals.

The criminal justice system, it is often suggested, must strike a balance between due process and crime control, the need to protect the rights of individuals while safeguarding collective security (see Royal Commission on Criminal Procedure 1981, ch. 1). The notion that individual rights and community interests can somehow be traded to achieve an optimal solution may be mistaken, not least because without assured individual rights there can be no collective security worthy of the name. Nevertheless, discussions about the practical organization of criminal justice usually reveal a tension between these considerations and nowhere is this tension more apparent than in debates about prison disciplinary systems.

Prisons, it is often pointed out, contain persons whose willingness and capacity to subvert order is proven: most prisoners have committed either serious or repeated offences. Whatever explanation for their behaviour is favoured, many prisoners, by virtue of their family or social background, or moral or mental deficiencies, are perceived to be at best socially inept and at worst asocial or anti-social (see Home Office 1984e: 14). Furthermore, all prisoners are persons held against their will in institutions which, because of their security functions, tend to be insular, inward-looking and restrictive. In prisons persons not noted for their regard for others have to live in close proximity, often for long periods: in prisons minor incidents can quickly be magnified to become major convulsions. Thus order in prisons, the argument runs, is precariously balanced: control requires special provisions to meet a threat which is pervasive and unpredictable. This reasoning leads to the proposition that prisons require specific disciplinary systems. And even though those systems deal with behaviour which on some occasions at least could be defined as criminal, they must incorporate modifications of those tenets and procedures which form the basis of criminal justice systems outside.

These assumptions have underpinned prison disciplinary arrangements historically in England and Wales (see also Fitzgerald Chapter 2) and are apparent in the terms of reference of the Prior Committee. While considering 'the disciplinary offences applying to prisoners, and the arrangements for their investigation, adjudication and punishment' the Committee is to have regard to 'the need within custodial institutions for a disciplinary system which is swift, fair and conclusive'. Significantly, speed comes first: and this priority involves a very particular interpretation of the maxim 'justice delayed is justice denied'.

There are, as the Prison Officers' Association (POA) has pointed out, three principal means by which prisoners are controlled: first, by the daily routine actions of prison officers; second, by administrative decisions of the Prison Department; and only finally by the invocation of the formal disciplinary system, which may include referral to an outside court (Prison Officers' Association 1984: 2). Resort to the latter, for which prison officers act as gatekeepers (the Prison Act 1952, s.8 invests prison officers with the powers of constables and the Prison Department Standing Order 3D 6 asserts that in most cases it is for the individual prison officer to lay charges), is for all but the most serious criminal offences discretionary, and can be avoided for either positive or negative reasons. If prison staff consider that discipline unresolved is discipline lost, then delays in formal disciplinary proceedings, for whatever reason, may simply reduce the degree to which they use that system. In so far as alternative methods of control are more covert, less easily reviewed and less subject to rules of due process, justice delayed may involve justice substantively denied.

The suggestion that the disciplinary system be swift is, therefore, not simply a constraint on the just investigation, preparation and trial of cases (though it is almost certainly that also) but a recognition of the relative powerlessness of prisoners and the interdependence and substitutability of control measures available to staff. This fact of prison life is tacitly recognized in the description of non-disciplinary methods for dealing with 'troublesome' prisoners – institutional transfers, security re-categorization, segregation under Rule 43, removal of privileges and the like – outlined for the Prior Committee by the Home Office (Home Office 1984d). These non-disciplinary methods of control are correctly though disingenuously described by the Home Office as 'entirely administrative in character': not 'punishments' however much prisoners may feel punished through their use (Home Office 1984d: 10). The POA, while disavowing any liking for the proposition, more honestly refers to these administrative mechanisms as an 'alternative' disciplinary system.

Two central questions, therefore, are, as the Prior Committee's terms of reference put it, 'the extent to which it is appropriate to use the ordinary criminal law courts and procedure to deal with serious misconduct by prisoners' and how, if they are not used, 'allegations by prisoners about their treatment' are to be investigated.

At present, both questions are resolved through the use of Boards of Visitors. Offences by prisoners are rarely brought before the criminal courts (though no numbers are published) and Boards of Visitors' hearings are quasi-judicial.

The hearings are supposedly inquisitorial (though 'accusatorial' has sometimes been said to be more apt a description) and the procedures are substantially different from those used in criminal courts. Prisoners have no right to representation, the accused has no right to cross-examine witnesses and may be prevented from calling his own, there is no requirement for a legally trained clerk to be present, and hearsay evidence may be admitted. Prisoners are said not to suffer disadvantages through the use of these private quasi-judicial proceedings because Boards of Visitors are held to be independent persons with considerable grievance-ventilation and inspectorial powers and duties. Thus, it is claimed, Boards not only adjudicate impartially but are able to put right any improprieties which adjudications bring to light. Board members have to authorize some of the 'alternative' controls (segregation under Rule 43 or use of restraints) and may bring other matters to the attention of the Governor, the Secretary of State or, in the last resort, the public at large. Above all, Boards of Visitors, by virtue of their multi-functional familiarity with prisons, are said to dispense speedy justice fully cognisant of the character and welfare interests of prisoners as well as the practical difficulties of prison management. That is the theory: scarcely anyone but Board members believe it to work in practice, and one in six of these has doubts (Maguire and Vagg 1984).

On one thing practically all groups which have submitted evidence to the Prior Committee are agreed: if a second tier of prison discipline (between governors' adjudications and charges in courts) is to be retained, it should not be composed of Boards of Visitors. This message is even apparent, though discreetly coded, in the Home Office evidence (see, for example, the suggestion that 'it seems natural to look to the ordinary criminal courts to provide the necessary machinery' for second-tier cases: Home Office 1984e: 20). The only persons expressing satisfaction with Boards' participation are individual Boards and Board members. Even the Association of Members of Boards of Visitors (to which a minority of Board members belong) is unequivocally opposed to maintenance of the existing system. Like the Jellicoe Committee ten years previously, and a more recent report from JUSTICE, AMBOV argues that Boards of Visitors' various duties are incompatible and mutually compromising rather than the reverse (Martin 1975; JUSTICE 1983; AMBOV 1984).

The argument about the compatibility or otherwise of Boards' duties has rumbled on for many years. Given the European Court of Human Rights' judgement in *Campbell and Fell* (1984) that

Board members may be considered independent of the prison administration for adjudication purposes, it seems unlikely that a mere swelling of the chorus claiming incompatibility will be considered sufficient reason to change the system. The conclusive factor is more likely to prove the POA's loss of confidence in Boards' capacity to cope (in a manner of which the POA approves) with the legal complexities forced on them by recent decisions of the Divisional Court (notably in *Tarrant*, see Fitzgerald this volume): Boards' lack of legal training, compounded by the absence of a legally qualified clerk, makes them prey to indecision and delay. This, the POA claims, is bringing about 'the final collapse of the system' (POA 1984: 9). Whatever the validity of this claim, the Chief Inspector of Prisons has stated that Boards now enjoy so little confidence that for justice in prisons to be seen to be done 'the balance of advantage lies in transferring the judicial function to another body' (HM Chief Inspector 1984f; para. 2). It will be surprising if the Prior Committee does not recommend this outcome.

If Boards of Visitors are no longer to be involved in adjudications (we presume that Boards, or some other group modelled on them, will continue to have inspection and prisoner complaint duties) then what other body will constitute the second disciplinary tier? It would of course technically be possible to dispense with a middle tier altogether so that cases were dealt with either by governors or the outside courts. This simplified arrangement, which would resolve many procedural difficulties, appears to work satisfactorily in most European countries. Yet the traditions and expectations of prison staff in England and Wales suggest this solution is unlikely to be adopted. In most European countries the punishment of loss of remission is not available to prison administrators. Governors here, however, already have the power to award up to twenty-eight days loss of remission. Were the middle disciplinary tier to be swept away, considerable pressure would almost certainly be brought to bear to increase governors' powers of punishment; otherwise, it would be argued, large numbers of relatively minor criminal offences would have to be referred to the courts, with all the delays and costs inevitably involved. Yet the grant of extra powers to governors would necessarily re-open the question of possible legal representation for prisoners at Governors' hearings. The 1979 Royal Commission on Legal Services recommended (para. 9.29) that in cases where prisoners were liable to seven or more days loss of remission they should have the right to legal representation. Both the Divisional Court in *Tarrant*, and the European Court of Human Rights in *Campbell and Fell*, stressed the important connection between legal representation and the possibility of serious penalties being imposed. Clearly, the administrative advantages of governors' hearings – their dispatch, their inquisitorial nature and all the procedural characteristics which flow from that – would substantially be lost (as, prison staff maintain, has happened already to Boards of Visitors' hearings) were legal representation to be introduced.

Thus though logic suggests there is no need for more than a single tier of internal prison discipline – with the vast majority of offences (disciplinary and criminal) being punished by way of fines, loss of privileges, and cellular confinement – the considerable powers of punishment already vested in governors and Boards of Visitors (the powers for the latter effectively being greater than those available to justices in summary criminal courts) are likely to result in the continuation of a multi-tier arrangement at least as, if not more, complex than that existing now. Significantly, none of the organizations giving evidence to the Prior Committee, including the civil liberties and penal pressure groups, appears to have considered it desirable or politic to advocate abolition of the second tier.

The body most favoured to replace Boards of Visitors for adjudications is a panel of local magistrates, though some groups propose the use of magistrates or lay persons as assessors alongside an itinerant judge or lawyer of standing (NCCL 1984; Howard League 1984). A panel of magistrates (its membership not overlapping with Boards of Visitors) could be formed from a bench or benches local to the prison; the members could be trained for the task as are justices for juvenile, domestic and licensing court work; it could operate with its own court clerk; and where the prison generated few adjudications, as do open prisons, a single panel could serve more than one institution to provide sufficient business for the acquisition of expertise and experience.

However, this recommendation still begs many questions which most submissions to the Prior Committee leave unresolved. First, are the proceedings to constitute a court – and thus be part of the criminal justice system – or a quasi-judicial tribunal, remaining part of the internal disciplinary system? Whatever the answer (and the answer does not necessarily follow from the decision as to membership) it will have implications for many other issues. Are the proceedings to be adversarial or inquisitorial? Are hearings to be within or without the prison, public or private, and, most importantly, are prisoners to have a right to legal representation or is the panel to exercise discretion?

It is not our purpose to anticipate answers to these questions or to propose a complete blue-print of our own. We are more concerned to argue that whatever solutions are framed will have consequences outside a strict reading of the Prior Committee's terms of reference. They will also have a bearing on the accountability of the prison system as a whole. In order to illustrate some of the issues involved, we offer one possible scenario of which we would broadly approve.

Given the history of prisons in England and Wales, and the expectations which flow from that, there would clearly be some merit in retaining a second-tier body which remained part of the internal disciplinary system. This might be composed of magistrates. However, magistrates have little experience of inquisitorial proceedings and might prove ineffective at prison adjudications: the manner in which they deal with search warrants (Lidstone 1984) and the record of the old prison Visiting Committees (Morris and Morris 1963: 130–1) does not inspire confidence. On these grounds it might be argued that a lawyer of standing, accompanied by two lay persons, not magistrates – the model for other tribunals – might be a more acceptable structure. Under such a system the proceedings would be more efficiently and speedily conducted, more 'due process' orientated than at present, and more able to cope with any legal issues which arose. Moreover, the tribunal would clearly be independent of the prison administration and the criteria of fairness and conclusiveness (the Prior Committee's terms of reference) better assured.

The question of the representation of prisoners at hearings might be solved either by adopting the criteria outlined by Mr Justice Webster in *Tarrant* (see Fitzgerald this volume; Morgan and Macfarlane 1984); or, more satisfactorily, by giving prisoners the right to be represented by duty solicitors or lay advocates. It seems reasonable to assume that the organization of duty solicitors operating within agreed time limits would prevent undue delay. Furthermore, since the majority of hearings are uncontested (Iles *et al.* 1984), it seems likely that many prisoners would wish to waive the right to be represented in order to get the matter over with as soon as possible.

This package sounds attractive. However, it should not be forgotten that the new structure would still comprise a quasi-judicial tribunal and not a court. For this reason it would seem right to reserve only to the courts the trial of serious offences which demand heavy penalties. The Prior Committee will have to wrestle with the complex and controversial question as to what offences should be retained in the Prison Rules and what penalties should be attached to them. That is a separate issue for which we have not space here. We do think, however, that the fact that internal hearings are quasi-judicial should certainly mean that the maximum punishment which can be imposed for any offence should be no greater, and almost certainly should be less, than that available to summary courts. Given that magistrates' courts are generally restricted to penalties of up to six months imprisonment, of which one-third is deducted for good behaviour, this should effectively mean a maximum penalty of less than 120 days loss of remission. We suggest that a maximum of 90 days would be reasonable.

It might be argued that reducing the maximum penalty would lead to many more cases going to the courts, and that there would be many more delays resulting from police investigation combined with the uncertainties as to whether or not a decision to prosecute will follow. In fact this is unlikely often to be the case. In 1982, Boards of Visitors imposed sentences of more than 180 days loss of remission on only two occasions out of 3,500. Awards in excess of 90 days were made on only 265 occasions. Were the new panels to have a maximum power of 90 days loss of remission, most cases currently dealt with internally, including those attracting more severe penalties, would almost certainly remain within the prison disciplinary system. Furthermore, commensurate with the reduction in second-tier maximum penalties, the possibility of legal representation at governors' hearings could virtually be banished by removing from governors the power to impose any loss of remission: the ability of a single person unilaterally to extend a prisoner's sentence will always be open to grave objection.

Yet it would be naive not to acknowledge that these proposals might increase the temptation on staff to make greater use of the 'alternative', 'administrative' controls. After all, the proposals do involve: certainly, a reduction in tribunals' powers of punishment; probably, some delay in dealing with a minority of cases; and, possibly, more incisive questioning by the panel of the circumstances surrounding offences.

These considerations suggest that the Prior Committee and subsequently Parliament should have regard to the desirability of creating countervailing accountability mechanisms. For example, assuming that Boards of Visitors, or some similarly constituted body, would retain inspection duties, they might have the right to be present at both first- and second-tier adjudications in order to monitor both the procedures and any improprieties revealed during them. Adjudications may, for example, bring to light background matters to do with the administration or regime of the prison which do not provide grounds for appeal. Nor may deficiencies in the way adjudications are conducted necessarily give rise to appeals which draw attention to them. Furthermore, to stress the new specialized and independent watchdog body's role it might be sensible for its members to be appointed by and be accountable to the local authorities rather than the Secretary of State; there would then be an obligation to report publicly on their work which would balance the closed, though not necessarily unreported, nature of disciplinary hearings.

As far as the Prison Department is concerned, there would be a case for altering the nature of the account it is statutorily required to lay before Parliament. The Prison Act 1952 s.5 requires only three aspects of the work of the Department to be recorded in its annual report: the accommodation and its occupation in each prison; the nature of the work done by prisoners, including the quantities of articles produced; and the details of punishments inflicted in each prison by offence, including precise particulars of the use of corporal punishment. Of course the latter punishment is no longer available, which perfectly illustrates the archaic irrelevance of much of the current Prison Act and the Rules deriving from it. What is required is a new legislative framework geared to the way prisons operate today. Much more appropriate would be a requirement placed on the Prison Department to account annually for such matters, *inter alia*, as the forcible use of drugs and segregation under Rule 43 or (pending an adjudication) under Rule 48, the prison equivalent of a refusal of bail.

The above is only one of many scenarios for which the Prior

Committee may settle. Furthermore, it has covered only a few of the issues with which the Committee will have to deal. But whatever solution it adopts for the disciplinary system it will have wider consequences for the accountability of the prison system in general. If the solution is to work, and to be fair, the Committee must have as much regard to these wider questions as to the technical matters in their terms of reference.

PART 5

OVERSEAS COMPARISONS

16
Grievance procedures in The Netherlands

Jan A. Nijboer and Gerhard J. Ploeg

Introduction

The topic treated in this chapter is the functioning of the grievance procedure for prisoners in Dutch penal institutions. Since the penitentiary situation in The Netherlands is different from other countries in certain respects, we shall first give a short description of the various types of institutions which exist and present some statistical data on the relative size and composition of the prison population. Furthermore, some recent developments in the prison system will be discussed since they influence the grievance procedure to a considerable degree.

In Section 2 we shall give a description of grievance procedures for prisoners in Dutch prisons. Section 3 contains a discussion of the results of a study concerning the actual functioning of the grievance procedure (Ploeg and Nijboer 1983). Finally, some concluding remarks will be made in Section 4.

1 The Dutch prison system

Dutch penal institutions can be divided into Houses of Detention and Prisons. Houses of Detention are similar to local prisons in the United Kingdom, their inmates being principally suspects in preliminary custody, although there are also prisoners with short-term sentences or awaiting transportation to another institution.

Prisons vary widely in type, as a result of the principle of individualization of treatment. According to this principle, each prisoner should be placed in the institution most suitable to his or her situation. There are special institutions for women, for juveniles to 23 years of age, for adult male prisoners with short-term sentences, and for those facing longer prison sentences.

A further distinction can be made between closed, half-open and open institutions. In closed prisons, where prisoners are not allowed to leave the premises, varying degrees of group interaction exist. Prisoners in half-open and open institutions enjoy a certain amount of personal liberty and contact with the outside world. They are in the final stage of their imprisonment. The idea is that a gradual return to society is made possible in this way. Rehabilitation, preparing the prisoner's comeback to everyday life, is also a basic principle of the Dutch prison system. We discuss below some recent developments in this way of thinking.

One of the most striking characteristics of the Dutch penitentiary system is the relatively small number of prisoners. On 1 February 1984 the number of prisoners per 100,000 population was only 31. This is the lowest of all members of the Council of Europe, apart from Malta. The median for all these member states was 68.6. The reason for this low number is mainly the fact that the average duration of prison sentences in The Netherlands is short: two months in 1982. A relatively large part – 22.7 per cent in February 1984 – of the prison population consists of juveniles under 23 years of age (Tournier 1984).

The number of foreigners in Dutch prisons increased markedly in the 1970s, yet has tended to stabilize, proportionally speaking, in the 1980s. In February 1984, 22 per cent of the prisoners were of a foreign origin. Foreigners are especially over-represented in the institutions for long-term imprisonment, and even outnumber native Dutch prisoners (Staatssecretaris van Justitie 1982–83). Communication, food and daily habits can be a source of misunderstanding and conflict.

A similar development, a stabilization after a rise, can be found with respect to the number of prisoners addicted to hard drugs. An exact figure cannot be given, but according to an estimate based upon statements of prison doctors, the percentage of drug-addicts in 1982 was 18.5 per cent for houses of detention and 12 per cent for prisons (Roorda 1984). In some houses of detention, one-third of the population was addicted, in the institutions for long-term imprisonment about 25 per cent (Moerings 1984). Evidently, drug-addicted prisoners form a significant problem.

The ratio between staff and prisoners in The Netherlands is high; there are 10 persons employed for every 7 prisoners. In England and Wales, for instance, every 10 officers have to deal on average with 19 prisoners. Also, prison management is relatively expensive in our country. The cost per prisoner per annum amounted to £19,000 in 1978, about three times as high as, for instance, that in England and Wales (Rijksbegroting 1981–82).

RECENT DEVELOPMENTS

The proportion of offenders sent to prison in The Netherlands decreased after 1972, yet has shown a tendency to increase again since 1980, especially with respect to medium- and long-term imprisonments (Rijksbegroting 1983). The number of prisoners per 100,000 inhabitants increased from 20 in 1975 to 31 in 1984. This development has led to capacity problems: in 1981 there was a shortage of 790 placements. Since then, a thousand new cells have been added, but a certain shortage remains. A number of measures have been taken, such as keeping persons in preliminary custody at police stations, and reopening closed or discarded buildings. In both cases the level of accommodation is quite inadequate, which leads to a great number of conflicts and problems.

In 1982, the Secretary of State for the Ministry of Justice, M Scheltema, wrote a white paper entitled 'Task and Future of the Prison System', in which a change in the way of thinking about the goals of imprisonment was proposed (Ministerie van Justitie 1982). The principle of rehabilitation was accorded less prominence, and the emphasis was placed instead upon carrying out imprisonments in as humane a manner as possible, with a minimalization of possible injurious effects. Consequently, certain programmes were created, which were aimed at a better adaption of the detention to the prisoners' own needs and interests.

It was proposed that prison labour be reduced in favour of things like study, creative activities and sports. The task of the prison officer should shift from strict guarding to a more personal contact with the prisoner. In practice, however, budget reductions have prevented the prisons from carrying out these measures. The number of officers decreased while the number of prisoners increased, necessarily leading to longer periods of cell confinement. The personal contacts between prisoners and officers have been reduced. An increase of tension within the institutions has resulted, demonstrated in conflicts between staff and inmates, but also in demonstrations by the former of their dissatisfaction with the situation.

2 Grievance procedures

In this section we shall give a brief historic survey of the developments of the legal status of prisoners in The Netherlands, paying special attention to grievance procedures.

HISTORICAL BACKGROUND

After the Second World War a change occurred in official thinking about prisons and imprisonment. This led to the introduction of a new Prison Act in 1953. Two important viewpoints illustrate these changes:

1 Imprisonment was no longer to be carried out as solitary confinement, but by involving the prisoner in various forms of group interaction.
2 The punitive thrust of imprisonment was to be reduced and emphasis was to be shifted towards a preparation for the offender's return to society.

At the same time, interest in the legal status of prisoners increased. Two aspects of this legal status must be distinguished: on the one hand, there is the whole issue of rights and duties, prohibitions and instructions to which the prisoner is subjected, the *material legal status*. On the other hand, there is control of the observance of legally established rights, the *formal legal status*. Our discussion is focused upon the latter.

In the Prison Act of 1953, the possibility was created for prisoners to turn to a Visiting Committee with their complaints or grievances. Such a committee – which has similarities with the English Boards of Visitors – was attached to every penal institution from that moment on. It consisted of three to eight members, each of them independent of the prison administration. The committee had a purely advisory capacity. It could bring certain matters to the attention of the prison Governor and advise on the decision to be made. The Governor was at liberty to follow the advice or to ignore it. There were practically no legal guarantees against possible arbitrariness.

The functioning of the Visiting Committees was criticized virtually right from the start. This criticism concerned the lack of power and expertise of the committees, their assumed dependent attitude, and the large social distance between members of the committee and prisoners. These factors were said to result in a lack of confidence on the part of the prisoners and to doubts about the independence of the Visiting Committee.

In 1964, a government committee was formed that was to create a draft proposal for a law dealing with the legal status of prisoners. After a discussion in Parliament the work of this committee resulted in the introduction in 1977 of a new Act regulating grievance procedures (Wet van 21 October 1976, Staatsblad 568).

THE NEW GRIEVANCE PROCEDURE

The 1977 Act provided for the establishment in each institution of a new Grievance Committee (GC). This GC consists of three members of the Visiting Committee. The latter continues to exist and still carries out the same task of general inspection of the situation inside the institution. The chairman of the newly formed GC is preferably a member of the legal profession who is already entrusted with the administration of justice. The idea behind this is quite simply to guarantee the presence of enough expert legal knowledge in the GC.

Fundamental to the formal regulation of grievance procedures were two points:

1 The grounds for complaints to be received by the GC were laid down in law.
2 The imposition of legal powers upon the decisions of the GC.

The general idea was to guarantee prisoners' rights by having their grievances judged upon by an independent group of people, and giving this judgement legal power. This meant that the prison Governors were obliged to accept the decisions of the GCs and to carry them out. In order to guarantee the discretionary powers of the prison Governors, on the other hand, the grounds for grievances had to be limited to a certain extent. If complaints could be lodged about every possible subject, the procedure would become overburdened and the institution would become unmanageable.

The grounds for grievances were formulated as follows: A prisoner in a prison or house of detention can lodge a complaint against:

1 a disciplinary punishment imposed upon him;
2 a refusal to hand over or send letters or other written or printed matter addressed to him or written by him, or to receive certain visitors in accordance with the prison rules;
3 any other measure imposed upon him by or on behalf of the Governor contrary to the rights the prisoner can derive from regulations considered to be valid in the institution.

In all cases a complaint can be admitted by the GC only when it concerns a decision made by or on behalf of the prison Governor. Decisions made by, for instance, the Public Prosecutor or the Minister of Justice are not handled by the GC.

A complaint has to be lodged within three days after the prisoner has learnt of the disputed measure or as quickly as can reasonably be expected. The prison Governor must give a written declaration of the measure within twenty-four hours in the case of grounds 1 and 2, and, if the complainant asks him to do so, also in the case of 3. The GC must decide upon the complaint within a period of three weeks.

The GC can make three possible decisions: it may decide not to admit the complaint because it does not deal with any of the above mentioned grounds, and it may declare the complaint either founded or unfounded. In all of these cases it is possible for both parties to appeal to a higher institution, the Central Board of Advice (CBA). This Board advises the Minister of Justice upon matters concerning the prison system, the organizations dealing with aid to discharged prisoners, and the care of psychiatric prisoners.

Such an appeal has to be made within eight days. Ultimately if the GC or the CBA has decided in favour of the complainant, the chairman of the GC has to examine with the prison Governor the possibilities of compensating the effects of the measure against which the complaint has been lodged.

As soon as the GC has received a complaint from a prisoner, its substance is brought to the attention of the Governor. The Governor supplies the GC with the necessary information concerning the case and may add his own remarks on the complaint and complainant. The GC sees to it that the complainant receives a written copy of this information and these remarks.

The possibility exists that the GC may judge a further hearing of the parties unnecessary because it is considered that the written material makes it sufficiently clear that the complaint is unfounded or not to be admitted. In all other cases, a meeting is held at which the complainant is given the opportunity to comment orally on his complaint. The prison Governor or one of his representatives will usually be there too, to present his view of the matter.

The GC can call witnesses, either on its own initiative or at the request of the complainant or the Governor. Further, the complainant may be accompained by an adviser. If he has none, he can ask the chairman of the GC to assign him one. In most cases this adviser will be a solicitor.

The GC can *revise* the decision made by the Governor if:

1 the decision is contrary to a regulation, considered to be valid in the institution;
2 the decision is unreasonable or unfair, considering all interests and circumstances.

The term 'revise' indicates that the GC can not only declare a Governor's decision to be invalid, but can also substitute a decision of its own. To complete this brief survey of the grievance procedure, we mention the possibility of suspension. The chairman of the GC can ask the Governor to suspend a certain measure, against which he has received a complaint. This possibility has been created in order to prevent a measure from being carried out during the period in which a complaint against it is being considered by the GC. For instance, a punishment of three days solitary confinement would have been served long before the GC decided upon the complaint against it. If the chairman of the GC judges, at first glance, a request for suspension to be reasonable, awaiting the meeting of the GC, he will contact the Governor. The Governor, however, need not comply with the request.

The grievance procedure for prisoners was established after

elaborate discussion in Parliament. Yet from the beginning, certain points of criticism came from several sides. Partly in consequence of this criticism, the Criminological Institute of the University of Groningen carried out a study, at the request of the Ministry of Justice, of the actual functioning of the procedure.

3 An evaluation of the functioning of the grievance procedure

Two questions were considered most important in our evaluation study:

1 Does the procedure represent an improvement over the old situation?
2 How does the procedure function in practice, and what problems arise?

In order to answer these questions two different projects were carried out, one in 1976 in which the situation before the introduction of the new law was studied, and one in 1982. By comparing the results, the first question could be answered. In order to obtain an idea of the practical functioning, we decided to speak to as many parties concerned as possible. There could be no question of a 'classical' evaluation, as the goals of the grievance procedure have never been stated explicitly enough to serve as measurable criteria. In addition, no agreement on these goals exists. We therefore made, as it were, an inventory of individual evaluations.

Meanwhile, we carried out an interim study in 1978, in order to find out which problems arose during and immediately after the introduction of the new procedure. It turned out that the most important drawback lay in ignorance about the procedures among prisoners and staff. Also, the definition of the roles of the Visiting Committee and the Grievance Committee created certain problems.

A number of recommendations resulted from this study, with respect to the provision of a better spread of information and some procedural improvements. Clearly, 1978 was too early for a definitive evaluation. This took place in 1982, and we will now describe the design of this study.

In order to obtain a clear image of the functioning of certain procedures, it was vital to speak with the parties concerned. For this reason we interviewed prisoners, prison officers, Governors, members of Grievance Committees and members of the appeal committee from the Central Board of Advice. First we drew a sample from the total number of penal institutions. Next, a sample was drawn from the prisoners and staff present in each institution at the time of interviewing. All prison Governors and members of all GCs in the first sample were approached for an interview.

The sample of institutions was not randomly drawn; we took certain factors into account, such as geographical distribution and character of the institution. Furthermore, we selected institutions known for their large numbers of complaint cases. The sample consisted of 22 penal institutions, 10 of which were houses of detention, 8 'closed' prisons and four (semi-) open prisons. All governors of these institutions were interviewed. In two cases the interviews with GC members could not take place. Four members of the Central Board of Advice, the committee of appeal, were also interviewed.

We imposed some restrictions as to the selection of prisoners: they were to be able to speak the Dutch language, over 18 years old and at least 4 weeks in prison. A random sample was drawn from this group. Apart from this group, we wanted to interview prisoners who had experience with the grievance procedure. Data for drawing this additional, 'purposive', sample were obtained from the prison records. Finally, a random sample was drawn from those officers present in the institution at the time of interviewing.

In all, we interviewed 176 prisoners in the random sample, 36 complainants in addition to the random sample, and 94 officers. The total number of complainants interviewed was 76, and this group had lodged a total of 196 complaints with the GC. The interviews with prisoners and staff were carried out with standardized questionnaires, consisting primarily of questions with precategorized alternatives for responses. Governors and members of GCs and CBA were interviewed in the form of a 'free conversation' with the help of a check-list of topics. These conversations were recorded on tape. In order to obtain a better view of some procedural aspects, we also carried out an analysis of the dossiers of roughly a quarter of all cases that were filed up to autumn 1982. We shall now discuss the results of our analysis of all these data.

RESULTS

1 Developments in the number of cases

The number of cases for the GC has increased dramatically since the introduction of the new procedure. In 1982, over four times as many complaints were lodged as in 1978. The percentage of complaints adjudged to be 'founded' remains about 15 per cent. The percentage of complaints not admitted fell from 25 per cent to 15 per cent, owing to a broader view of the ground 'violation of a right'. The number of complaints related to this ground has increased markedly as well, by a factor of seven from 1978 to 1982.

Prisoners appeal to the CBA more often than Governors in absolute numbers, yet proportionally it is the other way around. The CBA confirms the GC's decision in slightly over 50 per cent of the cases. Appeals by the Governor appear to be successful more often than prisoners' appeals. The above-mentioned tendency towards an increase in complaints admitted, especially with respect to violation of a right, can be found with respect to appeals as well.

2 Information, attitudes and experiences of prisoners and staff with respect to the grievance procedure

We found that 85 per cent of the prisoners knew of the existence of the Visiting Committee and 76 per cent knew of the Grievance Committee, yet only 21 per cent knew the difference between them. The composition of the GC was known to 91 per cent of those prisoners who knew of its existence. The grounds for grievance appeared to be poorly known. The best-known ground – a violation of rights (ground 3) – was mentioned by 17 per cent of all prisoners in the representative sample. Roughly one-third said they knew how to lodge a complaint, and 12 per cent knew the right time limit for doing so. Apart from certain details – compensation, suspension of a measure and appeal – prisoners were poorly informed about the way in which cases were actually handled. Of those prisoners who disagreed with a certain measure or punishment, a little over a third actually lodged a complaint about it. Yet 71 per cent appeared to prefer a less formal procedure for dealing with their complaints. Moreover, informal settlement produced more satisfied complainants than the formal procedure.

Prisoners placed little confidence in the GC. Its independence in particular was doubted. Furthermore, prisoners generally considered the procedure too lengthy, the GC to be lacking in expertise, and that redress was rarely forthcoming. This lack of confidence contributes to the fact that over 20 per cent of the prisoners had at some time deliberately not lodged a particular complaint.

Prisoners who had had contact with the GC were mostly dissatisfied with the meeting. They felt restricted in the possibilities for stating their case and thought that the GC was sympathetic toward the Governor. In 22 per cent of the relevant cases, the prisoners appealed to the CBA. The opinion of the CBA's meeting was considerably more favourable.

Only about one-third of the complainants appeared to be satisfied with the overall treatment of their complaint. Yet 76 per cent said that they would contact the GC again in the event of a new complaint arising. The overall conclusion was that the grievance procedure meets a certain need among prisoners, in spite of all the objections.

As might be expected, staff were better informed than prisoners on all points. However, there were some gaps in their knowledge with respect to certain details. We found misunderstandings about the grounds for complaint, time limits, and the possibilities for redress. Officers claimed not to be influenced by the grievance procedure in their way of working and their attitudes towards prisoners. They appeared to have a stereotyped idea of complaining prisoners, however, and considered them as trouble makers. Only a few officers had ever attended a meeting of the GC, and their impression was mostly negative. On the whole, the opinion among staff was that a grievance procedure is in itself a good thing, but that it is too often abused.

Our main conclusions, then, were that prisoners are insufficiently informed about their grievance procedure; that there is little confidence in the procedure among staff as well as among prisoners; that the level of acceptance of the GC's decisions is not very high with any of the parties concerned; but that the general opinion about the CBA's decisions, on the other hand, is much more positive.

3 Criteria for decisions

Much of the criticism of the grievance procedure, especially from prison Governors, concerns the criteria used by GCs and the CBA in deciding upon the justness of a complaint and the preceding question of admittance. According to the law, a decision should be revised when it is 'unreasonable or unjust', considering all relevant interests and circumstances. This means that in such a case a new decision replaces the one under complaint.

The possibility of revising a Governor's decision is crucial to the grievance procedure and forms the solid foundation of the prisoner's rights. This foundation was not questioned by any member of the interviewed groups, but problems arose with the interpretation of the grounds for complaint. We have the impression that some of the principles basic to the procedure may well be quite manageable separately, yet have unexpected effects when they interact with one another. The broad interpretation of 'violation of a right' has led, together with the standards applied for judgement and the principle of revising a decision, to a situation in which it is not unreasonable for a prison Governor to feel impaired in his authority.

A step in the right direction would be to bundle the rights and duties of a prisoner, now spread among several laws and instructions, into a more convenient form. The obscurity on this point was mentioned regularly by the various respondents.

4 Time limits

The Grievance Committees take a very lenient attitude with respect to the time limits mentioned in the law. This is true of the time limit for lodging the complaint as well as for the deadline for deciding upon it. In almost a third of all cases the GC exceeds the latter term of three weeks. We consider this an undesirable situation.

5 Suspension and redress

There is a strong relationship between the problems concerning suspension and those of redress or compensation. In our opinion at least one of these two matters ought to be effectively taken care of so as to guarantee satisfactory treatment of a complaint. A well-functioning suspension procedure can prevent compensation difficulties, and the other way around. In practice, it appears that a disciplinary punishment is seldom suspended. The reason is that, in the case of a short-term punishment, it has often already been undergone by the time a request for suspension reaches the Governor; in the case of a longer punishment, the Governor has considered the matter to be serious enough to justify such a long-term punishment and, consequently, will not easily comply with the GC's request. In our opinion the situation would be improved by making the chairman of the GC easier to reach and giving him the authority to decide about suspension.

None of the parties concerned is very enthusiastic about the functioning of the principle of redress. It appears to be very hard to find a way of satisfactorily compensating the experienced wrong. Many problems arise, especially when it is decided to award financial compensation. An alternative which we believe is worth thinking about is to compensate in the form of remission of some days of the sentence being served, even though many legal obstacles would have to be cleared before this is possible. Within the possibilities of the procedure as it now exists, it would appear that the best alternative is to search for redress in fields where the punishment had its primary effects: extra recreational time, sports, compensation for lost wages, and so forth.

Finally, according to the law the chairman of the GC and the Governor must discuss the possibility of redress or compensation every time a complaint is found grounded and the consequence of the measure cannot be undone. In several cases this apparently did not happen.

6 Judicial advisers

The absolute number of cases in which the complainant receives judicial assistance has risen since the introduction of the new procedure; relatively, however, it has more or less stabilized around 15 per cent. In the bulk of these cases the judicial adviser was a solicitor. We found no differences in the outcome of cases with and without judicial advisers. Cases involving a judicial adviser, however, did appear to be more complicated and take more time.

Several objections were made – especially by prison Governors – against having a fellow prisoner as judicial adviser. The objections mostly concerned their lack of expertise.

The increase in cases with judicial advisers obviously leads to an increase in costs. Although this should not be a reason for refusing judicial assistance in certain cases, it might play a part in assigning a solicitor. We found that chairmen of GCs adopted a pragmatic way of dealing with this matter. If the complainant had not come up with an adviser of his own, the chairman often tried, when he considered an adviser to be needed, to assign a solicitor known to be experienced in the field of penitentiary law. The presence of a solicitor is especially valued in cases concerning matters of principle which might have more general consequences. Finally, opinions varied with respect to the quality of the judicial advice. Solicitors who specialized in grievance procedures were valued most.

7 *Foreign prisoners*

Foreign prisoners who were not able to speak Dutch were excluded from the sample because of expected language problems. Therefore we gave special attention to their position in the interviews with Governors and members of the GC and CBA. The problems with foreign prisoners were mostly in the fields of deportation, cultural differences and religious matters. Foreign prisoners had relatively less contact with the GC than Dutch prisoners. The complaints they lodged did not seem to differ in content from those of Dutch prisoners. The level of knowledge among this group was even lower than among Dutch prisoners, although most institutions have information folders, translated into the most current languages. A foreign prisoner has the right of assistance by an interpreter when his complaint is dealt with. This did not appear to produce many problems, although it is sometimes hard to find capable interpreters in the case of less common languages within the limit of three weeks for deciding upon the complaint.

4 Discussion

EFFECTS OF THE GRIEVANCE PROCEDURE ON LIFE IN THE INSTITUTIONS

One of the conclusions of our study is that the developments in grievance procedures have led towards a polarization and a hardening of the atmosphere in the institutions. Polarization, because the fact that conflicts are 'taken to court' puts the parties in formal adversary positions; hardening of the atmosphere because after one of the parties is put in the wrong, they have to continue living together. Moreover, fear of creating a precedent makes the prison Governors take up a very formal position with respect to granting certain favours. On the other hand, the grievance procedure has produced greater equality before the law and legal security. One of the aims of the introduction of the formal grievance procedure was to clarify the material legal status of the prisoner through decisions of GCs and CBA. These committees have indeed gained a considerable reputation in the field of establishing the rights and duties of prisoners in substantial detail.

The question is, however, to what extent the jurisprudence of, notably, the CBA is effective. In principle a decision applies only to a specific prisoner in a specific case and has no general validity because the institutions vary too much in character. Nevertheless, certain tendencies can be distilled from its decisions. Some Governors, however, claim to continue taking certain measures even though they know they will probably lose if the prisoner lodges a complaint. The Ministry of Justice has been known in some cases to deal in another way with CBA decisions which they consider unfavourable. They simply change certain rules, so that the decision will go against the complainant in the next similar case. In this way jurisprudence has negative consequences for the prisoners.

On the whole, however, from the point of view of legal status, the negative effects of juridification do not seem to weigh against the progress made in reducing the opportunities for arbitrariness, clarifying the material legal status of the prisoner and banning the system of personal favours. We believe, however, that certain improvements can be made which would reduce the negative effects of these developments.

AN ALTERNATIVE WAY OF DEALING WITH PRISONERS' COMPLAINTS

There can be no doubt that the merits of the grievance procedure justify its existence. Therefore it should not be altered, apart from certain details. In our opinion, it should, however, be supplemented by a preliminary informal procedure in which those who are most directly involved try to resolve their conflicts. The parties or their representatives would attempt to settle their conflict in the presence of a neutral arbitrator. Only if they failed to reach a solution would the matter be referred to the GC. One of the advantages of such a procedure would lie in the fact that a solution to the conflict had been sought which was satisfactory to all parties, instead of having a judgement made which labels one party as the victor and the other as the loser.

Moreover, the complaint could be handled much more quickly so that problems concerning suspension and compensation could be avoided. The feeling of responsibility with respect to one's own life-situation would be stimulated, which would increase confidence among prisoners as well as guards. There are more opportunities here for creative solutions than in the formal procedure, where the emphasis is on being put in the right. However, it is necessary to provide an informal procedure with sufficient guarantees of fair treatment. It should not function as an empty, conciliatory gesture or as an instrument of social control. The idea is to achieve a greater degree of enfranchisement and sense of responsibility.

In addition, it must be realized that not all kinds of complaints are suited for seeking settlements through informal procedures. The latter seem less suitable with respect to questions of lawfulness or matters concerning material accommodations. On the other hand, conflicts concerning internal prison policy are especially eligible to be handled using these procedures, because a certain discretionary authority is the matter at issue. Informal procedures can also be useful in the case of conflicts between staff and prisoners, especially at a stage in which these conflicts have not yet escalated. In this way disciplinary punishment could possibly be avoided.

We propose a procedure in which a committee is formed, consisting of prisoners and prison officers. The members of this committee would be chosen by the parties they represent. The members themselves would choose a technical chairman or arbitrator who would not have the right to vote. If a solution was not reached, or if the solution did not satisfy the complainant, the matter could still be put before the GC or the Visiting Committee. Such a procedure would have to be tested in a practical experiment. In that way it could be determined whether it would contribute towards a meaningful improvement of the legal status of prisoners.

17

Accountability in Canadian penitentiaries: disciplinary procedures and judicial review

Charlene C. Mandell and Arthur L. Mandell

Introduction

Penitentiaries in Canada are controlled, operated and financed by the federal government. Not all offenders sentenced to imprisonment serve their sentences in a penitentiary; some serve their sentences in provincial institutions. The general rule, which is found in section 659 of the *Criminal Code* of Canada, is that a person sentenced to imprisonment for a term of two years or more, or for two or more terms that total two years or more, serves his or her time in a penitentiary. This chapter deals only with discipline in penitentiaries.

In this chapter we will first examine the disciplinary procedures to be employed within penitentiaries to deal with charges of flagrant or serious misconduct laid against inmates. We will then examine judicial review of the decisions of penitentiary disciplinary courts. We will be particularly concerned with the effect to date of the new *Canadian Charter of Rights and Freedoms* which is expected to have a significant impact in many areas of Canadian law and with the effect to date of judicial interpretation of the common law duty to act fairly in the context of penitentiary disciplinary decisions.

Disciplinary procedures

The *Penitentiary Act* and the *Penitentiary Service Regulations* (made pursuant to section 29 of the Act) provide the legislative and regulatory authority upon which the system of inmate discipline in Canadian penitentiaries is based. The operational detail is provided by Commissioner's Directive 600-7-03.1 (issued pursuant to the *Penitentiary Act*) and Divisional Instruction 600-7-03.1 (issued pursuant to the *Penitentiary Service Regulations*) both of which became effective on 31 August 1984 revoking the 1979 Directive, Annex 'A' to it and the 1982 amendment. The cases discussed in this chapter were decided under those, now revoked, administrative directives.

It was decided by the Supreme Court of Canada in *Martineau and Butters* v. *Matsqui Institution Inmate Disciplinary Board* (hereinafter referred to as *Martineau (No. 1)*) that the *Penitentiary Service Regulations* have the force of law but that the Commissioner's Directives do not. The reasoning in *Martineau (No. 1)* leads to the conclusion that the Divisional Instruction also does not have the force of law.

Section 39 of the *Penitentiary Service Regulations* lists the types of conduct which constitute disciplinary offences. Paragraphs 11 and 12 of the Divisional Instruction provide guidelines to assist penitentiary staff in categorizing disciplinary offences as flagrant or serious offences, or alternatively as minor offences. However, these are only guidelines and each case is to be assessed on its own merits. This chapter examines only the disciplinary procedures to be employed with respect to flagrant or serious offences.

The sole provision in the *Penitentiary Act* respecting inmate discipline is section 24.1 which states:

24.1

1 Every inmate who, having been credited with earned remission, is convicted in disciplinary court of any disciplinary offence is liable to forfeit, in whole or in part, the earned remission that stands to his credit and that accrued after the coming into force of this section, but no such forfeiture of more than thirty days shall be valid without the concurrence of the commissioner or an officer of the Service designated by him, or more than ninety days without the concurrence of the Minister.

2 The Governor in Council may make regulations providing for the appointment by him or by the Minister of a person to preside over a disciplinary court, prescribing the duties to be performed by such a person and fixing his remuneration.

Subsection 38.1(1) of the *Penitentiary Service Regulations* empowers the Minister, who is the Solicitor General of Canada, to appoint persons to preside over disciplinary courts. In exercising this power, the Minister usually appoints lawyers to those positions. The Commissioner's Directive refers to these appointees as 'Independent Chairpersons'.

Subsection 38(1) of the *Penitentiary Service Regulations* provides that the institutional head (also referred to as the Director or the Warden) is responsible for the disciplinary control of inmates confined within the institution. Subsection 38(2) provides:

38.(2)
No inmate shall be punished except pursuant to
- (a) an order of the institutional head or an officer designated by the institutional head; or
- (b) an order of a disciplinary court.

Paragraph 11 of the Directive instructs the Director to assign an Independent Chairperson to hear charges of flagrant or serious misconduct. However, it also provides that if no Independent Chairperson has been appointed to the institution, the Director may himself hear such charges and that if the inmate is scheduled to be released or transferred within twenty-four hours and an Independent Chairperson is not available, either the Director or Acting Director may hear the charges.

Before an inmate is required to appear before the Independent Chairperson he must have been charged with a flagrant or serious offence. The *Penitentiary Act* and the Regulations say nothing about the 'charging' process. However, Commissioner's Directive 600-7-03.1 and Divisional Instruction 600-7-03.1 set out extensive procedures respecting the 'charging' process.

The process of holding an inmate accountable for an alleged misconduct begins when a member of the institutional staff who has witnessed what he considers to be an act of misconduct completes a misconduct report. Paragraph 7 of the Divisional Instruction specifies that the report must contain:

> . . . a precise description of the alleged misconduct, and the date, time and location. Reports shall include the names of witnesses, an indication of what the witness can testify to, a list of exhibits, the disposition of physical evidence and what immediate action has been taken (such as use of force), allowing the designated officer to classify the misconduct.

The report must be submitted to the Director or his designate who decides whether to charge the inmate with a minor offence, or with a flagrant or serious offence, or to inform the police. The possible charges are set out in subsections (a) to (o) of section 39 of the Regulations and include such offences as possession of contraband, assaulting or threatening to assault another person, disobeying a lawful order of a penitentiary officer, and doing an act calculated to prejudice the discipline or good order of the institution. Subsection (o) makes it an offence to attempt to do anything listed in subsections (a) to (n) of section 39.

If the alleged offence is one which clearly constitutes an offence under the *Criminal Code* or any other Act of Parliament, the Director must inform the police unless the circumstances do not require such action. Once the police have been informed, the inmate's institutional charge must not be dealt with in disciplinary court unless and until the Crown declines to prosecute. This protects an inmate from being tried twice for the same alleged misconduct and avoids problematic questions about whether evidence given by an inmate at his disciplinary hearing or the fact of his conviction by a penitentiary disciplinary court can later be used against him in criminal court proceedings.

The Commissioner's Directive requires that an inmate charged with an offence be provided with notice in writing of the date, time and place of his hearing and of the charge as well as a summary of the evidence against him. It also requires that the hearing must take place not less than twenty-four hours from the time the notice is served unless the inmate waives the twenty-four hour notice requirement. The Divisional Instruction requires that the misconduct report must also be served on the inmate at least twenty-four hours prior to his hearing. If the misconduct report is completed as required then it satisfies the notice requirements in the Directive.

If the inmate does not understand the content of the notice, the Directive places on him the onus to request an 'interpretation'. However, the Divisional Instruction provides:

> In cases where because of reading, language or other deficiency, the accused inmate may not be able to fully understand the written notice, all necessary measures shall be taken by the member delivering the notice to assure a complete understand-

ing by the inmate. Failing the above the officer shall notify the Director.

What onus does the Divisional Instruction place on the person serving the notice? Must he inform himself about whether the inmate has a reading, language or other deficiency? There has been no litigation as yet to assist us in answering these questions. However, it could be argued that the person delivering the notice had failed to discharge his obligation to assure a complete understanding of the notice by the inmate where there was evidence which would have led a reasonable person to suspect or to conclude that there was some impediment such as a reading, language or other deficiency and where he does not take steps to assure himself that the inmate has a complete understanding of the notice.

The inmate must be given reasonable opportunity, without interfering with his institutional programme, to prepare his defence and to contact, in person or in writing, witnesses he wishes to call.

An inmate charged with a flagrant or serious offence normally appears before a disciplinary court presided over by an Independent Chairperson who conducts a hearing to determine the accused's guilt or innocence. Subsection 38.1(2) of the *Penitentiary Service Regulations* provides that the Independent Chairperson shall:

(a) conduct the hearing;
(b) consult, in the presence of the accused inmate, with two officers designated by the institutional head;
(c) determine the guilt or innocence of an accused inmate appearing before him; and
(d) on finding an accused inmate guilty, order such punishment authorized by these Regulations as he deems suitable.

Again, specific policies respecting the procedures to be employed at the hearing are found in the Commissioner's Directive and Divisional Instruction and not in the *Penitentiary Act* or Regulations.

The Directive provides that, as far as is practicable, the hearing shall commence within seven working days from the date the charge was laid unless a justifiable reason warrants delay and that the hearing may be adjourned when circumstances require.

Independent Chairpersons grant adjournments for, *inter alia*, the following reasons:

1 because the institution's witnesses are not available at that time; or
2 because the accused wishes to consult a lawyer before proceeding.

The Directive requires that priority be given to cases of accused inmates being held in administrative segregation while awaiting a hearing.

The Directive requires that these disciplinary hearings be recorded either electronically or by stenographic means so that a transcript can be produced, if required. Tapes must be preserved for at least twenty-four months. If legal proceedings are commenced the relevant tape must be preserved until the proceedings are completed.

The Commissioner's Directive entitles the accused to have his disciplinary hearing in English or French. An accused who does not understand and speak either language is entitled to an interpreter.

As stated above, *Penitentiary Service Regulation* 38.1(2)(b) requires the Independent Chairperson to 'consult, in the presence of the accused inmate, with two officers designated by the institutional head'. However, the Directive requires the Director to appoint one or two officers to assist the Chairperson. The Instruction permits the Chairperson, during the hearing, to consult with the officer or officers to obtain relevant details or documents. It also states that the officer or officers appointed shall not intervene during the hearing unless they have asked for and been granted permission to do so by the Chairperson.

At the beginning of the hearing, the Chairperson is required by paragraph 21 of the Directive to satisfy himself that the accused understands the content of the notice he received, and is required by paragraph 19 of the Instruction to ensure the charge is read to the accused.

The accused is then asked to plead. The Instruction provides that no questions shall be asked about a not guilty plea. The accused must be informed that he will have the opportunity to give evidence after all the witnesses against him have been heard and must be asked for the names of witnesses he wishes to call. He must also be asked if he has documents to produce.

If the accused refuses to plead, or pleads *nolo contendere*, the Instruction requires that a hearing be conducted as if he had pleaded not guilty. If the accused pleads guilty the Chairperson need only review a summary of the evidence.

If, at the hearing, the accused asks to be represented by a lawyer, the officer or officers assisting the Chairperson are required to request an adjournment to enable the institution to make submissions. The Directive instructs the Chairperson that: 'Representation is granted . . . solely where the Chairperson believes that such representation is necessary for a fair hearing'. The Directive provides no more explicit criteria to assist the Chairperson in making a decision respecting representation.

The Instruction states that the accused shall appear in person at the hearing until a verdict is rendered 'so that the evidence against him is given in his presence'. However, the Chairperson is given no instruction to follow if an inmate refuses to attend the hearing or attends but behaves in such a manner that he must be removed. All that is said is that institutional staff are responsible for initiating disciplinary action against inmates who behave in an unacceptable manner during a hearing.

When the accused pleads not guilty or refuses to plead, or pleads *nolo contendere*, the Independent Chairperson must conduct a hearing and make a finding. First, he hears the evidence of the witnesses against the accused. The Instruction provides that 'the technicalities of the rules of evidence in criminal matters do not apply in disciplinary hearings' and that the Chairperson 'may admit any evidence which he considers reasonable or trustworthy and base his decision on the evidence'. The Instruction requires that the accused be given an opportunity to test the evidence against him through the Chairperson and directs the Chairperson to allow the accused's questions 'unless there are very clear reasons for disallowance'. No guidelines respecting what would constitute 'very clear reasons' for not allowing a question are provided.

After hearing all the evidence against the accused, the Instruction directs the Chairperson to ask the accused if he wishes to give evidence and if he wishes to call witnesses. If the accused gives evidence the Chairperson may question him. If the accused requests that witnesses be called on his behalf, the Instruction sets out criteria to be used by the Chairperson in determining how many witnesses, if any, to permit and requires him to provide written reasons for his decision to refuse to hear a witness.

The Directive provides that incriminating evidence given by an accused or a witness at a disciplinary hearing 'shall not be used as evidence in a subsequent disciplinary hearing of another charge'.

After hearing the evidence the Chairperson must make his finding. The Directive requires that the finding be based solely on the evidence adduced at the hearing. The Directive provides that no finding shall be made against the accused unless prior to the hearing he has been given notice of the charge as required and permitted a reasonable opportunity to prepare his defence and unless at the hearing:

> the inmate has been given an opportunity to be heard, including the presentation of relevant documents, the questioning of witnesses through the Chairperson and where the Chairperson deems it appropriate and necessary, the calling of witnesses on behalf of the inmate. Reasons for the denial of any aspect of this opportunity shall be recorded and available to the accused inmate.

If the Chairperson finds the accused guilty then he must impose punishment. The punishments that may be imposed are set out in subsection 38(4) of the *Penitentiary Service Regulations*:

(a) a forfeiture of statutory remission or earned remission or both;
(b) dissociation for a period not exceeding thirty days;
 (i) with a diet, during all or part of the period, that is monotonous but adequate and healthful, or
 (ii) without a diet;
(c) loss of privileges.

The Chairperson may impose more than one of these punishments upon a single conviction but he may not impose any other punishment. Subsection 24.1(1) of the *Penitentiary Act* in conjunction with paragraph 38 of the Directive limits the amount of remission the Chairperson can order forfeited, on his own authority, to 30 days. A forfeiture of up to 90 days may be ordered with the concurrence of the Commissioner or an officer of the Service designated by him. A forfeiture of more than 90 days requires the concurrence of the Solicitor General.

In *Re Davidson and The Queen*, the Chairperson convicted the inmate on the same day of three separate offences. She imposed sentences of 30 days dissociation for each offence to run consecutively for a total of 90 days' dissociation. The question before the Federal Court, Trial Division was whether the Chairperson had the power to impose consecutive sentences. The court held that she did. This decision was followed by the British Columbia Supreme Court in *Re William Vigue*.

Before imposing punishment the Chairperson is required by the Directive to:

1 review the inmate's past conduct and decide whether the misconduct was committed deliberately or on impulse; and
2 give the inmate the opportunity to make submissions as to punishment.

The Directive requires the assisting officers to inform the Chairperson of:

1 any administrative action taken against the inmate respecting the misconduct and the reasons for the action; and
2 any minor disciplinary court sentence imposed on the inmate for a conviction relating to the same incident.

If the accused is acquitted, the Instruction requires that no record of the charge be maintained. If the accused is convicted, a summary of the charge, the punishment awarded and the reasons therefor are recorded.

An inmate convicted of a disciplinary offence by a Chairperson may seek redress in a number of ways. He, or a staff member on his behalf, may ask the Chairperson to reopen the hearing to consider new evidence. The inmate may use the institutional grievance procedure to grieve the procedures followed prior to the hearing. However, a successful grievance will not, in itself, alter the Chairperson's finding.

The inmate may also ask the Correctional Investigator to inquire into any aspect of the hearing including pre-hearing procedures. The Correctional Investigator is a Commissioner appointed under the *Inquiries Act* to investigate inmates' complaints. The Investigator may make recommendations but does not have the power to alter the Chairperson's decision.

The inmate may also seek the assistance of the courts and in a number of cases this has been done successfully. The provisions of the Commissioner's Directive and Divisional Instruction respecting inmate discipline, recently put into effect, seem to reflect and to take account of some of these successful cases.

Judicial review

The *Federal Court Act* established the Federal Court of Canada which consists of two divisions: the Federal Court, Trial Division and the Federal Court of Appeal. By virtue of sections 18 and 28 of the *Federal Court Act* these two federal courts were given exclusive jurisdiction with respect to certain remedies available against federal boards, commissions or other tribunals.

For a time it was unclear which, if either, of the two federal courts had jurisdiction to review the decision of an Independent Chairperson presiding over a penitentiary disciplinary court. In *Martineau (No. 1)*, the Supreme Court of Canada decided that the Federal Court of Appeal did not have the jurisdiction. In *Martineau* v. *Matsqui Institution Disciplinary Board (No. 2)* (1979) (hereinafter referred to as *Martineau (No. 2)*), the Supreme Court of Canada decided that a disciplinary court is subject to the common law duty to act fairly and that remedies for breach of this duty could be granted by the Federal Court, Trial Division pursuant to section 18 of the *Federal Court Act* which states:

18. The Trial Division has exclusive original jurisdiction
    (a) to issue an injunction, writ of *certiorari*, writ of prohibition, writ of *mandamus* or writ of *quo warranto*, or grant declaratory relief, against any federal board, commission or other tribunal; and
    (b) to hear and determine any application or other proceeding for relief in the nature of relief contemplated by paragraph (a), including any proceeding brought against the Attorney General of Canada, to obtain relief against a federal board, commission or other tribunal.

Although section 18 makes available a number of remedies, the remedy most often sought against a disciplinary court and its Independent Chairperson is *certiorari* to quash a conviction.

In April 1982 the *Constitution Act* 1982 came into force. Part 1 of that Act is the *Canadian Charter of Rights and Freedoms* (hereinafter referred to as the Charter). Subsection 24(1) of the Charter provides that:

24. (1) Anyone whose rights or freedoms as guaranteed by this Charter, have been infringed or denied may apply to a court of

> competent jurisdiction to obtain such remedy as the court considers appropriate and just in the circumstances.

It is our opinion that an inmate whose rights under the Charter have been denied or infringed by an Independent Chairperson may apply to the Federal Court, Trial Division pursuant to subsection 24(1) for 'such remedy as the court considers appropriate and just in the circumstances' by applying under section 18 of the *Federal Court Act* for the appropriate remedy and joining to it an application for relief under subsection 24(1) of the Charter.

Cases decided by the Federal Court, Trial Division since the *Martineau (No. 2)* decision have further illuminated the grounds on which the court is prepared to grant remedies on review of decisions of Independent Chairpersons.

In *Minott* v. *Presiding Officer of the Inmate Disciplinary Court of Stony Mountain Penitentiary and the Director of Stony Mountain Penitentiary* (1982), an application was made to the Federal Court, Trial Division for prohibition to prevent the Chairperson from continuing the applicant's disciplinary hearing or for such order as may be just. The applicant had requested that his counsel be allowed to appear at his disciplinary hearing with him. The Chairperson relied on the Annex to the Commissioner's Directive and denied the request. At that time, the Annex to the Directive stated:

> Such demands shall be met with the response that he is not entitled to counsel, and that the hearing will proceed without the accused person being represented.

Mr Justice Nitikman held that discretion is vested in the Chairperson to allow or not allow counsel and that the Chairperson had failed to exercise his discretion because he failed to give proper consideration to the effect of subsections 38(1) and (2)(b) and subsections 38.1(1) and (2) of the *Penitentiary Service Regulations* and because he failed to give any consideration to the principle of fairness. His Lordship remitted the matter to the Chairperson to be reconsidered in light of the court's decision.

The identical issue came before the Federal Court, Trial Division again in *Re Davidson and Disciplinary Board of Prison for Women and King* (1981) on an application for *certiorari* to quash the applicant's conviction for a disciplinary offence. Mr Justice Cattanach held that in light of the principle of fairness the

Chairperson has discretion to allow or not allow counsel and that the paragraph of the Annex to the Directive which purports to fetter that discretion offends a fundamental principle of natural justice and is, therefore, invalid.

The new Directive, effective 31 August 1984, appears to take account of the decisions in *Minott* and *Davidson*. It provides that representation is granted at the request of an inmate solely where the Chairperson believes it necessary for a fair hearing.

In *Re Blanchard and Disciplinary Board of Millhaven Institution and Hardtman* (1982), the applicant applied for *certiorari* to quash several convictions for disciplinary offences. At issue was whether the Chairperson breached his duty to act fairly in refusing the applicant's request to be represented by counsel at the hearing. Mr Justice Addy held that an inmate has no right to be represented by counsel at a disciplinary hearing and that the question of whether to allow representation is to be left to the discretion of the Chairperson. His Lordship held that the Independent Chairperson had exercised his discretion fairly and stated at 174:

> 'Unless the exercise of any such discretion is patently unfair, this court should not interfere.'

After the Charter came into force it was argued that section 7 and subsection 11(d) of the Charter now gave an inmate appearing before a disciplinary court the right to be represented by counsel. These sections state:

7. Everyone has the right to life, liberty and security of the person and the right not to be deprived thereof except in accordance with the principles of fundamental justice.

11. Any person charged with an offence has the right
    (a) to be presumed innocent until proven guilty according to law in a fair and public hearing by an independent and impartial tribunal.

This 'right to representation' issue was argued before Mr Justice Nitikman in *Re Howard and Presiding Officer of Inmate Disciplinary Court of Stony Mountain Institution* (1983). The applicant sought an order prohibiting the inmate disciplinary court from continuing or concluding his disciplinary hearing in the absence of legal counsel and relied on the above quoted sections of the Charter. The application was dismissed. His Lordship held that the principles of fundamental justice are equivalent to the principles of natural justice and that section 7 and subsection 11(d), quoted above, do not create any new principles of law. His Lordship also held that the term 'offence' as it is used in section 11 does not include a penitentiary disciplinary offence and that, therefore, subsection 11(d) did not guarantee any rights to an inmate charged in disciplinary court. His Lordship stated that, as he had held in *Minott*, the matter was one for the discretion of the Chairperson and if the discretion was properly exercised the court should not interfere.

In *Re Michael McLeod* (1982), the inmate, charged with a disciplinary offence, had pleaded *nolo contendere*, a plea unknown to Canadian law. Although the inmate did not at any time acknowledge his guilt, the Chairperson entered a plea of guilty and convicted him without hearing any evidence. An application was made to the Federal Court, Trial Division for *certiorari* to quash the conviction. Mr Justice Décary held in his unreported reasons:

> 'That plea of nolo contendere, in accordance with the duty to act fairly, should have been considered as there being no plea entered, in which instance a plea of not guilty was required to be entered and evidence heard.'

The new Instruction now makes this explicit.

In *Re Emile Joseph Phillips* (1984), the inmate, charged with a disciplinary offence, claimed that it was impossible for him to have committed the offence because of a medical problem he had at the material time. The Chairperson undertook to make inquiries with respect to this and adjourned the hearing. On a subsequent day he again adjourned the hearing to complete these inquiries. At the final reconvening of the hearing the Chairperson convicted the applicant. In his unreported reasons the Associate Chief Justice held:

> 'Since the Chairman undertook to make inquiries into this matter, it seems to me that I must have some evidence that the undertaking was either fulfilled by the Chairman or that opportunity was given to the accused to produce his own evidence on that point.'

Because there was no evidence available to satisfy his Lordship he quashed the conviction and remitted the matter to the Chairperson for a new hearing.

The Commissioner's Directive respecting inmate discipline has been held, in a number of cases, to provide guidelines respecting the scope of the duty to act fairly. The reasons given for the decision in *Phillips* may therefore respectfully be questioned. Since the Directive requires that the accused be provided with an opportunity to produce relevant evidence, it seems clear that in any case where the accused indicates that he has relevant evidence to produce, the Chairperson must give him an opportunity to produce it even when the Chairperson has given no undertaking to attempt to obtain the evidence himself.

In other cases the Federal Court, Trial Division has, on consent of the parties, quashed disciplinary convictions, on the ground that the Chairperson breached his duty to act fairly where, *inter alia*, the Chairperson either:

1 refused to allow an accused to call a relevant witness; or
2 did not advise an accused he had the right to call witnesses and afford him an opportunity to call them; or
3 disregarded the accused's defence.

In *Belmont and Disciplinary Court at Millhaven Institution and Hardtman* (1984), the inmate was charged with doing an act calculated to prejudice the discipline or good order of the institution. The witness against the accused testified that from the dining room he observed an inmate, not the accused, pour something into two cups and take the cups to a picnic table where the accused and another inmate were sitting. The witness said he and another officer proceeded toward the picnic table, that they observed the accused and the other inmate throwing something on the ground and that the other officer later retrieved three cups in which there was evidence of brew. The accused testified that while sitting at the table he was asked if he wanted some, that he said he did not and he denied knowing the jug of brew was thereabouts. On this evidence the Chairperson convicted. On application to the Federal Court, Trial Division for *certiorari*, Mr Justice Dubé quashed the conviction and held that the standard of proof required to convict an inmate of a disciplinary offence as established by the Directive is the same as for a criminal offence, namely, that the Chairperson must not convict the inmate unless satisfied of his guilt beyond a reasonable doubt. His Lordship held in his unreported reasons that it is clear

> 'that *certiorari* will issue to quash a decision of an inferior tribunal if that decision is made in the absence of any evidence to support it'

and that the evidence

> 'must have some probative force which would tend to show the existence or the non-existence of the facts in issue'.

His Lordship held that the charge requires that the applicant plan and do something deliberately for the very purpose of prejudicing the good order and discipline of the institution and concluded that 'there is not a scintilla of evidence' to support a conviction on this charge.

In *Belmont*, the applicant was able to rely on decisions which had held that the Commissioner's Directive provides guidelines to procedures required by the common law duty to act fairly. The old Commissioner's Directive provided that the standard of proof required for conviction of a disciplinary offence was the criminal law standard of proof beyond a reasonable doubt. The new Commissioner's Directive does not provide a standard of proof.

In *Lasalle* v. *The Disciplinary Tribunals of the Leclerc Institute* (1983), the applicant applied for *certiorari* to quash several convictions for disciplinary offences. All charges arose out of the same incident although not all were laid or tried at the same time. The applicant had not been given a summary of the evidence and twenty-four hours' written notice prior to the hearing as required by the Commissioner's Directive respecting the two charges heard first. There was evidence before the court that the applicant waived the notice requirement. Mr Justice Walsh held that the burden of proving that the inmate waived the requirement is on prison authorities. His Lordship did not quash these convictions because the applicant had pleaded guilty to them and there was no reasonable doubt about his guilt.

At the hearing respecting the other charges, the applicant requested legal assistance. The Chairperson refused the request without exercising his discretion. His Lordship, relying on the *Minott* and *Davidson* decisions, held that the Chairperson thereby breached his duty to act fairly. In addition, at this hearing the applicant was allowed to enter the hearing room only after the witnesses and the Chairperson had conferred and at the conclusion of the hearing the applicant was excluded but the witnesses and the penitentiary representatives remained with the Chairperson while he reached a decision. His Lordship found this to be unfair and observed that although the Directive states that it is common practice to have two staff members at the hearings, in this case it was not only staff members but witnesses who were in the room. His Lordship quashed the convictions registered at this hearing.

After the Charter had come into force, an inmate challenged the jurisdiction of the Independent Chairperson to conduct the disciplinary hearing. The inmate argued that pursuant to subsection 11(d) of the Charter he had a right to a hearing before an independent tribunal and that the Chairperson was not independent because of the way in which the Chairperson was appointed, remunerated and assigned to hear charges.

In his decision on this point in *Bolan* v. *Disciplinary Board at Joyceville Institution* et al. (1983), the Chairperson held that he was not independent as required by subsection 11(d) of the Charter and therefore had no jurisdiction to hear the charge.

The Department of Justice sought *mandamus* in the Federal Court, Trial Division to compel the Chairperson to hear the charges but subsequently withdrew the application. Meanwhile, other inmates at their disciplinary hearings before other Chairpersons were raising the 'independence' challenge. Chairpersons dealt with the challenge in different ways. One decided he had no jurisdiction to decide the question of his own independence. Another adjourned *sine die* all hearings in which the 'independence' challenge was raised.

In *Russell* et al. v. *Radley* (1984), two inmates whose hearings were adjourned *sine die* when they raised the 'independence' challenge applied to the Federal Court, Trial Division for prohibition to restrain the Chairperson from continuing their hearings. They argued, *inter alia*, that by delaying the hearings the Chairperson had denied them the right to be tried within a reasonable time that is guaranteed by subsection 11(b) of the Charter. In addition, they argued the Chairperson was not independent as required by subsection 11(d) and therefore had no jurisdiction.

In his decision Mr Justice Muldoon held that section 11 applies to penitentiary disciplinary offences. In *Howard*, discussed above, Mr Justice Nitikman had held that section 11 does not apply to these offences and that it applies only to offences tried in a court of law. Mr Justice Muldoon held that there is no such qualification in section 11 or elsewhere in the Charter and that the word 'tribunal' in subsection 11(d) includes bodies other than courts.

His Lordship held in *Russell* at 66:

> 'The disciplinary "court", being in reality an administrative tribunal, performing an administrative function, is not required by any standard to evince the plenitude of independence possessed by true courts'

and held at 67:

> 'As constituted, this administrative tribunal surely raises no reasonable apprehension . . . about the independence of the respondent, and others in his position'.

His Lordship concluded that the Chairperson was independent. However, his Lordship also held that by adjourning the hearings *sine die* the Chairperson had effectively denied the applicants their right to be tried within a reasonable time as required by subsection 11(b) of the Charter and held that subsection 24(1) of the Charter enabled him to invoke the provisions of the *Federal Court Act* to prohibit anyone from conducting a hearing on the charges.

In *Re Blaquiere* et al. *and Director of Matsqui Institution* et al. (1983), Mr Justice Collier quashed the sentences imposed on the applicants and referred the matter back to the Chairperson for sentencing because the Chairperson had not invited or given the applicants an opportunity to make submissions respecting punishment after convicting them of a disciplinary offence. His Lordship found that by this omission the Chairperson had breached his duty to act fairly.

The Commissioner's Directive now states that the Chairperson shall give the convicted inmate an opportunity to make submissions respecting punishment before imposing it.

Conclusion

It is too early to assess the impact of the Charter on the penitentiary disciplinary process. On the one hand, in *Howard*, the Federal Court, Trial Division held that section 7 and section 11 of the Charter do not create any new principles of law or any new rights for an inmate facing a penitentiary disciplinary court. The court held that the term 'offence' in section 11 of the Charter does not include penitentiary disciplinary offences and therefore, that section 11 cannot be seen as creating or preserving for inmates any of the rights set out therein.

On the other hand, in *Russell*, the same court held that the term 'offence' in section 11 of the Charter includes penitentiary disciplinary offences. Therefore, the court held that although penitentiary disciplinary hearings are administrative rather than judicial or quasi-judicial in nature, certain of the rights guaranteed in section 11 can reasonably be allowed in a penitentiary disciplinary hearing and are to be protected to the extent that it is reasonable to do so.

Apart from the Charter, the Federal Court, Trial Division has not been reluctant to grant redress to inmates when the Independent Chairperson has been shown to have breached the common law duty to act fairly. In interpreting this duty the court appears to have imposed a high standard of procedural fairness on the disciplinary process. Decisions such as those discussed above have benefited the individual applicants. They have also benefited inmates generally. In these decisions the Federal Court, Trial Division has begun to unpack the content of the duty to act fairly. Some of this content has already been explicitly incorporated in the new Commissioner's Directive and Divisional Instruction and to the extent that they take account of the jurisprudence these administrative documents have become a better guide to procedural fairness.

Addendum

Since this paper was written, in a decision released on 1 March 1985, and as yet unreported, Mr Justice Nitikman's decision in the *Howard* case has been overturned by the Federal Court of Appeal. The Court of Appeal granted a declaration that the appellant, Howard, was entitled to counsel for the defence of the disciplinary charges against him. In his reasons, Chief Justice Thurlow stated that:

> 'the enactment of section 7 has not created any absolute right to counsel in all such proceedings. . . .
>
> Once that position is reached it appears to me that whether or not the person has a right to representation by counsel will depend on the circumstances of the particular case, its nature, its gravity, its complexity, the capacity of the inmate himself to understand the case and present his defence. The list is not exhaustive . . . whether or not an inmate's request for representation by counsel can lawfully be refused is not properly referred to as a matter of discretion but is a matter of right where the circumstances are such that the opportunity to present the case adequately calls for representation by counsel'.

The Chief Justice also held that an Independent Chairperson's decision to disallow counsel

> 'cannot be regarded as an adjudication of the right and cannot prevent a superior court in the exercise of supervisory jurisdiction from determining the question on its own'.

We are advised that an application for leave to appeal the decision will be made to the Supreme Court of Canada.

18
Prisoners and the courts: the US experience

Rod Morgan and Alvin J. Bronstein

Background: imprisonment in the USA

The US has no prison system as such. Consistent with its federal constitution it has a large number of loosely interlocking local, state and federal systems which, for foreign observers, are of bewildering complexity. Surveying the use and administration of imprisonment in the USA involves encompassing systems possibly as diverse as those found throughout Europe. Criminal codes, incarceration rates, sentence lengths, parole and remission policies, physical conditions, regimes, the organization of staff and the character of prisoner populations – all differ so greatly from one county and state to another that generalizations are usually misleading. The two processes which have begun to bind this diverse decentralized field together, namely judicial intervention in prison administration and the development and certification of minimum prison standards, are those aspects of imprisonment in America which are currently attracting most interest in Europe. For this reason it should be made clear at the outset that the fragmented nature of US prisons policy has lent both judicial review and the prison standards movement a significance there which neither process was or is likely to have in most countries on the other side of the Atlantic.

The US prison population is by European standards enormous (United States Department of Justice 1984). Approximately two-thirds of a million US citizens are currently in prison, representing an incarceration rate (300 per 100,000 population) more than double the highest found in any western European country (there are currently 88 prisoners per 100,000 in England and Wales, and 31 per 100,000 in Holland). Furthermore, the American prison population has recently grown at a rate which makes concern in Britain about increasing numbers seem insignificant by comparison. Between 1972 and 1982 the US prison population doubled; in 1982 alone the increase was 12.5 per cent. These national statistics mask substantial inter-state variations however – variations larger than those to be found between European nations. For example, during the period 1960–82 whereas 47 states incarcerated proportionately more persons, 3 states recorded stable or declining rates. Some states, such as Nevada or South Carolina, have incarceration rates five times that found in other jurisdictions (for example, New Hampshire and North Dakota).

The contrasts between US states go beyond the structural dimensions of penal policy. Prison conditions differ also. Most of the quarter of a million untried, unsentenced and short-term prisoners (serving less than a year) are held in the more than 3,000 county and municipal gaols. Administered usually by elected sheriffs, these gaols are subject to little state or federal control. They range from small rural cell units capable of housing only a handful of prisoners to the huge urban institutions like Los Angeles County's Central Gaol which accommodates over 5,000 prisoners. By common consent, the worst prison conditions in the USA are found in the local gaols. Alongside the relatively few and lauded 'new generation' institutions, like California's Contra Costa County Gaol at Martinez, are the many overcrowded, squalid and dangerous gaols which, with large numbers of prisoners herded into dormitory cages, would have been familiar to John Howard two centuries ago.

Most medium- and long-term sentenced prisoners (454,136 in 1984) are housed in the more than 1,600 prisons which make up the 50 state correctional departments, the District of Columbia system and what is generally regarded as the best-equipped American agency, the Federal Bureau of Prisons. Again, conditions vary enormously. The biggest state systems, like Texas, California and New York, are comparable in size to the national prison systems of France or England and Wales. Ten states, on the other hand, had a prison population of fewer than 1,000 prisoners in 1983. Given such diversity, one cannot speak of the typical American prison. There are the vast forbidding back-to-back nineteenth-century steel-constructed cell blocks, the huge penitentiary farm colonies of the South, the new urban high-rise holding goals and the recently constructed unit-management prisons which, whether geared to industrial, therapeutic or maximum security purposes, are now attracting European interest. A modern De Tocqueville can find prisons in the US that are grotesquely overcrowded, rife with violence, architecturally brutalizing and poorly staffed. Elsewhere are institutions which by all physical or managerial standards would bear favourable comparison with any prison in the world.

Each part of this huge patchwork quilt is accountable, financially and administratively, to widely differing authorities and communities. The only institution to which the whole American prison panoply can be said legally to be accountable is the Constitution of the USA. Recently, the pressure on the courts to review prisons policy has been considerable. Our purpose here is to examine the extent, nature and impact of judicial intervention on prisons policy.

Prisoners' rights

Until the 1960s the prevailing view in the USA was that on becoming prisoners criminals forfeited almost all their rights. A prisoner was taken to be 'the slave of the state' (*Ruffin* v. *Commonwealth* 1871). The courts adopted what became known as the 'hands off' doctrine. Prison conditions and decisions were said not to be susceptible to judicial scrutiny and the courts' refusal to interfere with the administration of prisons meant that constitutional rights were neither interpreted nor enforced as far as prisoners were concerned.

During the 1960s, as a logical political extension of the civil rights and civil liberties movements, the *de facto* position of prisoners – that they had no rights – began to be questioned. The fact that such a high and growing proportion of the US prison population is drawn from the ethnic minorities (just over 50 percent in 1983) was undoubtedly an important factor in this process. Public attention was further focused by the bloody events at Attica in 1971, where 43 prisoners and staff were killed when police stormed the prison in which prisoners had taken control (Attica Commission 1972; Wicker 1975). Judicial attitudes changed markedly. The courts held that though prisoners rights and civil liberties were unavoidably diminished to some extent by the very fact of incarceration, nevertheless it was recognized that 'there is no iron curtain drawn between the Constitution and the prisons of this country' (*Wolff* v. *McDonnell* 1974). There was an explosion of litigation by or on behalf of prisoners and the courts embarked on a penetrating and detailed examination of what went on behind the curtain. In numerous judgements across the country the courts set limits on the governments' restriction of prisoners' rights and civil liberties. By 1980 the majority of the state prison systems were subject, *in toto* or in part, to court orders regarding some aspect of their conditions or decision-making process. Directly or indirectly, the administration of every prison in the country was affected by judicial review.

The profound impact of this intervention on prison administration in the US is not contested. James Jacobs' case study of Stateville Prison in Illinois provides the most illuminating analysis of the transition from an authoritarian/patrimonial to a bureaucratic/legalistic authority structure which stemmed in large measure from court intervention (Jacobs 1977). And in one of the few attempts systematically to appraise the overall impact of the prisoners' rights movement, Jacobs has elsewhere argued that 'prison litigation may be the peaceful equivalent of a riot in bringing prisoners' grievances to public attention and in mobilizing political support for change' (Jacobs 1980: 460). Prison administrators have agreed with him. Norman Carlson, the Director of the Federal Bureau of Prisons, has maintained that 'the federal judiciary as a whole is the most effective force for constructive change in prisons' (Carlson 1983).

This is not to say that prison administrators have welcomed particular judgements or seen judicial review as an unmixed blessing. They complain vociferously that many court rulings are inconsistent or impractical, and there is no doubt that many officials have rejoiced at the clear signals which the Supreme Court has recently sent out enjoining if not a return to 'hands off' then certainly supporting greater judicial restraint against involvement in prison affairs. In a series of cases since 1976 the majority of the Court seems to have been bent on halting the expansion of prisoners' rights law. In *Meachum* v. *Fano* (1976, a case concerning the transfer of a prisoner to different regime conditions) there was reference to a 'wide spectrum of discretionary actions that traditionally have been the business of prison administrators rather than the federal courts', leading to the opinion that 'the day-to-day functioning of state prisons' involves 'issues and discretionary decisions that are not the business of the federal judges'. In *Rhodes* v. *Chapman* (1981, a case concerned with overcrowding) the court considered what limitations the Eighth Amendment (prohibiting 'cruel and unusual punishment') imposed on the conditions in which prisoners might be held. The court concluded that prison administrators must have considerable discretion and added that 'to the extent that such conditions are restrictive or even harsh, they are part of the penalty that criminals pay for their offenses against society'. Most recently in *Hudson* v. *Palmer* (1984, a case involving a guard's destruction of a prisoner's personal and legal papers) a majority of the Supreme Court ruled that 'the Fourth Amendment proscription against unreasonable searches does not apply within the confines of the prison cell', a judgement which led a dissenting justice to pronounce that the court 'declares prisoners to be little more than chattels . . . a view I thought society had outgrown long ago'.

Whatever their symbolic as well as legal impact, these Supreme Court judgements cannot put the clock back to the 1960s: prisoners' rights law has advanced beyond that point. The number of cases filed by prisoners continues to grow, and in any case Supreme Court decisions are not necessarily a very good guide to what the lower courts are doing. Furthermore, the administrative and social structure of prisons has changed fundamentally. Nevertheless, the current climate of Supreme Court opinion must give pause for thought as to whether gains in prison conditions will in future best be achieved through judicial review.

The Constitution and the end of 'hands off'

The courts first began to peer behind the iron curtain of prison secrecy in the 1960s, since when they have laid down various limits to the degree to which prisoners' civil liberties may be restricted. Some judgements have been based on state and federal statutes but most derived from the US Constitution. Actions based on the First Amendment (entitled 'Freedom of Religion, of

Speech and of the Press') established prisoners' rights to be free from arbitrary censorship of mail and publications. The courts also condemned restrictions on the free exercise of religion, particularly for non-traditional religions such as the growing and influential Black Muslim movement. Furthermore, prisoners were protected in their right to express political beliefs and, though the formation of prisoner unions was not sanctioned, prisoners were permitted to engage in limited forms of political activity.

Despite the recent setback in *Hudson* v. *Palmer*, the Fourth Amendment ('Security from Unwarranted Search and Seizure') has been used successfully in prisoners' claims against improper seizure of property. The 'due process' clauses of the Fifth and Fourteenth Amendments (for federal and state prisoners respectively) – prohibiting deprivation of 'life, liberty or property without due process of law' – have been used to establish more legalistic and just procedures in prison disciplinary proceedings, parole hearings and the transfer of prisoners to harsher conditions. The 'equal protection' clauses of the same Amendments have been used to prohibit practices involving direct or indirect racial discrimination. Prisoners' rights to correspond with lawyers and courts and to have access to legal advice and information led to a steady increase in the volume of litigation. Finally, successful use of the Eighth Amendment led to the abolition of corporal punishment, to restrictions on the length and conditions of solitary confinement, to a limited right to privacy and to freedom as regards personal appearance. There have also been judgements to protect prisoners from harm resulting from staff abuse, deliberate indifference to medical needs, the depredations of fellow prisoners, or the character of the physical environment.

It is sometimes argued that because legal actions depend on individual initiatives, their impact on fields of public policy tends to be arbitrary and piecemeal. Two aspects of the US process reduce, though they do not avoid, that likelihood. The first is that the US system permits 'class actions' in which the complaints of, and remedies for, persons similarly situated to the named litigant are considered. Such actions encourage processes of investigation, discovery and testimony more far-reaching in their depth and scope than is likely in cases dealing only with individual complainants.

The second aspect concerns the development of 'totality of

conditions' suits. In 1969, in *Holt* v. *Sarver*, a federal court took a new approach to prison conditions. It ruled that prison conditions and practices which might not be unconstitutional when viewed separately could, when viewed as a whole, make confinement 'cruel and unusual punishment'. As a logical extension of this approach, in 1975, a federal court in Alabama added a new dimension to the scrutiny of prison conditions and practices by examining virtually every aspect of prison life in the entire state prison system. After looking at overcrowding, environmental conditions, idleness, levels of violence, staffing, prisoner classification, medical and mental health care, and restrictions on visits, the court found that the totality of conditions violated the Eighth Amendment's prohibition against cruel and unusual punishment and that the 'prison conditions are so debilitating that they necessarily deprive inmates of any opportunity to rehabilitate themselves or even maintain skills already possessed' (*Pugh* v. *Locke* 1976).

The court then ordered the state of Alabama to comply with a package of various 'minimum constitutional standards'. Among other things, it required the state to reduce its prison population to the designed capacity of each institution (a reduction of 42 per cent); to provide each prisoner with a minimum of sixty square feet of living space, a meaningful job, the opportunity to participate in recreational, educational, vocational training, and pre-release transition programmes; to provide each prisoner with certain minimum personal articles, such as linens, toilet requisites, reading and writing materials and access to hot and cold water; to provide necessary medical and mental-health care according to certain published standards; to provide minimum staff in various specific locations, at all times, to prevent violence; and to provide certain minimum food, public health, correspondence, visits, and other physical standards.

In addition, the court set out a timetable for bringing each of the state prisons into compliance with the standards; a plan for the hiring of appropriately trained staff, whose racial and cultural background was more similar to those of the prisoners; and a plan for the reclassification of all Alabama prisoners to identify those for whom transfer to community-based facilities would be appropriate, ordering the state to establish those facilities. Finally, the Alabama court said that inadequate funding or claimed lack of resources was no answer to the existence of unconstitutional conditions, and warned that failure to comply with the minimum standards would necessitate the closing of those 'several prison facilities herein found to be unfit for human confinement'.

Other courts followed this lead and the Supreme Court, despite its generally conservative tone referred to above, subsequently endorsed the view that prison conditions 'alone or in combination, may deprive inmates of the minimal civilized measure of life's necessities' and thus constitute a violation of the Eighth Amendment (*Rhodes* v. *Chapman* 1981). Approximately two-thirds of the states are subject to similar court orders dealing with their entire system or one or more major prisons.

The knock-on effect of these court judgements for prisons administration generally can scarcely be overstated. Practically all correctional authorities have found it necessary formally to agree and publish – for staff, prisoners and outside agencies alike – precisely what are their management practices, decision-making procedures, prisoner rules and regime standards. Court intervention has, by implication, put an end to prison management by personal fiat. A key aspect of this process of staff professionalization has been the development of published prison standards, the growth of the American Correctional Association and the emergence of the Commission on Accreditation for Corrections (CAC). The CAC now publishes by far the most influential codes of prison standards and is engaged in a rapidly expanding programme for their promotion. The CAC's voluntary inspection and accreditation scheme, whereby individual institutions are accredited for meeting CAC standards, now involves the majority of states as well as the Federal Bureau of Prisons. The CAC maintains that the majority of its standards are derived in part from court judgements (Sechrest 1978). It also sells its accreditation programme partly on the basis of its 'potential for reducing the number and extent of lawsuits' brought against institutions (Fosen and Lucas 1983). 'Accreditation', the CAC argues, 'is a form of self-regulation that promotes internal accountability, as well as accountability to the criminal justice system, the judiciary and the public (Commission on Accreditation for Corrections 1982). Although some recent court judgements make it clear that CAC accreditation is neither a sure safeguard against litigation nor a guarantee that conditions within accredited prisons are constitutional, the connection between the judicial establishment of prisoners' rights, the reform of prison management and the development and application of prison standards is readily apparent.

The question mark which some commentators have set alongside CAC accreditation – that inspection is insufficiently independent, that it is largely a documentary audit and that fundamental deficiencies may be waived (Allinson 1979; Gettinger 1982; Bazelon 1982) – highlights the fact that those rights that are guaranteed by the courts often prove illusory for prisoners in practice. Litigation, particularly the large-scale 'totality of conditions' class actions, is immensely costly and time consuming. Years of preparation and hearings often precede judgement, and the implementation of judgements rests primarily in the hands of prison officials, who often resist change. Furthermore, the rapid increase in the size of the prison population of recent years, and a more conservative political climate, have made it increasingly difficult for even the most well-meaning administrators to obtain the resources needed to accomplish change. Court judgements are one thing, compliance by correctional authorities another.

Obtaining and implementing court judgements

Despite the considerable volume of prison litigation, remarkably few studies have been made of the local impact of particular judgements (exceptions include: UCLA Law Review 1973; Champagne and Haas 1976; Harris and Spiller 1977; Harvard Law Review 1977). Where work has been done, the wider socio-political changes of which court judgements have been only one part, and the prolonged, almost open-ended, nature of many proceedings, have, as Jacobs has argued, created conceptual and methodological difficulties which make it difficult to draw general conclusions from narrow impact studies (Jacobs 1980). Nevertheless, the very fact that so many suits are protracted is evidence of the gap between gaining a court judgement and achieving policy changes in institutions. Some of the better known state-wide suits have comprised hearings – from the filing of an original complaint through to investigations, judgements or consent decrees, monitoring exercises, non-compliance suits and even contempt proceedings – spanning a decade or more. The courts have sometimes had to contend with prevarication or outright opposition from correctional departments or claims that the excessive demands made on departmental resources rendered compliance impossible. Unsurprisingly, it has frequently proved difficult to discern when non-compliance reflected unwillingness or inability to conform.

The courts have developed an array of new methods, albeit derived from traditional powers (see Nathan 1979), for arriving at decrees and implementing them. In the more complex 'totality of conditions' cases, hard experience has led prisoners' rights lawyers frequently to request, and courts to decide, that special masters (or some other monitoring agency) be appointed. These officers of the court, normally experts in the correctional field, have variously been charged with tasks of fact gathering, proposing feasible remedies, monitoring compliance, or resolving disputes arising out of changed circumstances following the making of a decree.

In some instances, failure to provide an effective means for settling disputes or monitoring decree compliance has resulted in tragic human and economic costs. In 1978, for example, the National Prison Project of the American Civil Liberties Union Foundation joined with local counsel in a case challenging the totality of conditions at the New Mexico State Penitentiary in Santa Fe. Although the New Mexico attorney general attempted to negotiate a settlement, he and the attorneys for the prisoners were hampered by a reluctant governor and state legislature. The federal judge assigned to the case, who had been active in state politics, appeared less than anxious to move the case along. In February 1980, after almost two years of little progress in the lawsuit, the prison exploded in a horrendous riot, which resulted in the deaths of 33 prisoners and gained world-wide publicity. The official report on the riot confirmed the appalling conditions in the prison which had formed the basis of the suit (New Mexico Attorney General 1980). In July 1980, motivated by the adverse publicity, a comprehensive agreement was entered into by state officials and incorporated in a consent decree.

By the spring of 1981, however, it became clear that the governor, the legislature, and the state corrections officials were not seriously interested in complying with the provisions of the settlement. The attorney general refused to represent state officials any further, believing them to have acted in bad faith. For the next year little progress was made with agreed reforms concerning, *inter alia*, the size of the prisoner population, disciplinary procedures, prisoner classification, prison facilities and staffing levels. In early 1982, while engaging in preparation for a trial at which the issue of non-compliance was to be heard, the attorneys for the prisoner discovered that the federal judge had received *ex parte* communications about some of the matters in controversy from a friend who was an employee of the defendant prison officials. A recusal motion was filed, and after a trial before a federal judge from another state appointed by the US Court of Appeals, the court decided that the judge's impartiality could reasonably be questioned. The case was transferred to another judge. In the autumn of 1982, a new governor and other state officials were elected and, with the presence of a new judge willing to act expeditiously, the state entered into a new agreement in the spring of 1983. This agreement also involved the appointment of a special master to monitor and oversee compliance.

The New Mexico litigation saga involved conspicuous tragedy. But the burst of violence at Santa Fe, matching the events at Attica in 1971, represented measures of official inertia and prisoner suffering possibly no greater than that experienced more covertly elsewhere. In Rhode Island a spate of custody conditions suits, preceded and followed by major prison disorders, were filed from 1969 onwards. Consent decrees were early agreed. But not until 1977 did the judge reluctantly agree that lack of progress required the appointment of a special master (BNA 1979). The history of prison litigation in Arkansas (Spiller 1976) and Alabama (BNA 1979) included similarly prolonged wrangles, and one of the most prominent current pieces of judicial intervention, in Texas, involved the appointment of a special master (*Ruiz* v. *Estelle* 1980) after a nine-year-long court battle and extensive evidence of intransigence on the part of the department of corrections (Levinson 1982).

Yet the device of appointing masters, or other monitoring agencies, is no panacea as far as implementation problems are concerned. Resources and politics often have more to do with the framing and enforcement of judgements than the spirit and letter of the Constitution. Thus masters inevitably occupy a sensitive and vulnerable role. In both the Rhode Island and Texas cases, the arrival of masters did not immediately bring peace to what had become a battlefield. In the former, contempt proceedings against the department of corrections ensued and in the latter the attorney general for the state moved for the dismissal of the master on the grounds of his alleged misconduct. In both cases resistance to change by the corrections department, and resentment against the interference represented by the activities of the master, were central. Nevertheless, there are grounds for arguing that in some complex and intractable cases, the appointment of monitors or masters has proved necessary and, in the long term, constructive.

It is not sensible, therefore, to talk in mechanistic terms of the relative efficacy of different decree enforcement mechanisms, any more than one can separate out the consequences of particular judgements from general changes in the penal climate. The evidence suggests that, in most cases, contrasting methods may serve equally well to establish facts and monitor compliance. The decrees studied by Harris and Spiller (1977) involved several enforcement approaches, from which the authors concluded that 'the impression the court conveyed about the speed and degree of compliance required outweighed all other factors'.

Nor should the appointment of special masters be viewed as an indicator of the incapacity of courts to achieve change. Though it has been suggested that the emergence of a new profession of court master has or will lead to incumbents protecting their own vested interests (see Levinson 1982), masters remain servants of the court and represent court powers. More importantly, whether there is judicial intervention in prisons or not, court judgements can never comprise more than one link in a complex chain of essentially political decisions which go to produce prison conditions. Both before and since the recent more conservative decisions of the Supreme Court, the most significant influence on the state of prisons in the US has been the explosion in the prisoner population. Most prison administrators, whatever their personal view of court intervention (and it should be noted that some privately welcome court decrees as a lever to press state legislatures into providing improved resources), have been swamped by increased numbers of prisoners. There has been a discernible hardening of public attitudes: the USA has become a very punitive society. In consequence, prison administrators have simultaneously had to cope with an increased prisoner population, had prison conditions increasingly declared unconstitutional, and encountered public and legislative unwillingness to provide funds to improve facilities. The complex relations between political, judicial and administrative decision-making are illustrated most simply by taking a case-study example.

Prison politics: the case of Rhode Island

Rhode Island is not a typical state: geographically it is the smallest in the Union and, by US standards, has a low incarceration rate. It also has a population of less than one million. Thus, almost uniquely, it has no county gaols and, traditionally, has housed all its prisoners, untried and sentenced, in adjacent buildings on one site. If anything, therefore, the links in the chain of Rhode Island's prisons policy are more simple and visible than in most states.

As indicated ealier, litigation began in Rhode Island in 1969. But in 1977, as a result of a class action brought by the National Prison Project on behalf of all 661 of Rhode Island's then prisoners, a far-reaching judgement was handed down in *Palmigiano* v. *Garrahy*. The case was based on the claim that the totality of conditions in the old maximum security prison ('Old Max') amounted to cruel and unusual punishment and that two groups of prisoners, the untried and those sentenced prisoners held in protective custody, were subject to even worse conditions in violation of the equal protection clause of the Fourteenth Amendment. The plaintiffs' case was upheld on all counts and the Rhode Island authorities were found additionally to be in breach of state statutes governing corrections.

The court ordered, *inter alia*, that: the Rhode Island authorities should, within three months, house pre-trial detainees separate from sentenced prisoners; 'Old Max' be closed within a year; all prisoners be accommodated in conditions meeting stated minimum standards; and that a special master be appointed, empowered to monitor compliance. Seven years later 'Old Max' remains in use, albeit not all of the building. Until January 1984, the Department of Corrections was subject to inspection by a special master and he can still be called upon by the court if needed. As recently as the summer of 1983, the Rhode Island Governor and Director of Corrections were held in contempt of earler decrees. Furthermore, court proceedings still continue on the basis that conditions for some prisoners remain below the constitutional minima set by the court in 1977.

There have been dramatic changes however. The director of corrections from 1977, to whom the judge was presumably referring in his opinion 'that there is a complete absence of effective leadership or management capability', has been dismissed by the state governor on the recommendation of the first special master.

Prior to 1977 there was virtually no written administrative policy; now there are agreed procedures and standards for almost every aspect of the prison regime with copies of manuals available to prisoners. Two entirely new prisons have been built and brought into use and a substantial work release centre opened.

Had the population of Rhode Island's prisons remained at the 1977 level, the hundred-year-old maximum security prison might have been closed, if not within the year ordered by the court then at least by 1982, by which time a new gaol and one new prison had been opened. Between them the new accommodation units provided almost as many prisoner places as 'Old Max'. But by 1982, Rhode Island's average daily prison population had risen by 50 per cent and has since exceeded the 1977 level by over 90 per cent. Within a matter of months of being opened the new gaol began double-celling pre-trial detainees. 'Old Max' has continued regularly to house more than 200 prisoners, a little more than half its rated but condemned capacity.

During the period since 1977, the court has held back from drastic remedies. The deadlines originally ordered for the closure of 'Old Max', and for the segregation of pre-trial prisoners, were repeatedly extended by the presiding judge. Despite written reports from the master to the effect that the defendants were dragging their feet, confident in the view that 'the court will not step in and order them to close the facility down forthwith', the judge was unwilling to decree measures which might prejudice the integrity of the criminal justice system. He could not, he announced in 1980, yet take measures which would, in effect, compel the release of 100–150 dangerous prisoners. Deadlines were variously extended: pending the outcome of a state referendum on the issue of a special bond to pay for the expansion of the new high security unit (it was overwhelmingly rejected by the voters); or the opening of a prison under construction; or on the basis of reports from the master indicating that though conditions were not fully in compliance with agreed standards, they had improved. In a revealing published interview, the judge confessed that his original deadlines had been fixed quite arbitrarily; designed, it appears, as starting guns rather than carefully measured courses to be run (BNA 1978). In the seven years since the *Palmigiano* judgement he had moderated his decisions out of sympathy with the plight claimed by the defendants and in recognition of their willingness to comply.

Matters changed substantially in 1983: the voters approved a state bond referendum which gave the department of corrections $5.5 million to renovate 'Old Max' completely. After a series of hearings, the court created a new timetable for bringing the prison into full compliance with the earlier court decrees as well as establishing a reporting mechanism to ensure that the various facilities do not fall below constitutional requirements because of population pressure.

The new cohort of administrators in Rhode Island look back on the litigation with mixed feelings. Conditions prior to 1977 were, they admit, indefensible. There was virtually no proper administration, there was minimal financial support from the legislature and, they confess, a small group of powerful prisoners ran a corrupt, violent and squalid system. In one sense they see the *Palmigiano* judgement as the best thing that could have happened; it swept the old guard away and for the first two years the department had virtually all its budgetry demands met. Events were triggered by the court decree which would almost certainly not have happened without it.

But for much of the period since 1977 the administrators also perceived their task to be unworkable. The dramatic rise in the number of persons committed by the courts, the product of tougher bail conditions and sentencing, made it unreasonable from their standpoint that 'Old Max' be closed. They argued that given the funds, conditions in parts of 'Old Max' could be brought up to an acceptable level. They saw themselves to be sandwiched between a legislature unwilling to increase the budget, sentencers increasingly committing offenders to custody, and counsel for the litigants pressing for full implementation of a seven-year-old decree which the administrators perceived to have been overtaken by events. They also saw the litigation process as sapping their time and managerial energies. But in 1983 their position changed again. Their funds increased substantially enabling them to plan, for the first time, to comply fully with the court decrees. And they began to work with counsel for the prisoners on a cooperative, rather than adversarial, basis with both sides having a common objective of a constitutional prison system.

As far as counsel for the plaintiffs are concerned, many of the problems faced by the department of corrections were self-inflicted or avoidable. The justification for the bond issue put to the voters in 1980 was, as the master wrote in his report at the time, 'riddled with inconsistencies and unsupported by convincing data': as such it failed and the determination of the defendants to provide a real solution to their accommodation problems was questioned. In 1981–82, the authority's plea that they be allowed to retain use of 'Old Max' if it were renovated was belied by their budget deficit which suggested they were incapable of funding a speedy renovation. Furthermore, crime statistics for Rhode Island provided no evidence that increases in crime explained the rise in the prison population: had the state and courts got together they could, counsel suggested, have controlled the size of the prison population. Nor, in counsel's view, had the department of corrections sought radically to reduce the excessive resort to high security accommodation by adjusting prisoner categorization policy. And, thus, counsel kept up pressure for full implementation of the court decree: they feel their stance to have been vindicated by the improvements since 1983.

Conclusions

The size and composition of any prison population, and the conditions in which that population is held, are ultimately political responsibilities. Legislatures either decide the questions directly, or they delegate authority and discretion to others to decide, be they the courts or correctional authorities. Thus judicial intervention in the management of prisons, either by upholding constitutional rights or enforcing compliance with prison statutes, does not change the political reality; rather it adds another channel through which political decisions may be transmitted or political influence may be brought to bear. In that sense, as the various state examples discussed above demonstrate, it is wrong to see judicial intervention as a means of breaking out of the political bind of policy making. Court judgements do not fix more certainly where the buck shall stop; indeed it could be argued that they provide yet another staging post on a circuit round which the buck rotates precariously.

The US experience should serve as a warning to those who argue naively for the adoption of a written constitution on the grounds that it makes certain the operational meaning of rights. It does not. There could be no better illustration of the fact than the very fundamental question of prison crowding. During the past decade, the US courts have handed down numerous judgements prohibiting correctional authorities from housing more than one prisoner in cells ranging from 35 to 88 square feet (National Institute of Justice 1980: 169). In *Rhodes* v. *Chapman* the Supreme Court held that the Eighth Amendment could not be translated into an entitlement to so many square feet per prisoner: in the same way that what constitutes 'cruel and unusual punishment' depends on the totality of conditions, so any definition of cell crowding should, in the court's view, depend in part on: the modernity of the prison; the amount of time prisoners have to spend in their cells; the opportunities for work and education and prisoners' access to other facilities. In the case concerned, the Supreme Court held that the double occupancy of 63 square feet cells designed for single occupancy was not unconstitutional *per se* because the contextual facilities were good.

Furthermore, court intervention is neutral as far as the expansion or contraction of prison system capacity and population is concerned. If the community, or legislature, is intent on incarcerating more offenders and is willing to pay the price, then court orders may stimulate a prison building programme which might otherwise be avoided. Equally, court judgements can serve as a break on population growth by holding down numbers in systems where the authorities cannot or will not provide funds for extra capacity.

The great merit of judicial intervention is that the reality of prison policy decisions are laid on the public line: the price of sentencing decisions and correctional rhetoric, both financial and in the quality of prisoners' lives, is laid bare. During hearings a vast amount of detailed evidence typically emerges about the minutiae of daily life in the prison. In anticipation of hearings, prison administrators prepare fuller accounts of day-to-day policy in order that their management practices have credibility. Directly or indirectly, the whole process stimulates greater accountability for what is done in prison in the name of the community. Judicial review of what happens in prisons has lifted a veil; in the USA at least it has ensured that if the political decision is made that more persons should go to prison, that object is not achieved simply by compressing more prisoners into worse and worse conditions.

Statutes, regulations, administrative directives, and cases

Canada

STATUTES

Constitution Act 1982 (enacted by the Canada Act 1982 (UK) c 11 Schedule B).
Criminal Code, RSC 1970, ch. C-34 as amended.
Federal Court Act, RSC 1970, ch. 10 (2nd supp.).
Penitentiary Act, RSC 1970, ch. P-6 as amended.

REGULATIONS

Penitentiary Service Regulations.

ADMINISTRATIVE DIRECTIVES

Commissioner's Directive 600-7-03.1.
Divisional Instruction 600-7-03.1

CASES

Belmont and Disciplinary Court at Millhaven Institution and Hardtman, an unreported decision of Mr Justice Dubé, FCTD 9 July 1984.

Bolan v. Disciplinary Board at Joyceville Institution *et al.* (1983), 2 Admin LR 107.

Lasalle v. The Disciplinary Tribunals of the Leclerc Institute (1983), 5 Admin LR 23 (FCTD).

Martineau and Butters v. Matsqui Institution Inmate Disciplinary Board (1977), 33 CCC (2nd) 366 (SCC).
Martineau v. Matsqui Institution Disciplinary Board (No. 2) (1979), 50 CCC (2nd) 353 (SCC).
Minott v. Presiding Officer of the Inmate Disciplinary Court of Stony Mountain Penitentiary and the Director of Stony Mountain Penitentiary, [1982] 1 FC 322 (FCTD).
Re Blanchard and Disciplinary Board of Millhaven Institution and Hardtman (1982), 69 CCC (2nd) 171 (FCTD).
Re Blaquiere *et al.* and Director of Matsqui Institution *et al.* (1983), 6 CCC (3rd) 293 (FCTD).
Re Davidson and Disciplinary Board of Prison for Women and King (1981), 61 CCC (2nd) 520 (FCTD).
Re Davidson and The Queen (1982), 67 CCC (2nd) 244 (FCTD).
Re Emile Joseph Phillips (1984), 11 WCB 383 (FCTD).
Re Howard and Presiding Officer of Inmate Disciplinary Court of Stony Mountain Institution (1983), 8 CCC (3rd) 557 (FCTD).
Re Michael McLeod (1982), 9 WCB 249 (FCTD).
Re William Vigue (1983), 9 WCB 187 (SCBC).
Russell *et al.* v. Radley (1984), 5 Admin LR 39 (FCTD).

Federal Republic of Germany

STATUTES

Gesetz über den Vollzug der Freiheitsstrafe und der freiheitsentziehenden Massregeln der Besserung und Sicherung 1976.

Netherlands

STATUTES

Wet van 21 October 1976, Staatsblad 568.

United Kingdom

STATUTES

Habeas Corpus Act 1816.
Official Secrets Act 1911.
Consolidated Fund Appropriation Bill 1938.
Criminal Justice Act 1948.
Prison Act 1952.

Mental Health Act 1959.
Factories Act 1961.
Offices Shops and Railway Premises Act 1963.
Parliamentary Commissions Act 1967.
Health and Safety at Work Act 1974.
National Health Act 1977.
Imprisonment (Temporary Provisions) Act 1980.
Criminal Justice Act 1982.
Mental Health (Amendment) Act 1982.
Mental Health Act 1983.

REGULATIONS

Prison Rules (1964), SI 1964 no. 388 as amended.

CASES

Anderson v. Home Office. In *The Times* 8 October 1965.
Anderson (1984) R v. Secretary of State ex parte Anderson (1984) 1 All ER 920.
Arbon v. Anderson (1943) KB 252.
Becker v. Home Office (1972) 2 QB 407.
Christofi v. Home Office. In *The Times* 31 July 1975.
D'Arcy v. The Prison Commissioners. In *The Times* 15–17 November 1955.
Davis v. The Prison Commissioners. In *The Times* 21 November 1963.
Egerton v. Home Office (1978). *Criminal Law Review*: 494.
Ellis v. Home Office (1953) 2 QB 135.
Findlay v. Secretary of State for the Home Department (1984) 3 All ER 801.
Fox-Taylor (1982) R v. Board of Visitors of Blundeston Prison ex parte Fox-Taylor (1982) 1 All ER 646.
Fraser v. Mudge (1975) 3 All ER 78.
Freeman v. Home Office (1984) 1 All ER 1036.
Gunnell (1984) R v. Secretary of State ex parte Gunnell, *The Times* 3 November 1983 and 7 November 1984.
King v. Deputy Governor of Camp Hill Prison (1984) (Divisional Court) Unreported.
King (1984) R v. Deputy Governor of Camp Hill Prison ex parte King (Court of Appeal). (1984) 3 All ER 897.
Malone v. Commissioner of Police of the Metropolis (No. 2) 1979.
McAvoy (1984) R v. Secretary of State ex parte McAvoy (1984) 3 All ER 417.
McConkey (1982) R v. Board of Visitors of Highpoint Prison ex parte McConkey. In *The Times* 23 September 1982.
McGrath (1984) R v. Board of Visitors of Swansea Prison ex parte McGrath, *The Times*, November 1984.
Mealy (1981) R v. Board of Visitors of Gartree Prison ex parte Mealy, *The Times* 14 November 1981.
Nahar (1983) R v. Commissioner of Police in the Metropolis ex parte Nahar and others. In *The Times* 28 May 1983.

O'Reilly v. Mackman (1982) 3 All ER 1124.
Payne v. Lord Harris of Greenwich (1981) 2 All ER 842.
Pett v. Greyhound Racing Association (No. 1) (1969) 1 QB 125.
Pullen v. The Prison Commissioners (1957) 3 All ER 470.
Raymond v. Honey (1982) 1 All ER 756.
Ridge v. Baldwin (1964) AC 40.
St Germain (1978) R v. Board of Visitors of Hull Prison ex parte St Germain (1978) 2 WLR 598 (Divisional Court).
St Germain (No. 1) (1979) R v. Board of Visitors of Hull Prison ex parte St Germain (1979) 1 All ER 701 (Court of Appeal).
St Germain (No. 2) (1979) R v. Board of Visitors of Hull Prison ex parte St Germain (1979) 3 All ER 545.
Sidaway v. Bethlem Royal Hospital (1985) 1 All ER 643.
Smith (1984) R v. Board of Visitors of Dartmoor Prison, ex parte Smith. In *The Times* 12 July 1984.
Tarrant (1984) R v. Secretary of State ex parte Tarrant and another (1984) 1 All ER 799 and (1984) 2 WLR 613.
Williams v. Home Office (No. 2) (1981) 1 All ER 1211.
Zamir v. Secretary of State (1980) 2 All ER 768.

United States of America

CASES

Holt v. Sarver (1969) 300 F Supp 825 (E D Ark 1969).
Hudson v. Palmer (1984)
Kaimowitz v. Michigan (1973) 42 USLW 2063.
Meachum v. Fano (1976) 427 US 215.
Palmigiano v. Garrahy (1977) 443 F Supp 956 (D R I 1977).
Pugh v. Locke (1976) 406 F Supp 318 (M D Ala 1976).
Rhodes v. Chapman (1981)
Ruffin v. Commonwealth (1871) 62 Va. 790.
Ruiz v. Estelle (1980) 503 F Supp 1263 (S D Tex 1980).
Wolff v. McDonnell (1974) 418 US 539.

European Commission and Court of Human Rights

CONVENTIONS AND RESOLUTIONS

Draft Convention on Torture and Other Inhuman Treatment (7.81).
Council of Europe Committee of Ministers (1973), Standard Minimum Rules for the Treatment of Prisoners. Resolution 73/5.
European Convention on Human Rights 1953.
Standard Minimum Rules for the Treatment of Prisoners (1973) Committee of Ministers Resolution 73/5.

APPLICATIONS, REPORTS, AND JUDGEMENTS

(DR – Decisions and Reports of the Commission)

A v. UK Application No. 6840/74.

Campbell and Fell v. UK 7819/77 and 7878/77. Report of Commission (7/5/82). Judgement no. 52 (28/6/84).

Golder v. UK 4451/70. Judgement no. 18 (21/2/75).

Ireland v. UK 5310/71. Report of Commission (1/10/72). Judgement no. 25 (18/1/78).

Kiss v. UK 6224/73. Report of Commission (16/12/76) 7 DR 55.

Schertenleib v. Switzerland 8339/78. Report of Commission (12/7/79) 17 DR 180.

Silver and others v. UK 2/1981/41/60–66. Judgement no. 61 (25/3/83).

X v. UK 6998/75. Report of Commission (14/5/77) 8 DR 106.

References

Advisory Council on the Penal System (1968) *The Regime for Long-term Prisoners in Conditions of Maximum Security* (the 'Radzinowicz Report'). Report of the Advisory Council on the Penal System. London: HMSO.

Allinson, R. (1979) The Politics of Prison Standards. *Corrections Magazine*, March: 54–62.

AMBOV (1984) *Evidence to the Departmental Committee on the Prison Disciplinary System*. London: Association of Members of Boards of Visitors, July 1984. Unpublished.

Anderson, S. (1978) Ombudsmen and Prisons in Scandinavia. *Nordisk Tidsskrift for Kriminalviderscab* 66: 211.

—— (1981a) The Corrections Ombudsman. In Fogel, D. and Hudson, J. (eds) *Justice as Fairness*. Ohio: Criminal Justice Studies, Anderson Publishing Co.

—— (1981b) The Prison Work of the New Zealand Ombudsman. *Ombudsman Journal* 1: 24.

—— (1982) *The Ombudsman Research: What Has Been Done and What Needs To Be Done*. Santa Barbara: Centre for the Study of Democratic Institutions, University of California.

Aronson, D.H. (1982) Prisoners' Rights. *Annual Survey of American Law*: 79–106.

Ashworth, A. (1983) *Sentencing and Penal Policy*. London: Weidenfeld.

Attica Commission (1972) *Official Report of the New York State Special Commission on Attica*. New York: Bantam Books.

Austin, C. and Ditchfield, J. (1985) *A Study of Prisoners' Applications and Petitions*. Home Office Research and Planning Unit Paper. London: HMSO.

Bassett, M. (1943) Newgate Prison in the Middle Ages. *Speculum* 18: 233.

Bazelon, D.L. (1982) The Accreditation Process. *Corrections Magazine*, December: 20–26.

Beaven, A. (1979) Prisoners' Access. *Law Quarterly Review* 96: 393–417.

Bedau, H.A. (1984) Why We Have the Rights We Do. *Social Philosophy and Policy* 1(2): 56–72.

Bentham, J. (1791) Panopticon: or the Inspection House. In Sir J. Bowring (ed.) *Works* vol. 4.

Birkinshaw, P. (1981) The Closed Society: Complaints Mechanisms and Disciplinary Proceedings in Prisons. *Northern Ireland Legal Quarterly* 32: 117–57.

—— (1983) Legal Order and Prison Administration. *Northern Ireland Legal Quarterly* 34: 269–91.

Blom-Cooper, L. and Zellick, G. (1982) Prisons. *Halsbury's Laws of England* 4th edn. London: Butterworths.

Bottoms, A.E. (1977) Reflections on the Renaissance of Dangerousness. *Howard Journal of Criminal Justice* 16: 70–96.

—— (1983) Neglected Features of Contemporary Penal Systems. In Garland, D. and Young, P. (eds) *The Power to Punish*. London: Heinemann Educational Books.

Brazier, M. (1982) Prison Doctors and Their Involuntary Patients. *Public Law*: 282.

Bureau of National Affairs (1978) Prison Reform: the Judicial Process – a BNA Special Report on Judicial Involvement in Prison Reform. *The Criminal Law Reporter* 23, 17: 977–96.

Brody, S.R. (1976) *The Effectiveness of Sentencing: A Review of the Literature*. Home Office Research Study 52. London: HMSO.

Burns, T. and Stalker, G.M. (1966) *The Management of Innovation* 2nd edn. London: Tavistock.

Calvatia, K. (1983) The Demise of the Occupational Safety and Health Administration: a Case Study in Symbolic Action. *Social Problems* 30, 4: 437–48.

Campbell, T.D. (1983) *The Left and Rights*. London: Routledge and Kegan Paul.

Canadian Correctional Investigator (1974) *Annual Report 1973/4*. Ottawa: Office of the Correctional Investigator.

Carlen, P. (1983) On Rights and Powers: Some Notes on Penal Politics. In Garland, D. and Young, P. (eds) *The Power to Punish*. London: Heinemann Educational Books.

Carlson, N. (1983) Monday Morning Highlights. *Federal Prison System*. Washington, DC: US Department of Justice.

Casale, S. (1984) *Minimum Standards for Prison Establishments*. London: National Association for the Care and Resettlement of Offenders (NACRO).

Champagne, A. and Haas, K.C. (1976) The Impact of *Johnson and Avery* on Prison Administration. *Tennessee Law Review* 43: 275–306.

Cohen, S. (1983) Social-Control Talk: Telling Stories About Correctional Change. In Garland, D. and Young, P. (eds) *The Power to Punish*. London: Heinemann Educational Books.

—— and Taylor, L. (1972) *Psychological Survival: the Experience of Long Term Imprisonment*. Harmondsworth: Penguin.

—— and —— (1978) *Prison Secrets*. London: National Council for Civil Liberties.

Collins, W.P. (1980) Public Participation in Bureaucratic Decision-Making: a Reappraisal. *Public Administration* 67: 465–77.

Commission on Accreditation for Corrections (1982) *Accreditation: Blueprint for Corrections*. Rockville, Maryland: CAC.

Cottingham, J. (1984) The Balancing Act: Weighing Rights and Interests in the Criminal Process. *Archiv für Rechts and Sozialphilosophie* 19: 97.

Council of Europe (1984) *Stocktaking on the European Commission on Human Rights*. Strasbourg: Council of Europe.

Cox Report (1973) *Report of the Working Party on Dispersal and Control.* Unpublished report: Home Office.

Cross, A.R.N. (1976) *Punishment, Prison and the Public*. London: Stevens.

Dean, M. (1973) The Law's Inside Job. *The Guardian* 2 February.

Dignan, J. (1984) The Sword of Damocles and the Clang of the Prison Gates. *Howard Journal of Criminal Justice* 23, 3: 183–200.

Douglas, G. (1984) Dealing with Prisoners' Grievances. *British Journal of Criminology* 24: 2.

Dubs, A. (1982) Prisoners' Rights. *Prison Service Journal* 47:9.

Du Cane, E. (1865) *The Punishment and Prevention of Crime*. London: Macmillan.

Dworkin, R. (1977) *Taking Rights Seriously*. London: Duckworth.

English, P. (1973) Prisoners' Rights: Quis Custodiet Ipsos Custodes? In Bridge, J.W. (ed.) *Fundamental Rights*. London: Sweet and Maxwell.

European Commission of Human Rights (1983) *Survey of Activities and Statistics*. Strasbourg: ECHR.

Fitzgerald, M. and Sim, J. (1982) *British Prisons* 2nd edn. Oxford: Basil Blackwell.

Floud, J. and Young, W. (1981) *Dangerousness and Criminal Justice*. London: Heinemann Educational Books.

Fosen, R.H. and Lucas, W. (1983) Why Jail Accreditation? *The National Sheriff* August–September: 8–12.

Foucault, M. (1977) *Discipline and Punish: the Birth of the Prison*. London: Allen Lane.

Galligan, D.J. (1982) Judicial Review and the Textbook Writers. *Oxford Journal of Legal Studies* 2: 257–76.

Garland, D. and Young, P. (eds) (1983) *The Power to Punish*. London: Heinemann Educational Books.

—— and —— (1983) Towards a Social Analysis of Penality. In Garland, D. and Young, P. (eds) *The Power to Punish*. London: Heinemann Educational Books.

Garrett, J. (1980) *Managing the Civil Service*. London: Heinemann.

Gellhorn, W. (1966) *Ombudsmen and Others: Citizen Protectors in Nine Countries*. Cambridge, Mass: Harvard University Press.

Gettinger, S. (1982) Accreditation on Trial. *Corrections Magazine* February: 7–19.

Gewirth, A. (1984) The Epistemology of Human Rights. *Social Philosophy and Policy* 1, 2: 1–24.

Gobert, J. and Cohen, N. (1981) *Rights of Prisoners*. New York: McGraw.

Gostin, L. (1977) *A Human Condition* vol. 2. London: MIND.

—— (1985a) *Mental Health Services and the Law*. London: Shaw and Sons.

—— (1985b) Sentencing and the Mentally Disordered Offender. In Gostin, L. (ed.) *Secure Provision: A Review of Special Services for Mentally Ill and Mentally Handicapped People*. London: Tavistock.

Gruner, H. (1982) *A Good and Useful Life*. London: The Howard League.

Gunn, J. (1985) The Prison Medical Service. In Gostin, L. (ed.) *Secure Provision: A Review of Special Services for Mentally Ill and Mentally Handicapped People*. London: Tavistock.

Guze, S.B. (1976) Criminality and Psychiatric Disorders. Oxford: Oxford University Press.

Hall-Williams, J.E. (1984) The Need for a Prison Ombudsman. *Criminal Law Review*, February: 87.

Hansard, Official Reports, Session 1979–80. London: HMSO.

Harlow, C. (1978) Ombudsmen in Search of a Role. *Modern Law Review* 41: 446.

—— (1980) Public Law and Private Law: Definition Without Distinction. *Modern Law Review* 43: 241.

Harris, M. Kay and Spiller, D.P. (1977) *After Decision: Implementation of Judicial Decrees in Correctional Settings*. Washington, DC: American Bar Association.

Hart, H.L.A. (1955) Are There Any Natural Rights? *Philosophical Review* 64: 175–91.

Harvard Law Review (1977) Implementation Problems in Institution Reform Litigation. *Harvard Law Review* 91: 428–63.

Hawkins, K. (1984) *Environment and Enforcement: Regulation and the Social Definition of Pollution*. London: Oxford University Press.

Hobhouse, S. and Fenner Brockway, A. (1922) *English Prisons Today*. London: private subscription.

Hohfeld, W.N. (1919) *Fundamental Legal Conceptions*. New Haven: Yale University Press.

Home Office (1951) *Committee to Review Punishments (etc.) Report* (the 'Franklin Report'). Cmnd 8256. London: HMSO.

—— (1964) *Report of the Working Party on the Organisation of the Prison Medical Service* (the 'Gwynn Report'). London: HMSO.

—— (1966) *Report of the Inquiry into Prison Escapes and Security* (the 'Mountbatten Report'). Cmnd 3175. London: HMSO.

—— (1972) *Report of the Committee of Privy Counsellors appointed to consider authorised procedures for the interrogation of persons suspected of terrorism*. Cmnd 4901. London: HMSO.

—— (1973) 'Report of the Working Party on dispersal and Control' (the 'Cox Report'). Untitled and unpublished: Home Office.

—— (1975) *Report of the Working Party on Adjudication Procedures in Prisons* (the 'Weiler Report'). London: HMSO.

—— (1977) *Report of an Inquiry by the Chief Inspector of the Prison Service into the Cause and Circumstance of the Events at HM Prison Hull During the Period 31 August to 3 September, 1976* (the 'Fowler Report'). London: HMSO.

—— (1979) *Committee of Inquiry into the UK Prison Services* (the 'May Report'). Report and 3 volumes of evidence. Cmnd 7673. London: HMSO.

—— (1982) *Home Office Statement on the Background, Circumstances and Action Subsequently Taken Relative to the Disturbance in 'D' Wing at HM Prison Wormwood Scrubs on 31 August 1979; Together with the Report of an Inquiry by the Regional Director of the South East Region of the Prison Department*. HC 199. London: HMSO.

—— (1984a) *Report on the Work of the Prison Department 1983*. Cmnd 9306. London: HMSO.

—— (1984b) *Managing the Long-term Prison System: the Report of the Control Review Committee*. London: HMSO.

—— (1984c) *Prison Department, Current Recommended Standards for the Design of New Prison Establishments*. Unpublished.

—— (1984d) *The Prison Disciplinary System, A Descriptive Memorandum. Evidence to the Committee on the Prison Disciplinary System.* Unpublished.

—— (1984e) *The Prison Disciplinary System, the Main Issues: A Discussion Paper, Evidence to the Committee on the Prison Disciplinary System.* Unpublished.

—— (1984f) *Government Reply to the First Report from the Education, Science and Arts Committee.* London: HMSO.

—— (1984g) *Criminal Justice – A Working Paper.* London: HMSO.

HM Chief Inspector of Prisons (1981) *HM Prison Cookham Wood.* Report by HMCIP. London: Home Office.

—— (1982a) *HM Chief Inspector of Prisons, Annual Report 1981.* Cmnd 8532. London: HMSO.

—— (1982b) *HM Prison Birmingham.* Report by HMCIP. London: Home Office.

—— (1982c) *HM Prison Leeds.* Report by HMCIP. London: Home Office.

—— (1982d) *HM Prison Gloucester.* Report by HMCIP. London: Home Office.

—— (1982e) *HM Prison Stafford.* Report by HMCIP. London: Home Office.

—— (1983a) *HM Chief Inspector of Prisons, Annual Report 1982.* HC 260. London: HMSO.

—— (1983b) *HM Remand Centre Ashford.* Report by HMCIP. London: Home Office.

—— (1983c) *HM Prison Manchester.* Report by HMCIP. London: Home Office.

—— (1983d) *HM Prison Brixton.* Report by HMCIP. London: Home Office.

—— (1983e) *HM Prison Wormwood Scrubs.* Report by HMCIP. London: Home Office.

—— (1983f) *HM Prison Nottingham.* Report by HMCIP. London: Home Office.

—— (1984a) *HM Chief Inspector of Prisons, Annual Report 1983.* HC 618. London: HMSO.

—— (1984b) *HM Prison Leicester.* Report by HMCIP London: Home Office.

—— (1984c) *The Maze Prison.* Incident report by HMCIP. London: Home Office.

—— (1984d) *Suicides in Prison.* Thematic report by HMCIP. London: Home Office.

—— (1984e) *Prison Categorisation Procedures.* Thematic report by HMCIP. London: Home Office.

—— (1984f) *Evidence to Departmental Committee on the Prison System.* Unpublished.

—— (1985) *HM Prison Canterbury.* Report by HMCIP. London: Home Office.

House of Commons Expenditure Committee (1978) *Fifteenth Report of the Expenditure Committee. The Reduction of Pressure on the Prison System.* London: HMSO.

Howard League (1984) *Submission to the Department Committee on the Prison Disciplinary System.* Unpublished.

Hunt, A. (1981) The Politics of Law and Justice. *Politics and Power* 4.

Ignatieff, M. (1978) *A Just Measure of Pain: the Penitentiary in the Industrial Revolution 1750–1850.* London: Macmillan.

Iles, S., Conners, A., May, C. and Mott, J. (1984) *Punishment Practice by Prison Boards of Visitors.* Home Office Research and Planning Unit Paper 26. London: Home Office.

Irving, B. and Hilgendorf, L. (1980) *Police Interrogation: the psychological approach.* Royal Commission on Criminal Procedure, Reasearch Study No. 1. London: HMSO.

Irwin, J. (1980) *Prisons in Turmoil.* Boston: Little Brown and Company.

Jacobs, J.B. (1977) *Stateville: the Penitentiary in Mass Society.* Chicago: University of Chicago Press.

—— (1980) The Prisoners' Rights Movements and its Impacts, 1960–1980. In Morris, N. and Tonry, M. (eds) *Crime and Justice: an Annual Review of Research* vol. 2. Chicago: University of Chicago Press.

Johnson, R. and Toch, H. (eds) (1982) *The Pains of Imprisonment.* Beverley Hills, Ca.: Sage Publications.

JUSTICE (1977) *Our Fettered Ombudsman.* London: JUSTICE.

—— (1983) *Justice in Prison.* London: JUSTICE.

Kamenka, E. and Tay, A.E.S. (1975) Beyond Bourgeois Individualism. In Kamenka, E. and Neal, R. (eds) *Feudalism, Capitalism and Beyond.* Canberra: Australian National University Press.

Kassebaum, G., Ward, D. and Wilner, D. (1971) *Prison Treatment and Parole Survival: an Empirical Assessment.* New York: Wiley.

Keating, J.M. (1975) *Grievance Mechanisms in Correctional Institutions: a Prescriptive Package.* Washington: US Department of Justice.

King, R.D. (1979) Dangerous Prisoners: Dispersal or Concentration. Evidence to the Committee of Inquiry into the UK Prison Services. Privately circulated.

—— and Elliott, K.W. (1978) *Albany: Birth of a Prison, End of an Era.* London: Routledge and Kegan Paul.

—— and Morgan, R. (1979) *Crisis in the Prisons: the Way Out.* A paper based on evidence submitted to the Inquiry into the United Kingdom Prison Service. Universities of Bath and Southamption.

—— and —— (1980) *The Future of the Prison System.* London: Gower.

Kittrie, N. (1971) *The Right to be Different.* Baltimore: Johns Hopkins Press.

Lee, B. (1983) Medical Advice to HM Inspectorate of Prisons. *AMBOV Quarterly* 9.

Levinson, M.R. (1982) Special Masters: Engineers of Court-ordered Reform. *Corrections Magazine* August: 7–18.

Lidstone, K.W. (1984) Magistrates, the Police and Search Warrants. *Criminal Law Review* August: 449–59.

Liverman, M.G. (1938) Prison Discipline. *Howard Journal of Criminal Justice* 96.

Logan, A.D.W. (1982) Prisoners' Rights. *Prison Service Journal* No. 47 (new series) 12.

Lynxwiler, J., Shover, N. and Clelland, D.A. (1983) The Organisation and Impact of Inspector Discretion in a Regulatory Bureaucracy. *Social Problems* 30, 4: 425–36.

MacDonagh, O. (1977) *Early Victorian Government.* London: Weidenfeld.

Maguire, M. (1985) Applications to Boards of Visitors. *AMBOV Quarterly* February 1985.

——, Pinter, F. and Collis, C. (1984) Dangerousness and the Tariff: the Decision-making Process in Release From Life Sentences. *British Journal of Criminology 24, 3.*

Maguire, M. and Vagg, J. (1983a) Who are the Prison Watchdogs? The Membership and Appointment of Boards of Visitors. *Criminal Law Review* 238.

—— and —— (1983b) Reflections on Effectiveness. *AMBOV Quarterly* 11.

—— and —— (1984) *The 'Watchdog' Role of Boards of Visitors*. London: Home Office.

Marin, B. (1983) *Inside Justice: a comparative analysis of practices and procedures for the determination of offences against discipline*. London: Associated University Press.

Martin, J.P. (1975) *Boards of Visitors of Penal Institutions* (the 'Jellicoe Report'). London: Barry Rose.

McConville, S. (1981) *A History of English Prison Administration 1750–1877*. London: Routledge and Kegan Paul.

McGillis, D., Mullen, J. and Studen, L. (1976) *Controlled Confrontation*. Washington: US Department of Justice.

Milligan, J.E., Rajcoomar, J., Lees, M.K. and Whelan, T.P. (1984) Litigation: the Case for Training. Unpublished paper presented to the 40th Assistant Governors' Training Course, Prison Service College, Wakefield.

Ministerie van Justitie (1982) *Taak en toekomst van het Nederlandse gevangeniswezen*. 's Gravenhage: Ministerie van Justitie.

Moerings, L.M. (1984) Recente Ontwikkelingen in het Gevangeniswezen. *Delikt en Delinkwent* 14, 3: 220–35.

Morgan, R. (1982) Segregation: Imprisonment Within a Prison. *AMBOV Quarterly* 6.

—— (1983) The Use of Resources in the Prison System. In *A Prison System for the 80s and Beyond*. London: NACRO.

—— and Macfarlane, A. (1984) *After Tarrant: Advice for Boards of Visitors Regarding Assistance for Prisoners at Adjudications* 2nd edn. London: Association of Members of Boards of Visitors.

Morris, N. (1975) *The Future of Imprisonment*. Chicago: University of Chicago Press.

Morris, T. and Morris, P. (1963) Pentonville. London: Routledge and Kegan Paul.

Mott, J. (1985) Adult Prisons and Prisoners in England and Wales 1970–82: A review of the findings of social research. Home Office Research Study no. 84. London: HMSO.

Nathan, V.M. (1979) The Use of Masters in Institutional Reform Litigation. *Toledo Law Review* 10, Winter: 419–64.

National Institute of Justice (1980) *American Prisons and Jails* 3 vols. Washington DC: National Institute of Justice.

NCCL (1984) *Evidence to Departmental Committee on the Prison Discipline System*. London: National Council for Civil Liberties.

New Mexico Attorney General (1980) *Report of the Attorney General on the February 2 and 3, 1980 Riot at the Penitentiary of New Mexico*. New Mexico.

Nozick, R. (1974) *Anarchy, State and Utopia*. New York: Basic Books.

Nuffield, J. (1979) *Inmate Grievance Procedure Pilot Project*. Saskatchewan Penitentiary. Unpublished.

Owen, T. and Sim, J. (1984) Drugs, Discipline and Prison Medicine: the Case of George Wilkinson. In Scraton, P. and Gordon, P. (eds) *Causes for Concern*. Harmondsworth: Penguin.

Packer, H.L. (1969) *The Limits of the Criminal Sanction*. Stanford: Stanford University Press.

Parliamentary All-Party Penal Affairs Group (1982) *The Role and Function of Boards of Visitors*. London: PAPPAG.

Plant, R. (1979) Justice, Punishment and the State. In Bottom, A.E. and Preston, R.H. (eds) *The Coming Penal Crisis*. Edinburgh: Scottish Academic Press.

Pennock, J.R. and Chapman, J.W. (1981) *Human Rights – Nomos 23*. New York: New York University Press.

Ploeg, G. and Nijboer, J. (1983) *Klagers Achter Slot en Grendel: een evaluatie van het funktioneren van de gewijzigde beklagregeling voor gedetineerden*. Groningen: Kriminologisch Instituut.

Prescott, J. (1976) Hull Prison Riot: Submissions, Observations, Recommendations. Private submission to Mr G.M. Fowler, Chief Inspector of Prison Services.

Prison Officers' Association (1984) *The Prison Disciplinary System: Submission to the Home Office Departmental Committee on the Prison Disciplinary System*. London: Prison Officers' Association.

Prison Service College (1984) Adjudications Training Package. Unpublished: Wakefield.

Prosser, T. (1982) Towards a Critical Public Law. *Journal of Law and Society* 9: 1–19.

Rawls, J. (1971) *A Theory of Justice*. London: Oxford University Press.

Rhodes, G. (1982) *Inspectorates in British Government: Law Enforcement and Standards of Efficiency*. London: Allen and Unwin.

Richardson, G. (1984) Time to Take Prisoners' Rights Seriously. *Journal of Law and Society* 11: 1–32.

—— (1985) Judicial Review of Parole Policy. *Public Law*.

Rijksbegroting (1981–82) *Heroverweging collectieve uitgaven. Deelrapport 38-Heroverweging Strafrechttoepassing*. 's Gravenhage, Ministerie van Justitie.

—— (1983) *Rijksbegroting voor het jaar 1983. Hoofdstuk VI Departement van Justitie*. Zitting 1982–83, 17600. 's Gravenhage, Ministerie van Justitie.

Roorda, P.A. (1984) *Registratie van Verslaafden in de Penitentiare Inrichingen: Vergelijking van de cijfers van 1981 en 1982*. 's Gravenhage, Ministerie van Justitie.

Rose, G. (1961) *The Struggle for Penal Reform*. London: Stevens.

Royal College of Psychiatrists (1979) The College's Evidence to the Prison Services Inquiry. *The Bulletin of the RCP*, May 1979: 81

Royal Commission on Legal Services (1979) *Final Report*. Cmnd 7684. London: HMSO.

Royal Commission on Criminal Procedure (1981) *Report*. Cmnd 8092. London: HMSO.

Rutherford, A. (1982) Minimum Physical Standards Regulating the Administration of Prisons. Unpublished paper, 18 January 1982.

—— (1983) Prison Justice. *Public Law* 568.

—— (1984a) *Prisons and the Process of Justice: the Reductionist Challenge*. London: Heinemann.

—— (1984b) Deeper into the Quagmire: Observations on the Latest Prison Building Programme. *Howard Journal of Criminal Justice* 23, 3: 129–37.

Samuels, G. (1983) Public and Private Law: a Private Lawyer's Response. *Modern Law Review* 46: 558.

Scheingold, S.A. (1974) *The Politics of Rights*. New Haven: Yale University Press.
Sechrest, D. (1978) The Legal Basis for Commission Standards. *American Journal of Corrections* November–December: 14–23.
Smith, D., Austin, C. and Ditchfield, J. (1981) *Board of Visitor Adjudications*. London: Home Office Research Unit.
Society of Civil and Public Servants, Governors' Branch. (1983) *Prison Standards*. Unpublished.
Spiller, D.P. (1976) *After Decision: a Case Study of Holt v Sarver*. Washington DC: American Bar Association.
Staatssecretaris van Justitie (1982–83) *Brief van de Staatssecretaris van het Ministerie van Justitie*. Zitting 1982–3, 17539, no. 3, p. 9. 's Gravenhage, Ministerie van Justitie.
Stewart, R.B. (1975) The Reformation of American Administrative Law. *Harvard Law Review* 88: 1682–83.
Taylor, P.J. and Gunn, J. (1984) Violence and Psychosis: 1. Risk of Violence among Psychotic Men. *British Medical Journal* 288: 1945–49.
Tettenborn, A. (1980) Prisoners' Rights. *Public Law* 74.
Thomas, J.E. (1972) *The English Prison Officer Since 1850*. London: Routledge and Kegan Paul.
—— and Pooley, G. (1980) *The Exploding Prison*. London: Junction Books.
Tournier (1984) *Statistics Concerning Prison Populations in the Member States of the Council of Europe*. Paris: Centre de recherche sociologique sur le droit et les institutions penales (CESDIP LA CNRS 313).
UCLA Law Review (1973) Judicial Intervention in Corrections: the California Experience – an Empirical Study. *UCLA Law Review* 20: 452–575.
Unger, R.M. (1976) *Law in Modern Society*. New York: Free Press.
United States Department of Justice (1980) *Federal Standards for Prisons and Jails*. Washington DC: US Department of Justice.
—— (1984) *Sourcebook of Criminal Justice Statistics*. Washington DC: Department of Justice.
von Hirsch, A. (1976) *Doing Justice: the Choice of Punishments*. New York: Hill and Wang.
Walker, N.D. (1980) *Punishment, Danger and Stigma*. Oxford: Basil Blackwell.
Wener, G. (1983) *A Legitimate Grievance*. London: Prison Reform Trust.
Wicker, T. (1975) *A Time to Die*. London: Bodley Head.
Wood, W.A. (1983) Dealing with Difficult Prisoners. *Informer*. London: Governors' Branch, Society of Civil and Public Servants.
Wright, M. (1982) *Making Good*. London: Barnett Books.
Yale Law Journal (1979) Note: 'Mastering' Intervention in Prisons. *Yale Law Journal* 88: 1062–91.
Zellick, G. (1978) The Case for Prisoners' Rights. In Freeman, J.C. (ed.) *Prisons Past and Future*. London: Heinemann.
—— (1981) The Prison Rules and the Courts. *Criminal Law Review:* 602.
—— (1982) The Prison Rules and the Courts: A Postscript. *Criminal Law Review*: 575.
—— (1982a) The Offence of False and Malicious Allegations by Prisoners. *British Journal of Criminology* 22, 1.

Name index

Note: Names associated with legal cases can be found in the subject index.

Subject index

Notes
1. Sub-entries are in alphabetical order except where chronological order is significant.
2. Legal cases, reports, applications and judgements are shown in italics.
3. All references are to the United Kingdom, unless otherwise stated.